Security and Diplomacy: Old Issues New Challenges

Security and Diplomacy: Old Issues New Challenges

A.K. Dixit

CYBER TECH PUBLICATIONS
4264/3, Ansari Road, Daryaganj, New Delhi-110002 (India)
Ph.: 011-23244078. Fax: 011-23280028
E-Mail: cyberpublicationsdelhi@yahoo.com

SECURITY AND DIPLOMACY: OLD ISSUES NEW CHALLENGES

A.K. Dixit

First Edition 2009

Published by :

G.S. Rawat for **Cyber Tech Publications**
4264/3, Ansari Road, Daryaganj, New Delhi-110002 (India)
Ph.: 011-23244078. Fax: 011-23280028
E-Mail: cyberpublicationsdelhi@yahoo.com

Printed at :

Preface

One hundred years ago the question of the future of diplomacy was raised as a result of technological progress—the invention of the radio and telegraph and the intervention of public into the domain of foreign policy. The first factor brought the apprehension that diplomats would become "honorary mailmen" and the second raised the issue of open diplomacy. However, the role of diplomacy in the twentieth century has not been restricted by these two factors. The functioning of diplomacy is influenced by a complicated combination of different interrelated factors. To begin with, there is a set of political factors. During most of the twentieth century, two world wars, the Cold War, the rivalry of two super powers, the ideologization of international affairs and military confrontation have made diplomacy a subsidiary instrument of power politics and ideology. As a result, diplomacy has very often executed the "dance of death." The end of the Cold War has radically changed the international political scene. Moreover, today we are facing the shift of the civilizational paradigm, which affects not only the major units of world polities - the states - but which also brings new actors into the forefront of international relations.

The major political factor influencing diplomacy is the relative decline of the role of the national governments. Today governments are facing stern competition from other actors. Private sector, religious groups, immigrants, media and other entities of the civil society are demanding from the government that their interests be taken into consideration and that they have a say in making and implementing foreign policy. People want to travel freely, to conduct business abroad or to be involved in various types of cultural exchange.

—*Author*

CONTENTS

1

An Agenda for Peace: Preventive Diplomacy and Related Matters

The General Assembly, Recalling the statement of 31 January 1992, adopted at the conclusion of the first meeting held by the Security Council at the level of Heads of State and Government, in which the Secretary-General was invited to prepare, for circulation to the States Members of the United Nations by 1 July 1992, an "analysis and recommendations on ways of strengthening and making more efficient within the framework and provisions of the Charter the capacity of the United Nations for preventive diplomacy, for peacemaking and for peace-keeping",

Welcoming the timely presentation of the forward-looking report of the Secretary-General entitled "An Agenda for Peace", in response to the summit meeting of the Security Council, as a set of recommendations that deserve close examination by the international community,

Recognizing the need to maintain the increased interest in and momentum for revitalization of the Organization to meet the challenges of the new phase of international relations in order to fulfil the purposes and principles of the Charter of the United Nations,

Stressing that the implementation of the concepts and proposals contained in "An Agenda for Peace" should be in strict conformity with the provisions of the Charter, in particular its purposes and principles,

Recalling also its resolution 2625 (XXV) of 24 October 1970, the annex to which contains the Declaration on Principles of

International Law concerning Friendly Relations and Cooperation among States in accordance with the Charter of the United Nations, and its resolution 43/51 of 5 December 1988, the annex to which contains the Declaration on the Prevention and Removal of Disputes and Situations Which May Threaten International Peace and Security and on the Role of the United Nations in this Field,

Emphasizing that international peace and security must be seen in an integrated manner and that the efforts of the Organization to build peace, justice, stability and security must encompass not only military matters, but also, through its various organs within their respective areas of competence, relevant political, economic, social, humanitarian, environmental and developmental aspects,

Stressing the need for international action to strengthen the socio-economic development of Member States as one of the means of enhancing international peace and security and, in this regard, recognizing the need to complement "An Agenda for Peace" with "An Agenda for Development",

Acknowledging that timely application of preventive diplomacy is the most desirable and efficient means of easing tensions before they result in conflict,

Recognizing that preventive diplomacy may require such measures as confidence-building, early-warning, fact-finding and other measures in which consultations with Member States, discretion, confidentiality, objectivity and transparency should be combined as appropriate,

Emphasizing the need to strengthen the capacity of the United Nations in the field of preventive diplomacy, through, inter alia, allocating appropriate staff resources and financial resources for preventive diplomacy, in order to assist Member States to resolve their differences in a peaceful manner,

Reaffirming the fundamental importance of a sound and secure financial basis for the United Nations in order, inter alia, to enable the Organization to play an effective role in preventive diplomacy,

Emphasizing the importance of cooperation between the United Nations and regional arrangements and organizations for preventive diplomacy within their respective areas of competence,

Emphasizing also that respect for the principles of sovereignty, territorial integrity and political independence of States is crucial to any common endeavour to promote international peace and security,

Recalling further other resolutions adopted by the Assembly during its forty-seventh session concerning various aspects of "An Agenda for Peace",

Emphasizing the need for all organs and bodies of the United Nations, as appropriate, to intensify their efforts to strengthen the role of the Organization in preventive diplomacy, peacemaking, peace-keeping and peace-building and to continue the discussion of the report of the Secretary-General with a view to adequate action being taken,

Stressing the need for adequate protection of personnel involved in preventive diplomacy, peacemaking, peace-keeping and humanitarian operations, in accordance with relevant norms and principles of international law,

Noting the definition of preventive diplomacy provided by the Secretary-General in his report entitled "An Agenda for Peace",

PEACEFUL SETTLEMENT OF DISPUTES

Emphasizing the need to promote the peaceful settlement of disputes,

1. Invites Member States to seek solutions to their disputes at an early stage through such peaceful means as provided for in the Charter of the United Nations;
2. Decides to explore ways and means for a full utilization of the provisions of the Charter whereby the General Assembly may recommend measures for the peaceful adjustment of any situation, regardless of origin, which is deemed likely to impair the general welfare or friendly relations among nations;

3. Encourages the Security Council to utilize fully the provisions of Chapter VI of the Charter on procedures and methods for peaceful settlement of disputes and to call upon the parties concerned to settle their disputes peacefully;
4. Encourages the Secretary-General and the Security Council to engage at an early stage in close and continuous consultation in order to develop, on a case-by-case basis, an appropriate strategy for the peaceful settlement of specific disputes, including the participation of other organs, organizations and agencies of the United Nations system, as well as regional arrangements and organizations as appropriate, and invites the Secretary-General to report to the General Assembly on such consultations;

EARLY-WARNING, COLLECTION OF INFORMATION AND ANALYSIS

Recognizing the need to strengthen the capacity of the United Nations for early-warning, collection of information and analysis,

1. Encourages the Secretary-General to set up an adequate early-warning mechanism for situations which are likely to endanger the maintenance of international peace and security, in close cooperation with Member States and United Nations agencies, as well as regional arrangements and organizations, as appropriate, making use of the information available to these organizations and/or received from Member States, and to keep Member States informed of the mechanism established;
2. Invites the Secretary-General to strengthen the capacity of the Secretariat for the collection of information and analysis to serve better the early-warning needs of the Organization and, to that end, encourages the Secretary-General to ensure that staff members receive proper training in all aspects of preventive diplomacy, including the collection and analysis of information;
3. Invites Member States and regional arrangements and organizations to provide timely early-warning

information, on a confidential basis when appropriate, to the Secretary-General;

4. Encourages the- Secretary-General to continue, in accordance with Article 99 of the Charter of the United Nations, to bring to the attention of the Security Council, at his discretion, any matter which in his opinion may threaten the maintenance of international peace and security, together with his recommendations thereon;
5. Invites Member States to support the efforts of the Secretary-General in preventive diplomacy, including by providing assistance he may require;
6. Encourages the Secretary-General, in accordance with the relevant provisions of the Charter, to notify the General Assembly, as appropriate, of any situation which is potentially dangerous or might lead to international friction or dispute;
7. Invites the Secretary-General to bring to the attention of Member States concerned, at an early stage, any matter which in his opinion may adversely affect relations between States;

FACT-FINDING

Recalling the statements made by the President of the Security Council, on behalf of the Council, on 29 October and 30 November 1992, and its own resolutions 1967 (XVIII) of 16 December 1963, 2104 (XX) of 20 December 1965, 2182 (XXI) of 12 December 1966 and 2329 (XXII) of 18 December 1967 on the question of methods of fact-finding,

1. Reaffirms its resolution 46/59 of 9 December 1991, the annex to which contains the Declaration on Fact-finding by the United Nations in the Field of the Maintenance of International Peace and Security, particularly its guidelines;
2. Recommends to the Secretary-General that he should continue to utilize the services of eminent and qualified experts in fact-finding and other missions, selected on as wide a geographical basis as possible, taking into

account candidates with the highest standards of efficiency, competence and integrity;

3. Invites Member States to submit names of suitable individuals whom the Secretary-General might wish to use at his discretion in fact-finding and other missions;
4. Recommends that a request by a Member State for the dispatch of a fact-finding mission to its territory should be considered expeditiously;
5. Invites the Secretary-General to continue to dispatch fact-finding and other missions in a timely manner in order to assist him in the proper discharge of his functions under the Charter of the United Nations;

CONFIDENCE-BUILDING MEASURES

Recognizing that the application of appropriate confidence-building measures, consistent with national security needs, would promote mutual confidence and good faith, which are essential to reducing the likelihood of conflicts between States and enhancing prospects for the peaceful settlement of disputes,

Recalling its resolutions 43/78 H of 7 December 1988 and 45/62 F of 4 December 1990, as well as its resolution 47/54 D of 9 December 1992 on the implementation of the guidelines for appropriate types of confidence-building measures,

Recognizing that confidence-building measures may encompass both military and non-military matters, including political, economic and social matters,

Stressing the need to encourage Member States, and regional arrangements and organizations where relevant and in a manner consistent with their mandates, to play a leading role in developing confidence-building measures appropriate to the region concerned and to coordinate their efforts in this regard with the United Nations in accordance with Chapter VIII of the Charter of the United Nations,

1. Invites Member States and regional arrangements and organizations to inform the Secretary-General through appropriate channels about their experiences in confidence-building measures in their respective regions;

2. Supports the intention of the Secretary-General to consult on a regular basis with Member States and regional arrangements and organizations on further confidence-building measures;
3. Encourages the Secretary-General to consult with parties to existing or potential disputes, the continuance of which is likely to endanger the maintenance of international peace and security, and with other Interested Member States and regional arrangements and organizations, as appropriate, on the possibility of initiating confidence-building measures in their respective regions and to keep Member States informed thereon ln consultation with the parties concerned;
4. Commends such confidence-building measures as the promotion of openness and restraint in the production, procurement and deployment of armaments, the systematic exchange of military missions, the possible formation of regional risk reduction centres, arrangements for the free flow of information and the monitoring of regional arms control and disarmament agreements;

HUMANITARIAN ASSISTANCE

Recalling its resolution 45/100 of 14 December 1990 on humanitarian assistance to victims of natural disasters and similar emergency situations and its resolution 46/182 of 19 December 1991 on the strengthening of the coordination of emergency humanitarian assistance of the United Nations,

Welcoming the increasing role of the United Nations system in providing humanitarian assistance,

Noting that, in certain circumstances, programmes of impartially-provided humanitarian assistance and peace-keeping operations can be mutually supportive,

1. Encourages the Secretary-General to continue to strengthen the capacity of the Organization ln order to ensure coordinated planning and execution of humanitarian assistance programmes, drawing upon the specialized skills and resources of all parts of the

United Nations system, as well as those of non-governmental organizations, as appropriate;

2. Also encourages the Secretary-General to continue to address the question of coordination, when necessary, between humanitarian assistance programmes and peace-keeping or related operations, preserving the non-political, neutral and impartial character of humanitarian action;
3. Invites the Secretary-General to bring to the attention of appropriate organs of the United Nations any situation requiring urgent humanitarian assistance in order to prevent its deterioration, which might lead to international friction or dispute;

RESOURCES AND LOGISTICAL ASPECTS OF PREVENTIVE DIPLOMACY

Recognizing the need for adequate resources in support of the United Nations efforts in preventive diplomacy,

1. Invites Member States to provide political and practical support to the Secretary-General in his efforts for the peaceful settlement of disputes, including early-warning, fact-finding, good offices and mediation;
2. Also invites Member States, on a voluntary basis, to provide the Secretary-General with any necessary additional expertise and logistical resources that he might require for the successful execution of these functions of increasing importance;

ROLE OF THE GENERAL ASSEMBLY IN PREVENTIVE DIPLOMACY

Emphasizing that, together with the Security Council and the Secretary-General, it has an important role in preventive diplomacy,

Recognizing that, having an important role in preventive diplomacy, it has to work ln close cooperation and coordination with the Security Council and the Secretary-General in accordance with the Charter of the United Nations and consistent with their respective mandates and responsibilities,

Decides to explore ways and means to support the recommendations of the Secretary-General ln his report entitled "An Agenda for Peace" to promote the utilization of the General Assembly, ln accordance with the relevant provisions of the Charter of the United Nations, by Member States so as to bring greater influence to bear in pre-empting or containing any situation which is potentially dangerous or might lead to international friction or dispute;

FUTURE WORK

Bearing in mind that owing to time constraints lt could not examine all the proposals contained ln the report of the Secretary-General entitled "An Agenda for Peace",

1. Decides to continue early in 1993 its examination of other recommendations on preventive diplomacy and related matters contained in the report of the Secretary-General entitled "An Agenda for Peace", including preventive deployment, demilitarized zones and the International Court of Justice, as well as implementation of the provisions of Article 50 of the Charter of the United Nations, in conformity with the Charter and taking into account the relevant developments and practices ln the competent organs of the United Nations;
2. Also decides to discuss and consider other proposals contained in "An Agenda for Peace".

The General Assembly, Recalling its resolution 47/120 A of 18 December 1992 entitled "An Agenda for Peace: preventive diplomacy and related matters",

Reaffirming its resolution 46/59 of 9 December 1991, the annex to which contains the Declaration on Fact-finding by the United Nations in the Field of the Maintenance of International Peace and Security,

Recalling also its resolution 46/182 of 19 December 1991 on the strengthening of the coordination of humanitarian emergency assistance of the United Nations,

Recalling further its resolution 47/71 of 14 December 1992 on the comprehensive review of the whole question of peace-keeping operations in all their aspects,

Emphasizing that, together with the Security Council and the Secretary-General, it has an important role in preventive diplomacy,

Recognizing that it has to work in close cooperation and coordination with the Security Council and the Secretary-General in accordance with the Charter of the United Nations and consistent with their respective mandates and responsibilities,

ROLE OF THE GENERAL ASSEMBLY

Recalling the relevant provisions of the Charter of the United Nations relating to the functions and powers of the General Assembly,

Recalling also the report of the Secretary-General entitled "An Agenda for Peace", which refers to the utilization of these functions and powers,

1. Resolves to make full and effective use of the functions and powers set out in Articles 10 and 14 of the Charter of the United Nations, in conformity with other relevant provisions of the Charter;
2. Decides to consider the use of existing or new machinery, including subsidiary organs under Article 22 of the Charter, to facilitate consideration of any situation coming within the scope of Article 14 of the Charter, with a view to recommending measures for the peaceful adjustment of such a situation;
3. Also decides to consider appropriate ways and means consistent with the Charter to improve cooperation among the competent United Nations organs in order to strengthen the role of the United Nations in the promotion of peace, including the possibility that the General Assembly receives reports, as appropriate, from the Secretary-General on matters related to the items on its agenda or on other matters within its competence;

PREVENTIVE DEPLOYMENT AND DEMILITARIZED ZONES

Taking note of paragraphs 28 to 33 on preventive deployment and demilitarized zones contained in the report of the Secretary-

General entitled "An Agenda for Peace", within the larger context of preventive diplomacy, as well as the views expressed on these issues by Member States,

Stressing that the implementation of any concepts and proposals on preventive deployment and demilitarized zones contained in "An Agenda for Peace" should be undertaken in accordance with the provisions of the Charter of the United Nations, in particular its purposes and principles, and other relevant principles of international law,

Welcoming the instances of effective use of United Nations preventive deployment and the establishment of demilitarized zones,

Stressing the importance of appropriate consultations with Member States and transparency in any decision-making concerning the undertaking of preventive deployment or the establishment of a demilitarized zone,

Recognizing that a United Nations preventive deployment or the establishment of demilitarized zones could promote the prevention or containment of conflicts, the continuance of which is likely to endanger the maintenance of international peace and security,

Emphasizing that respect for the principles of sovereignty, territorial integrity and political independence of States and non-intervention in matters which are essentially within the domestic jurisdiction of any State is crucial to any common endeavour to promote international peace and security,

Bearing in mind that, as each situation in which preventive deployment may be undertaken or a demilitarized zone established has its own special characteristics, it is of the utmost importance to make decisions on such measures on a case-by-case basis with due regard to all relevant factors and circumstances, including consultations with Member States,

Recognizing the need to preserve the impartiality of the United Nations when engaged in preventive deployment or in the establishment of demilitarized zones,

Recognizing also that preventive deployment and the establishment of demilitarized zones are evolving concepts,

1. Acknowledges the importance of considering, on a case-by-case basis, the use of preventive deployment and/or the establishment of demilitarized zones as a means to prevent existing or potential disputes from escalating into conflicts and to promote efforts to achieve the peaceful settlement of such disputes, the continuance of which is likely to endanger the maintenance of international peace and security;
2. Reaffirms that a United Nations preventive deployment and/or the establishment of a demilitarized zone should be undertaken with the consent of and, in principle, on the basis of a request by the Member State or Member States involved, having taken into account the positions of other States concerned and all other relevant factors;
3. Also reaffirms that a United Nations preventive deployment and/or the establishment of a demilitarized zone should be undertaken in accordance with the provisions of the Charter of the United Nations, in particular its purposes and principles and other relevant principles of international law, also taking into account relevant General Assembly and Security Council resolutions;
4. Invites the competent organs of the United Nations, within their respective mandates, to consider implementing preventive deployment and/or the establishment of a demilitarized zone with the objective of preventing conflict and of promoting efforts to achieve the peaceful settlement of disputes, and to continue to examine practical, operational and financial aspects of such preventive deployment and demilitarized zones with a view to increasing their efficacy and effectiveness;

USE OF THE INTERNATIONAL COURT OF JUSTICE IN THE PEACEFUL SETTLEMENT OF DISPUTES

Emphasizing the role of the International Court of Justice under the Charter of the United Nations in the peaceful settlement of disputes,

1. Encourages States to consider making greater use of the International Court of Justice for the peaceful settlement of disputes;
2. Recommends that States consider the possibility of accepting the jurisdiction of the International Court of Justice, including through the dispute settlement clauses of multilateral treaties;
3. Notes that the use of chambers of the International Court of Justice for dealing with particular cases submitted to the Court by the parties is a means of providing increased use of the Court for the peaceful settlement of disputes;
4. Requests States to consider making, if possible on a regular basis, contributions to the Trust Fund of the Secretary-General to assist States in resolving their disputes through the International Court of Justice, and invites the Secretary-General to report periodically both on the financial status and the utilization of the Fund;
5. Recalls that the General Assembly or the Security Council may request the International Court of Justice to give an advisory opinion on any legal question, and that other organs of the United Nations and specialized agencies, which may at any time be so authorized by the General Assembly, may also request advisory opinions of the Court on legal questions arising within the scope of their activities;
6. Decides to keep under examination all the recommendations of the Secretary-General concerning the International Court of Justice, including those related to the use of the advisory competence of the Court;

SPECIAL ECONOMIC PROBLEMS ARISING FROM THE IMPLEMENTATION OF PREVENTIVE OR ENFORCEMENT MEASURES

Recalling Article 50 of the Charter of the United Nations, which entitles States that find themselves confronted with special economic problems arising from the carrying out of preventive or enforcement measures taken by the Security Council against any other State, to consult the Council with regard to a solution to those problems,

Recalling also the recommendation of the Secretary-General in his report entitled "An Agenda for Peace" that the Security Council devise a set of measures involving the financial institutions and other components of the United Nations system that can be put in place to insulate States from such difficulties and his view that such measures would be a matter of equity and a means of encouraging States to cooperate with decisions of the Council,

Recalling further the statement made on 30 December 1992 by the President of the Security Council, in which the Council expressed its determination to consider this matter further and invited the Secretary-General to consult with the heads of international financial institutions, other components of the United Nations system and Member States of the United Nations, and to report to the Council as early as possible,

Recalling its resolution 47/120 A entitled "An Agenda for Peace: preventive diplomacy and related matters", in which it decided to continue early in 1993 its examination of other recommendations contained in the report of the Secretary-General entitled "An Agenda for Peace", including implementation of the provisions of Article 50 of the Charter, in conformity with the Charter and taking into account the relevant developments and practices in the competent organs of the United Nations,

Stressing the importance of economic and other measures not involving the use of armed forces in maintaining international peace and security, in accordance with Article 41 of the Charter,

Recalling Article 49 of the Charter, which requires the Members of the United Nations to join in affording mutual assistance in carrying out the measures decided upon by the Security Council,

Noting that the implementation of Article 50 of the Charter has been addressed recently in several forums, including the

General Assembly and its subsidiary organs and the Security Council,

Recognizing that, in the conditions of economic interdependence that exist today, the implementation of preventive or enforcement measures under Chapter VII of the Charter against any State continues to create special economic problems for certain other States,

Recalling that Member States have engaged previously in consultations with bodies established by the Security Council regarding special economic problems confronted by them as a result of the implementation of preventive or enforcement measures against Iraq and the Federal Republic of Yugoslavia (Serbia and Montenegro),

Concerned that certain States continue to be confronted with adverse economic problems owing to the implementation of preventive and enforcement measures under Chapter VII of the Charter,

Recognizing the need for appropriate means to find solutions to these problems as soon as possible,

1. Decides to continue its examination of ways to implement Article 50 of the Charter of the United Nations, with a view to finding solutions to the special economic problems of other Member States when preventive or enforcement measures are decided upon by the Security Council against a State;
2. Invites the Security Council to consider what could be done within the United Nations system and involving international financial institutions with regard to solutions to the special economic problems of States arising from the carrying out of the measures imposed by the Council and to consider, inter alia, the following measures:

(a) Strengthening of the consultative process for studying, reporting on and suggesting solutions to the special economic problems, with a view to minimizing such economic problems through consultations with States adversely affected or, as appropriate, with States likely to be adversely affected as a result of their implementing the preventive or enforcement measures, as well as with the Secretary-General, the principal organs, programmes and agencies of the United Nations, and international financial institutions;

(b) Other measures, in consultation with Member States and, as appropriate, with international financial institutions, such as voluntary funds to provide assistance to States experiencing special economic problems arising from carrying out the measures imposed by the Security Council, additional credit lines, assistance for the promotion of exports of the affected countries, assistance for technical cooperation projects in such countries and/or assistance for the promotion of investment in the affected countries;

3. Also invites the committees of the Security Council and other bodies entrusted with the task of monitoring the implementation of preventive and enforcement measures to take into account, in discharging their mandates, the need to avoid unnecessary adverse consequences for other Member States, without prejudice to the effectiveness of such measures;
4. Requests the Secretary-General to report annually to the General Assembly on the implementation of Article 50 of the Charter;

POST-CONFLICT PEACE-BUILDING

Noting that post-conflict peace-building is a new and evolving concept,

Recognizing the need for sustained cooperative efforts by the United Nations to deal with the underlying economic, social, cultural and humanitarian causes and effects of conflicts in order to promote a durable foundation for peace,

Recalling the provisions of Article 55 of the Charter of the United Nations,

Recognizing also that the concept of post-conflict peace-building is aimed at the creation of a new environment to forestall the recurrence of conflicts,

Bearing in mind that each situation in which post-conflict peace-building may be undertaken is unique and therefore should be considered on a case-by-case basis,

Bearing in mind also that post-conflict peace-building should complement efforts at peacemaking and peace-keeping in order to consolidate peace and advance a sense of confidence and well-being among people and States,

1. Acknowledges the usefulness of the proposals of the Secretary-General contained in paragraphs 55 to 59 of his report entitled "An Agenda Peace", particularly in relation to the range of activities for post-conflict peace-building;
2. Emphasizes that post-conflict peace-building should be carried out in accordance with the Charter of the United Nations, in particular the principles of sovereign equality and political independence of States, territorial integrity, and non-intervention in matters that are essentially within the domestic jurisdiction of any State;
3. Recalls that each State has the right freely to choose and develop its political, social, economic and cultural systems;
4. Stresses that activities related to post-conflict peace-building should be carried out within a well-defined time-frame;
5. Also stresses that post-conflict peace-building be undertaken on the basis of agreements ending conflicts or reached after conflicts, or at the request of the Government or Governments concerned;
6. Emphasizes the need for measures to promote peace and cooperation among previously conflicting parties;
7. Stresses the need for coordinated action by relevant components of the United Nations system, including the contributions that the international financial institutions can make in the area of socio-economic development in post-conflict peace-building;

8. Also stresses the importance for post-conflict peace-building of contributions from diverse sources, including components of the United Nations system, regional organizations, Member States and non-governmental organizations;
9. Requests the Secretary-General to inform the General Assembly of requests relating to post-conflict peace-building by the Government or Governments concerned, or emanating from peace agreements ending conflicts or reached after conflicts by parties concerned;
10. Affirms its readiness to support, as appropriate, post-conflict peace-building;

COOPERATION WITH REGIONAL ARRANGEMENTS AND ORGANIZATIONS

Recognizing the importance of the role of regional organizations and arrangements in dealing with such matters relating to the maintenance of international peace and security as are appropriate for regional action, and the need to enhance, in this respect, cooperation between such organizations and arrangements and the United Nations,

Recalling Chapter VIII of the Charter of the United Nations and its acknowledgement of the role of regional arrangements and agencies in dealing with such matters relating to the maintenance of international peace and security as are appropriate for regional action, provided that such arrangements or agencies and their activities are consistent with the purposes and principles of the United Nations,

Taking into account the experience gained and the favourable results achieved by regional organizations in the peaceful settlement of disputes in different parts of the world,

1. Recognizes that regional organizations, arrangements and agencies can, in their fields of competence and in accordance with the Charter of the United Nations, make important contributions to the maintenance of international peace and security, preventive diplomacy, peacemaking, peacekeeping and post-conflict peace-building;

2. Encourages regional organizations, arrangements and agencies to consider, as appropriate, in their fields of competence, ways and means for promoting closer cooperation and coordination with the United Nations with the objective of contributing to the fulfilment of the purposes and principles of
3. Also encourages the Secretary-General to continue his efforts at promoting cooperation between the United Nations and regional organizations, arrangements and agencies, in accordance with the Charter;

SAFETY OF PERSONNEL

Recalling its resolution 47/72 of 14 December 1992 on protection of peace-keeping personnel, and all other relevant resolutions,

Bearing in mind the concern expressed by the Secretary-General over the safety of United Nations personnel in his report entitled "An Agenda for Peace",

Also recalling the relevant resolutions of the Security Council,

Taking note with appreciation of the statement made on 31 March 1993 by the President of the Security Council on the protection of United Nations forces and personnel,

Noting with appreciation the work done by the Special Committee on Peace-keeping Operations on the issue of the status and safety of United Nations peace-keeping personnel,

Gravely concerned about the growing number of fatalities and injuries among United Nations peace-keeping and other personnel resulting from deliberate hostile actions in dangerous areas of deployment,

1. Welcomes the report of the Secretary-General on the security of United Nations operations;
2. Decides to consider further steps to enhance the status and safety of United Nations personnel involved in United Nations operations, taking into account the need for concerted action by all relevant bodies of the United Nations in this regard.

2

Knowledge and Diplomacy

INTRODUCTION

Diplomatic knowledge consists of both information and other elements of knowledge. Perhaps it is true to say that diplomatic information, can be distinguished from all the other elements of diplomatic knowledge by whether it is recordable. If this is so then the best recorded form of diplomatic knowledge is the diplomatic information contained in Diplomatic Documents.

Much greater emphasis needs to be placed on primary sources of diplomatic knowledge: on the diplomatic document. Because of the increasing glut of information scholars, diplomats, international negotiators, international lawyers, international civil servants, journalists and other cognoscenti of international relations rely much more on commentaries, which are, by definition, secondary.

Moreover they are known to find themselves at a greater loss on how to acquire wider unrecorded diplomatic knowledge- if they are lucky enough to realize that they do not have it!

Since only recorded diplomatic information is normally accessible, (and not always, or all of it!), it is proposed therefore to develop a method which re-integrates the primary importance of the diplomatic document.

Starting from analysing the diplomatic document, diplomatic knowledge which is clearly more than the diplomatic information contained in the document itself can be gained. This method therefore not only re-asserts the primary importance of the diplomatic information in diplomatic documents but also leads to acquiring elements of unrecorded diplomatic knowledge.

First this can be done by dissecting or unpacking the diplomatic document itself, attributing clauses to their sponsors, be they domestic or international, and then drawing a balance of strategic, political, economic interests displayed. This is all carried out in a static time-frame. At a second level the time factor is introduced. In this dynamic dissection, the "diplomatic trail" of an international agreement is analysed. Diplomatic knowledge is thus undoubtedly enhanced.

Digitalization and information technology makes this method much more user-friendly, all the more imperative for a better understanding of international relations and diplomacy, as well as an essential teaching tool.

KNOWLEDGE, INFORMATION AND DIPLOMACY

Diplomats' knowledge differs from that of ordinary citizens. The diplomat's essential relationship to knowledge is access to other knowledge and to others' knowledge. It is about that other knowledge.

The diplomat must not only know his country's agenda. He must also know the agenda of the other country. Most importantly, however, he must identify and get to know very well which factors at both ends can be reliably used for his (country's) purposes. It is this third exercise which reveals the interaction between knowledge and diplomacy par excellence.

Too much diplomacy without enough knowledge may prove fatal. Too much knowledge with too little diplomacy may be disastrous. Discovering a judicious mix amounts to a basic survival kit for diplomats.

The types of knowledge the diplomat might want to access might be oral or written, public or confidential, lay or technical, past or present.

Since administrative matters became more complex, masses of technical material increasingly found their way into diplomatic documents. Technical appendices however, and the best knowledge of them, do not, have not and cannot replace diplomacy. It is the skilful juxtaposition of these technical chunks of knowledge which demonstrates the art of diplomacy.

Thus the diplomat's real intentions, motives, and strategy would not necessarily be on file at the Ministry! Moreover, the media coverage of diplomatic meetings might be even further afar from the diplomatic version of the truth contained in the official files.

A wealth of knowledge about diplomacy and diplomats' handling of knowledge is also maintained by way of oral tradition binding generations of diplomats together. Knowledge of this tradition sharpens the young diplomat's critical sense of trial and error.

Elements of the old and the new can be confirmed in numerous diplomats' biographies. But Autobiographies must be taken with a pinch of salt. Even official records may be glossed over. A particular Permanent Secretary's choice of which diplomatic documents to downgrade and which to highlight might not be totally disinterested. Peeling the gloss away from official documents is an essential preliminary to diplomatic analysis.

KNOWLEDGE AS INFORMATION

Knowledge is not only information. Information has the advantage of being recorded. Knowledge, in general, is not easily recorded. Knowledge as information enjoys another characteristic: it travels. However, even when recorded, knowledge as information does not flow unhindered in the real world.

The free flow of information is much more of an ideal than a true picture of reality. A number of obstacles exist. Some are easily surmounted. Others are more difficult and costly, if not impossible to overcome. Many are the obstacles which (still?) hinder the free flow of information universally.

This truth also applies to the free flow of information in the same nation state. Within the State this truth also applies to the Governmental Administrative apparatus itself. There is hardly a free flow of information within a bureaucracy: the mandarins know only too well that knowledge is power or influence at the very least, they do not part with any scrap of knowledge completely or all the time.

On an even more domestic level this truth is not unknown to apply within the same Ministry including the Foreign Ministry. Perhaps this is where this truth is at its strongest: between the very members of the same cabinet or secretariat or desk. Most paradoxically these are the diplomats entrusted with the UNESCO task of enshrining the principle of the free flow of information into an International Convention!

The management of knowledge as information in diplomacy can be illustrated quite succinctly. A clear example is the case of handling relations with the United Nations Organization and its Agencies.

Since its foundation the UN and its Agencies have developed a veritable international bureaucracy. Their numerous initiatives in their 50-year history produced volumes of paperwork. This demands much more than what a medium sized multilateral section in a medium sized foreign Ministry can manage.

However, some Foreign Ministries will insist on retaining total control of relations with all the branches of the UN. In these extreme cases, relations remain the Foreign Ministry's domain not only with the General Assembly and its Committees but also with the World Health Organization, the International Labour Organization, the Food and Agriculture Organization and the United Nations Education Science and Culture Organization to name a few.

At the other extreme a Foreign Ministry will have delegated or been slowly relieved of all these particular duties by the respective Health, Agriculture, Labour, or Education Ministries.

In reality a "modus vivendi" between the Foreign Ministry and the other ministries will have evolved somewhere in between these two extremes. Generally the Foreign Ministry will have kept control of what is political, though that might prove difficult to define sometimes; the Ministries controlling what is eminently theirs by subject matter and keeping the relevant files.

DIPLOMATIC DOCUMENTS.

Diplomacy could be circuitously defined as the activity of the diplomat. The focus of diplomacy is usually an international agreement, past, present or future. It need not be a written agreement, although it usually is.

The Vienna Convention on the Law of Treaties explicitly recognizes this definition of international agreements. This realistic admission helps to define the domain of diplomacy.

Diplomatic activity between one international written agreement and its successor is punctuated by a series of verbal agreements which, in turn, are built upon various exchanges contained in diplomatic documents.

Form has been known to pre-occupy some diplomats unduly. Form has also pre-occupied a number of scholars and writers about diplomacy.

In Sir Ernest Satow's classic work, "A Guide to Diplomatic Practice", diplomatic documents are categorized. Thus diplomatic documents could contain demands or offers as in a Memoir and in an Aide-Memoir, or in the more official Note Verbale, signed or unsigned, or in other diplomatic Notes. Once agreement is reached in part or in toto this is either implicit or explicitly stated as in an exchange of Notes Verbal constituting an international agreement.

The more manifest form of an agreement could be held to start with an agreement initialled between lower officials "ad referendum" to higher governmental authority. Diplomatic documents range in importance from the unofficial Proces Verbal of a meeting, to Protocols, to Treaties. Similarly, Sir Harold Nicholson's reference work on "Diplomacy" classifies diplomatic documents too.

Is a hierarchical order of diplomatic documents useful or necessary? By giving more or most importance to fully fledged treaties and the least importance to the modern "non-paper" a diplomatic primer for students is at hand. But is this enough?

This traditional method of assessment of diplomatic documents does not really much to knowledge. It does not amount to proper diplomatic analysis. It is superficial as it only treats diplomatic documents at face value. Students emerge all the poorer for it, obsessed with form for form's sake.

DISSECTING DIPLOMATIC DOCUMENTS

Instead, it is proposed to dissect diplomatic documents. This should enable students of diplomacy-as well as diplomats themselves-to sharpen their sense of diplomacy by developing analytical diplomatic talents. However greater the complexity of the data of their future cases these can be crunched better with these more mature analytical diplomatic talents.

Dissection of diplomatic documents can take place on a number of different levels. Dissection results open up more fruitful dimensions of analysis.

First the "balance of interests" approach. A diplomatic document concluded between two governments, say an international agreement of ten paragraphs, can be dissected by unpacking it into its substantive points.

This unfolding can then be developed further by attributing paternity to each of the various inputs into the treaty. Inputs may be whole Articles, paragraphs, clauses or sub-clauses of the agreement. They may also be side-letters, ancillary exchanges of Notes Verbale, Agreed Minutes of interpretation etc. Usually paternity corresponds to the interests of a particular government. Each input is thus tagged according to whose interest is best served by it. Which party secured, input by input, more plusses and least minuses, for its national interest?

The balance of interests is thus the result of a rough quantification of each side's score.

In trying to attribute points to the two sides then, not only will the number of clauses count. Further refinements of this diplomatic analysis are in order. Definitions and meanings of each input will have to be re-assessed.

It will be necessary to assess for example whether a favourably tagged clause were seen in one country to count for more than one clause in the given circumstances. In other words whether a degree of diplomatic ambiguity in meaning in a particular clause-or even a single word-gave it a different value in the two different countries.

See for example the concession of U.N. Scretary General Kofi Anan to Iraqi Deputy P.M. Tariq Aziz in para. 3 of the 23/2/98 Memorandum of Understanding that UNSCOM would respect the "dignity" of Iraq; a term which means much, much more in Arabic than in English.

This method of analysis might, at the limit, be totally irrelevant in say a treaty of unconditional surrender. There is hardly any "balance" of interests there. Without resorting to such far-fetched examples is this method of analysis useful in contemporary diplomacy?

There is hardly any balance of interests noticeable in a number of standard treaties. Take for example standard treaties on visa abolition, cultural and sports co-operation, and the like. When a standard treaty contains a clause or two bearing only one party's interest then there is a clear imbalance of interests. Indeed this provides the student with a starting point for this method of analysis.

PURSUING A "DIPLOMATIC TRAIL"

The Second level of analysis of diplomatic documents is not static. It is a dynamic analysis generated by pursuing the "diplomatic trail" of an international agreement.

The student will be asked to examine a National issue that overwhelmed his country's foreign policy agenda for example ten years ago. This could have been an international issue which festered for a number of years. It could even have reached crisis point before a diplomatic agreement settled the issue.

Students are invited to identify and follow the agreement's diplomatic trail. The diplomatic trail is tracked from the files and various related records kept internally in the Foreign Ministry.

As with a series of flashbacks in a film this method starts from the diplomatic agreement and moves backwards in time. By studying file after file on how each paragraph was developed and bargained for, precious diplomatic knowledge is gleaned.

Diplomatic levers are observed in action, at work, not in theory but as they were actually applied in this particular case-study. These observations will then constitute valid contributions to others' diplomatic knowledge too.

By going right back to the start of negotiations, the students' inside knowledge of their chosen National issue will be immensely improved.

By encouraging students to refer to the actual sources in their own Foreign Ministry Archives, gaps between folkloristic or media versions of the crisis and the real story and issues involved might be discerned much more clearly.

More importantly, the student will be accessing a wealth of diplomatic knowledge otherwise buried in the archives. Actual exchanges of diplomatic notes, the various memoranda presented or not, the proces-verbales of numerous diplomatic meetings, together with the rubrics-the marginal notes in the archive files-all leading up to the final international agreement are a hidden treasure of diplomatic knowledge for any student, but most particularly for that country's young diplomats.

The young diplomat will also be able to note whether parts of (and which parts of) that international agreement where developed properly or shoddily. This might be relevant to a corresponding exercise to discover whether parts of an agreement are more precarious than others, rendering perhaps the whole agreement unstable.

This method is also appropriate for analysing international resolutions. See for example the notorious U.N. Security Council 242 adopted unanimously on the "withdrawal of Israeli armed forces from territories occupied" after the 1967 war. As the French version had "the" territories, this encouraged the optimistic Palestinian interpretation that it included the 1948 territories too. Whether this ambiguity defuses or kindles a time-bomb remains a moot point.

It might also be possible and useful to identify the original motivations and factors causing certain clauses to be inserted into an international agreement and whether these were now redundant and superseded by events. Conversely interesting would be an analysis of why certain terms are found to be inconvenient and removed from a diplomatic document.

This is of utmost importance in the founding document, the establishment of wide-ranging long-term international initiatives. The European Union's "Euro-Med initiative" is a case in point.

Few if any analysts have been able to answer the fundamental question of why the security clauses the preliminary editions of the Euro-Med terms of reference were dramatically downscaled. Contrast the 1994 debate realistically emphasising the security dimension which is then whittled down in the communication of the E.C. Commission COM (95) 72 and finally disappears in the Council of Ministers mandate (10/4/1995).

Similarly useful would be to study whether meanings originally attributed to particular sections of the agreement (if not to the whole agreement itself) had changed by force of circumstance; whether the old meanings had been revalued or devalued by the new meanings evolved.

Other nuggets of diplomatic knowledge could be found in unutilised drafts of treaties or parts of them. They might have been discarded as too hot or because of domestic political rivalries, though still appropriate. Or they could have been abandoned out of neglect just because of changes of personnel or changes of circumstances.

Undoubtedly they remain invaluable if brought back into circulation as diplomatic knowledge for potential use. Similarly enlightening would be the commentaries or inputs received in correspondence from the Ambassadors and embassies involved directly.

DIGITALIZED KNOWLEDGE, INFORMATION AND DIPLOMACY

Digitalization has changed a lot of this, not everything, but a substantial number of critical matters have altered. some for the better others for worse. What has not changed is the need for diplomacy, for its style, its human factor.

In other words digitalization, like other historic advances in transport and communications, is yet another tool in the diplomat's arsenal, not his replacement.

In dissecting a diplomatic document in digitalized form at the Ministry, the paternity exercise is made simpler through hyperlinks. The score of each side in the simple two party negotiating model where all inputs clear instantly into the final agreement is thus more easily arrived at.

Standard treaties. Databases have already been developed for them thus permitting diplomats to avoid the task of re-inventing the wheel. They only have to add the few relevant, if any, additions or amendments to make the particular treaty as tailor-made to their country at that particular moment in time as possible.

These "standard treaties" are unlike and in sharp contrast to totally customized treaties arising out of a particular crisis. [See the Exchange of Letters between Tariq Aziz and Kofi Anan 13/11/1998 and pursue its "diplomatic trail".]

A. Following the "diplomatic trail" in digitalized form is also made easier. In the more complex model where the two parties take time, rack their adviser's brains and strain the general public's tolerance, disturb NGO's patience and wreck MNC's cash-flows. Here all these inputs are available, can be accessed quicker, if not immediately, and given their relative weighting much more precisely than before. This is a research luxury compared to the previous position where one would have had to compare different files kept in different Ministries or Libraries.

At the more textual level, the trade-offs occurring between clauses as the final agreement is developed can be recorded more easily and influencing factors noted. Also, compromise formulae can be shown to have been derived from their parent clauses, according to or even against given written advice as the case may be.

Organization

Digitalization with its networking possibilities has vastly helped to overcome the inter-ministerial, inter-departmental or inter-agency problem. Where is the file? Who has the file? are (should) no longer remain a problem. Modern Foreign Ministries supervise other ministries' conduct of foreign relations with e.g. U.N. Agencies by dividing responsibilities on a regulator/operator basis.

The Human Factor

However it remains doubtful to what extent digitalization will be a perfect substitute for the human factor. Style, to put it mildly, is rather cramped in digital form. On the other hand can cyber-sex be too far from boudoir diplomacy? Influence, charm, bloody-mindedness, bluff, are factors not easily conveyed in full on the internet, though approximations have been recorded already.

Rubrics

The internal Preliminary diplomatic discussions by e-mail now recorded, and immediately available, are a further rich source of diplomatic knowledge. Their instant hyper-links replace the value of rubrics in old files. Moreover the advantage of opening up a draft or final diplomatic document for comments and discussion between the diplomatic community (existing and retired) are a boon for distance learning via the internet. They will be a further recorded source of diplomatic knowledge.

To conclude, the method sketched only in outline here demands further development to increase the opportunities for Diplomatic solutions as alternatives to the use of force.

3

Security Sector Reform: Defence Diplomacy

INTRODUCTION

The aftermath of the Cold War and the tragic events of 9/11 have forced western nations to re-examine the principles according to which they manage the international environment. The conflicts in the Balkans during the 1990s taught that ethnic hatred can still be a far stronger motivator than reason. 9/11 taught North America that its once-vaunted security is far more vulnerable than it had thought. In addition, the world has also had to come to grips with a variety of so-called "non-traditional" security threats, including environmental degradation, global warming, potential pandemics, failed states, transnational crime, etc.

When George F. Kennan penned "the Long Telegram" in 1946(1) outlining his views on how best to meet the growing Soviet threat, he realized that military might, although essential, would not in itself prove sufficient. While Moscow was "impervious to the logic of reason" but "highly sensitive to the logic of force," in the long run the principal tools required were to be economic, political, cultural and diplomatic. In order to be effective, the strategy of "containment" would have to comprise much more than military superiority.

Kennan proved the major architect of U.S. foreign policy during the Cold War. It was because of his profound understanding of the complexity of the strategic environment, and the views of others like him, that the post-World War II period saw the development and growth of a variety of multilateral institutions. Along with a strong military, these institutions helped the West confront the moral and strategic challenges of the Cold War.

A NEW DISCOURSE

Today, the world faces equally serious challenges and has begun to develop "appropriate" mechanisms and concepts for dealing with them. Just as Kennan and his generation of visionaries understood, our generation too will need to use a mixture of military and civilian means. Indeed, we have adopted a discourse informed by a broader and more subtle set of concepts than previously possible. We speak of human security, capacity building, the sanctity of the individual, multilateralism, and the need to hold the authority of states themselves accountable.

It is no longer accepted that the pursuit of genuine security for human beings, as individuals, is necessarily subversive of the foundations of international society. Intervention in the behaviour of states to protect individuals is now deemed an accepted principle of international relations. In fact, Rwanda has taught that it can, at times, be an obligation. These views entail far more than the musings of disaffected intellectuals and idealists. They are attempts to come to terms with a reality that is not fully comprehended or accepted. What is certain is that today "security" means coming to terms with forms of domination and insecurities that had long been ignored or sacrificed on the altar of "realpolitik."

The primacy of the state in strategic thinking permitted a gap to develop between the meaning of the term security as applied to individuals and its meaning for the state. For security to make sense at the international level, it must make sense at the basic level of the individual human being. Thus, attempts to understand the complexities of security threats need to look not only to the perceptions and histories of statesmen and diplomats; they also need to take into account the experiences of those rendered insecure by the present world order. While developed nations continue to speak of the importance of foreign aid, they now also accept the fact that the principle of state sovereignty can be breached in order to save those victimized by the state and its agents. Human security, first and foremost, entails physical security-the basic security of the individual. Without such security, foreign aid remains little more than a cheap meal on the road to continuing despair.

The language of realpolitik is slowly giving way to the more nuanced and humanitarian principles of "soft" power and human security. This new lexicon has enabled the West to widen its horizons and to put on the table security concerns formerly relegated to subsidiary, if any, relevance. It is, in part, because of this rethinking that we can seriously ponder the implications of a variety of so-called non-traditional threats for our long-term "common security" interests.

Needless to say, attempts to deal with the dislocations of the post-Cold War era have not been particularly successful. When looking at the failures of Rwanda and Somalia, the continuing struggle in Afghanistan, failed states like Haiti, and the fiasco in Iraq, western nations are led to wonder whether events have run ahead of our understanding or whether we simply lack the institutional capabilities for dealing with them. If our understanding is such that we cannot really grasp what is transpiring, then our ability either to construct or to restructure relevant institutions will be seriously hampered.

A NEW MISSION

Defence diplomacy is one of the organizing principles used to help the West come to terms with the new international security environment. It has become an increasingly important component of the "whole of government" approach, and in the United Kingdom defence diplomacy has been made one of the military's eight "defence missions." The United Kingdom began work on security sector reform in 2000. Early in the process, planners realized that new policy frameworks would be required if Britain's efforts in conflict prevention were to be effective. While relevant ministries drew up policy papers, it soon became clear that a joint approach to security sector reform required a common policy framework. The government went on to set up a security sector reform policy committee and an informal interdepartmental strategy was then developed.

Planners also created two interdepartmental funding pools, the Global Conflict Prevention Pool and the Africa Conflict Prevention Pool, in order to improve the United Kingdom's conflict prevention policy and effectiveness through joint analysis, long-term strategies, and improved coordination with international partners. Much of the U.K. security sector reform work is financed through these two pools, which receive both overseas development assistance (ODA) and non-ODA funds for programs based on agreed Ministry of Defence (MOD), Department for International Development (DFID) and Foreign and Commonwealth Office (FCO) strategies. In order to promote stronger adherence to the common framework, the U.K. Treasury contributes additional resources to the pools beyond those committed by the foregoing ministries. The Netherlands has also established a "Stability Fund" in order to provide for coherence through pooled funding, as well as an integrated policy-driven approach to security and development issues.

The consensus seems to be that U.K. interventions have proven more effective when based on a shared analysis of a conflict and a joint response. Such an approach also makes for a better synergy between government policy and operations. The conflict prevention pool approach has also been helpful in giving the Treasury a better understanding of the issues faced by the departments on the ground. Both pools have a peacekeeping and a program component. The peacekeeping component covers the United Kingdom's assessed and voluntary contributions to international peacekeeping and related operations. The program component is further subdivided into country or regional strategies and thematic strategies, like security sector reform. A parliamentary vote decides the settlement figure given to pools, which incorporates an extra top-up amount to encourage interdepartmental collaboration.

Money contributed to the Global Pool by the four departments is managed by the FCO, and funding for the Africa Pool is managed by the DFID. Once activities are agreed upon, they are examined by the DFID for ODA eligibility. The strength of this approach lies in the fact that "distinct roles remain for development and security sectors, [while] working under one overarching security system reform policy in a coherent way with relevant departments." Also, under such a scheme, development agencies can better comprehend and have an increased impact on security-related issues when they are vital for development goals. It is important that development agencies establish effective partnerships with their defence and security counterparts, especially when operating in areas where their effectiveness might be restricted because of security issues.

It is then easy to see how defence diplomacy fits into the overall policy framework. Its basic aim is "to provide forces to meet the varied activities undertaken by the MOD to dispel hostility, build and maintain trust and assist in the development of democratically accountable armed forces, thereby making a significant contribution to conflict prevention and resolution." Included in the mission are a number of military tasks, e.g.:

- arms control, non-proliferation, and confidence and security building measures;
- outreach (advice and assistance to countries);
- other defence diplomacy activities.

Recognizing the importance of security sector reform and defence diplomacy, the United Kingdom also established what is called the Defence Advisory Team (DAT) in 2001. Today the DAT provides advice and assistance on governance and civil military relations, defence reviews, defence organization, force structures, procurement and logistics, and change management, financial and human resource management and development in the defence sector. Since the DAT's inception, the U.K. government has significantly increased its funding.

The British approach to security reform and defence diplomacy might prove a useful model for Canadian policy makers. The integrated policy framework and pooled funds provide an important degree of flexibility and efficiency when addressing security concerns. The type of approach envisaged would, of course, require both cooperation and coordination among several government departments and agencies, including the Canadian International Development Agency, the Department of National Defence, Foreign Affairs Canada,

Finance, and the Privy Council Office. Given Canada's ongoing commitment to peacekeeping and the 3D approach (Defence, Diplomacy, and Development), policy makers might do well to look at the British model as a way of organizing our "whole of government" approach to security matters.

ACTIVE DIPLOMACY FOR A CHANGING WORLD: THE UK'S INTERNATIONAL PRIORITIES

In a world of global communications and markets, our security and prosperity depend more than ever on what happens in other parts of the world. We have to be active internationally to shape global developments for the benefit of our citizens and because we are committed to a safer, more just and prosperous world.

We live in a period of rapid change-we have moved from the relative certainties of the Cold War to a more complex and uncertain world. More issues are cutting across national boundaries and new global actors are emerging. Our open economy, diverse society and international responsibilities offer opportunities in the next decade, working with others, to shape the future for our citizens and the world.

Active diplomacy for a changing world-the UK's International Priorities updates the Strategy published by the FCO in 2003. It identifies the trends we expect to shape the world in the next 10 years. It sets out the UK's role in the international system and our main partnerships. Based on this analysis it identifies the strategic international priorities for the Government as a whole. And it describes the FCO's role in pursuing them.

THE WORLD IN THE NEXT TEN YEARS

We cannot know the future, but we can prepare for it and so help to influence it. Based on extensive consultation with partners around Government and beyond, some of the broad trends and their implications for the UK outlined in the White Paper are:

The gathering pace of globalisation: the flow of people, goods, money and knowledge and the rapid growth of Asia are driving globalisation. This presents new opportunities and risks.

How countries react to these will have important implications for us. We must adapt our economy, work with others to support global economic openness and integrate new powers fully into the international system. We must also help build effective states able to provide security, opportunity and justice for their citizens.

Pressures on natural resources: rising economic demand, population growth and climate change are putting the world's natural resources under new pressure. We will need to manage increasing competition for energy in particular, through more effective markets, cleaner technologies and dialogue between major consumers and producers.

An uncertain security environment: terrorism will remain the primary security threat to the UK. New proliferation pressures make the next 10 years critical in the fight to control the spread of nuclear, biological and chemical weapons. There will be new risks to fragile states and uncertainty about developments in key parts of the Middle East, Africa and Asia. Building stronger relationships with the Muslim world and countering the message of extremists will be a top priority.

Our key conclusions are:

we must be engaged around the globe to shape developments at a time of rapid change

we must strengthen our partnerships and international institutions to build a future based on common values and interests

closer co-operation across Government and with others will be essential as the impact at home of events overseas continues to grow.

WORKING WITH OTHERS

No country can tackle this agenda alone. So we have to work with others in the UN, the EU, the G8, NATO, the Commonwealth and other groups. We must work to reform international institutions in the face of new challenges. Our most important partnerships will remain within the EU, and with the United States. We will also need to build on our strategic relationships with China, India, Japan, Russia and others. Relations between these major and developing actors will influence the international system for the next decade and beyond and set the context in which we will promote our interests and values. As the links between domestic and international issues grow, co-operation between Departments of Government and with the private sector, NGOs and the public must deepen.

INTERNATIONAL PRIORITIES FOR THE UK

Based on our analysis, we have identified the following nine strategic international priorities for the UK over the next five to ten years. They underline how closely domestic and international policies are now linked.

making the world safer from global terrorism and weapons of mass destruction

reducing the harm to the UK from international crime, including drug trafficking, people smuggling and money laundering

preventing and resolving conflict through a strong international system

building an effective and globally competitive EU in a secure neighbourhood

supporting the UK economy and business through an open and expanding global economy, science and innovation and secure energy supplies

promoting sustainable development and poverty reduction underpinned by human rights, democracy, good governance and protection of the environment

managing migration and combating illegal immigration

delivering high-quality support for British nationals abroad, in normal times and in crises

ensuring the security and good governance of the UK's Overseas Territories

Role of the FCO

The FCO is a network of people working in the UK and in over 250 diplomatic posts abroad. We have a total staff of around 16,000, of whom 6,000 are recruited in the UK and 10,000 recruited overseas. Our purpose is to work for UK interests in a safe, just and prosperous world. To do that we:

develop and deliver the Government's international policies

identify and influence developments overseas which affect the UK

provide consular, visa and commercial services to British nationals, business and others

maintain a global network of Posts and work closely with our partners in the rest of Government to pursue our priorities.

Our role is not to report on events or pursue good relations for their own sake. It is to exercise judgement and influence in order to shape the future for the benefit of our citizens and others. To do so, we must be engaged on the ground with the knowledge, experience and skills to effect change.

Our network of Posts must continue to adapt to new opportunities and risks-moving resources to priorities in Asia and the Middle East; tackling issues such as conflict, energy security or economic and political reform in key regions; developing rapid deployment teams for crisis response; using information and communication technology to deliver better services and manage the network more flexibly.

Worldwide Services to British Nationals

International travel by British nationals for business and leisure continues to rise. Providing high quality services to the public and businesses around the world is a core function of the FCO and as important as anything else we do. For most people, these services are the part of the FCO's work that they experience most directly. Around 2,000 staff are engaged in our visa operations, and around 1,000 on consular services. In total, over a quarter of our staff worldwide work directly in service delivery. High quality support to British nationals abroad is now a strategic priority in its own right, reflecting the importance the UK public and we attach to it.

More Open, Flexible and Diverse

The FCO needs to adapt to the challenges of the 21st century. Delivering services, influencing others and shaping change needs a flexible and targeted diplomatic network. The strategic priorities provide the framework for deploying our efforts as resources remain tight and demand for our services grows.

We will build on our core strengths-regional expertise, negotiating, communicating, language and influencing skills and a strong tradition of service. We will develop further the specialist, management and finance skills needed to run a complex and diverse organisation and provide the quality services our citizens expect. And we will draw on the talent of people of different backgrounds, better reflecting the country we represent.

PREVENTIVE DIPLOMACY AND PEACEKEEPING

Since the termination of the Cold War and the resulting alterations in the global and regional power balances, the world has witnessed a proliferation of low intensity conflicts. The international response, mainly via the United Nations, has been to promote preventive diplomacy and, in a number of cases, to implement peacekeeping operations. This new world order trend is obviously a most welcome and positive development. Through peacekeeping, military assets that have been originally designed and deployed to destroy human life, are now being used, albeit on a limited scale, to prevent conflict and to save lives. The peacekeeping revolution is a significant step towards increased human co-operation and the development of a functional international society. Although peacekeeping operations may require significant commitments on the part of participating states, specifically the willingness to accept financial costs and casualties, all governments should seriously consider taking part in these operations in the interest of promoting international and regional stability.

Post-Cold War conflicts may be largely divided into two categories. The first category includes civil wars caused by long standing historical differences, or new nationalism. The second category, which dominates on the African continent, are conflicts based on ethnic, national or religious divisions. Africa is additionally affected by a complex array of problems which have not been remedied over the last three decades. Many problems can be traced to colonialism, while other difficulties are part of the socio-political systems which have evolved in the post-colonial era.3 The specific nature of each dispute consequently requires appropriate responses in order to limit or to prevent conflict.

A great deal has been written on both preventive diplomacy and peacekeeping, and an increasing number of conferences have been held to address these issues in recent years. This intellectual process, while in some cases far removed from the reality of international diplomacy and military operational activity, is to be welcomed as a way of further promoting the use of diplomacy and war machinery to serve peaceful and positive ends. Research in the field of peacekeeping has focused on a wide range of issues and, as is the fashion in the nineties, has attracted a large and impressive academic following. Regrettably, much of this research has concentrated on what is theoretically desirable, while the political and practically possible has been neglected. This approach has promoted enormous expectations of the UN, which clearly cannot be met.

In the African context, South Africa has been identified by many observers as the one state able to execute effective peacekeeping operations on the continent. On paper, South Africa's military capabilities appear impressive, but in reality there are many impediments to a major role for the South African National Defence Force (SANDF) in peacekeeping. However, these impediments are not unique to South Africa and apply to all democratic countries. There are a number of central issues which the promoters and supporters of preventive diplomacy and peacekeeping have not paid sufficient attention to in their analyses.

KEYS FOR SUCCESS

The four important issues which have not received adequate attention by peace operations studies and which are of critical importance to any government contemplating involvement in preventive diplomacy or peacekeeping are:

- early warning and the early response to a crisis-the key to preventive diplomacy;
- adequate financial support for peacekeeping;
- an accurate assessment of casualty tolerance in peacekeeping operations; and
- sufficient information for successful peacekeeping.

The above issues are fundamental to any political leader's decision-making process. Without dealing adequately with these issues, no decision-maker can realistically be expected to make a major contribution to crisis diplomacy, or to undertake an even more risky peacekeeping operation.

EARLY WARNING AND PREVENTIVE DIPLOMACY

The idea of 'early warning' as "information that can provide a timely alert to potential conflicts" has been emphasised by a number of scholars as an important component in conflict resolution.4 In the African context, the Organisation of African Unity (OAU) has sought to develop an effective early warning system in an effort to deal with continental conflict. The OAU Secretary-General appears to favour a system which would provide sufficient information of an impending inter-state conflict, or internal political crisis. Once the problem has been tabled at the OAU, a high-level mediation mission can be mandated to initiate discussions with the objective of resolving the crisis.

Any successful early warning system should involve the synthesis of a range of information inputs from different sources, including governments, non-government organisations (NGOs), academic and research institutions.

By implication, any early warning system or activity may be perceived to be infringing on a state's sovereignty and could be rejected as an unwelcome form of foreign intervention. Nevertheless, crisis management and resolution have the best chance of success if action is taken early. A continental early warning system, as proposed by the OAU is extremely ambitious and is unlikely to be successful in the short term. The OAU's

Conflict Management Centre (CMC) in Addis Ababa is a major step towards the prevention of conflict in Africa, but lacks the funding and resources to provide an effective continental service. Rather, individual African countries, armed with sufficient early warning information, should be able to initiate regional crisis diplomacy, while the OAU mobilises broader support. The OAU's 1993 resolution on Conflict Prevention, Management and Resolution serves as the foundation and guiding light for preventive diplomacy on the African continent, but the difficulties in mobilising sufficient support for speedy action necessitates a more streamlined procedure.

In the former UN Secretary-General's An Agenda for Peace, member states were asked to mobilise regional organisations and actors in co-operation with the UN to lighten the burden of peacekeeping.5 The OAU Early Warning Seminar, held in January 1996, acknowledged the importance of the 'sub-regional level' in early warning and preventive diplomacy processes.6 A multinational organisation located far from the crisis area can never compete with the speed and co-ordination of a national government. Former UN Secretary-General Boutros-Ghali had plans to abdicate some or all of the UN's peacekeeping functions to regional organisations. In November 1996, the UN's Joint Inspection Unit (JIU) indicated that there was a need for the UN to find partners "who would share responsibilities in collective security." In addition, the JIU study suggested that regional organisations "should be the first port of call for the prevention and pacific settlement of local disputes."7 There is a growing international consensus that conflicts could more easily be prevented or resolved through regional initiatives.

A recent British proposal to the UN on conflict prevention and peacekeeping in Africa has stressed that early warning is vital for successful preventive action.8 In most cases, especially conflicts in Africa over the last few years, there is no shortage of information indicating an impending crisis. However, the complex causes of conflict and the difficulty of processing and analysing different pieces of information require a co-ordinated and concentrated intelligence effort. Moreover, the sharing of processed information among all potential peace operation participants is a necessity for a timely and appropriate response. The UN, as well as its specialised agencies, should improve their information collection, analysis and distribution capabilities. Specifically, real time information should be readily available to the OAU headquarters, supplied by the UN and available to all OAU members involved in any regional peace operation.

In support of international efforts to provide information for preventive diplomacy, individual states should allocate intelligence assets for early warning. Indications and warning (I&W) or 'warning intelligence' are based on an interdisciplinary approach incorporating current, estimative intelligence with broader political, historical and geographical analyses. The warning intelligence process results in the production of an accurate warning statement for decision-makers. The peace operation warning process, however, requires some modification to the traditional approach of attempting to identify and predict possible surprise attacks by regional or ideological opponents.9 Traditionally, the raison d'être of an early warning system was to ensure that the nation's decision-makers were not surprised by an enemy attack.

The peace operations early warning system requires a different approach with less emphasis on direct threat analysis. In order to respond adequately to a regional crisis, decision-makers require strategic warning and tactical warning. Strategic warning ensures that the decision-makers have a clear overall picture and sufficient quality time to make the necessary decision. Strategic warning should provide decision-makers with regular updates on regional developments with specific emphasis on the potential for internal or inter-state conflict, thereby ensuring an opportunity to prepare effectively for a decisive peace support intervention. Tactical warning requires more detailed and specific information for the decision-maker willing to commit a direct response. In this context, the leaders of the conflicting parties, as well as the central issues in dispute should be identified and analysed in detail. Psychological and biographical profiles of the leaders concerned should be provided along with possible diplomatic solutions. Tactical warning should also provide the decision-maker with a number of options which could be pursued if preventive diplomacy is to be initiated.

States should allocate key defence and intelligence assets to the prediction of conflict and thereby provide the means for an early settlement. The warning analyst should be trained to think in terms of probabilities, predictions and possible short term courses of action. The goal is to discern the intentions of major players in any potential regional conflict. Military and other reconnaissance satellites should be more directly used in providing early warning and support for diplomacy. For example, Russia's earth observation satellite, the Resurs-F3 is capable of delivering film negatives of 2,2 metre in diameter.

Images, costing between $3 000 and $5 000, would be adequate to identify the movement of troops, or refugees. The United States Air Force white paper entitled Global Presence 1995, outlined the US' ability to maintain 'virtual' presence via space-based and air-breathing reconnaissance systems along with other information gathering technologies. The use of these technologies to support preventive diplomacy, rather than simply to promote the national interests of the US, would be a major contribution to conflict resolution. The mobilisation of satellite observation platforms for peace operations could be decisive in empowering early warning organisations. Last year, then US Defence Secretary William Perry undertook to provide Israel with near real time satellite early warning information from Colorado Springs via secure US military downlink stations in Europe. A similar service, with the emphasis on information for preventive diplomacy, would be extremely useful for the UN and OAU. Details on the positioning, or movement of military forces combined with other open sources of information may be the key in preventing the initial outbreak of conflict and accompanying loss of life. At the same time, any early warning system should respect the sovereign equality and territorial integrity of all states.

The key factor in the success of any early warning system is an early response, not simply the ability to identify an impending problem: in other words, the earliest possible application of preventive diplomacy. The former UN Secretary-

General defined preventive diplomacy as "the action required to prevent existing disputes from escalating into conflict and to limit the spread of the latter when they occur." The method of choice for preventive diplomacy is based on intensive 'shuttle diplomacy' to organise one-to-one meetings with all stakeholders. In addition, the involvement and support of regional leaders is clearly important for the success of such an exercise. The institution of preventive diplomacy early in 1994 in response to the growing political instability in Lesotho, serves as a useful model for this form of activity.

The co-ordination of a regional initiative combined with a rapid response to an impending crisis were the keys to success. Moreover, the willingness of the protagonists to accept external intervention cannot be overemphasised. In the ideal case, regional crisis negotiators should be invited, rather than impose themselves, to lead negotiations for a peaceful diplomatic settlement. Events preceding the Rwandan crisis of April-June 1994 provided extensive evidence of an impending outbreak of violence. For more than a year prior to the eruption of the crisis on 6 April 1994, the increasing tension and violence in the country pointed towards a disaster. There is strong evidence to suggest that the UN was in possession of information indicating an impending outbreak of major conflict. The failure to respond appropriately and speedily to early warning information allowed the genocide to occur. The spark of the recent Zairian crisis occurred on 7 October 1996 when the deputy governor of Zaire's South Kivu province demanded that the 300 000 strong Banyamulenge community (ethnic Tutsis) leave Zaire within a week, or "be hunted down as rebels."

Within fourteen days, serious conflict erupted between the Banyamulenge and Zairian troops leading to the flight of over 250 000 refugees into Zaire. It took almost one month before an emergency summit was held to discuss the crisis. By this time, the refugees were faced with severe problems and the conflict had escalated significantly. An effective early warning system should have been able to warn of the impending conflict and should have facilitated the launch of a diplomatic initiative before the crisis began on 7 October 1996, or immediately thereafter.

Thus, the appropriate standby arrangement for crisis management and resolution are experienced and respected 'shuttle diplomats', supported by the necessary secretariat and rapid transport. Additional requirements include satellite telephones, IT support, data communication systems, along with the necessary technical skills to manage a complex negotiation process. In this context, South Africa could play a leading role on the African continent. South African diplomats, complemented by President Mandela's immense prestige, along with the necessary secretarial personnel and executive aircraft could provide the means for African solutions to continental conflict without the intrusion of external powers.

THE FINANCIAL COSTS OF PEACEKEEPING

Preventive diplomacy should always be the chosen option for resolving a crisis. However, if diplomacy is insufficient, a peacekeeping operation is the next best option. Peacekeeping presents a range of different problems, the first of which is finding the necessary funds to finance the operation. As a consequence of growing scepticism with regard to the effectiveness of peacekeeping operations, the UN has been forced to reduce its peacekeeping budget. This marks an unfortunate reversal of an earlier trend. The UN's peacekeeping budget increased from $379 million in 1990 to a high of $3,5 billion in 1994. However, 1995 saw a decrease to $3,2 billion, while 1996 recorded the lowest expenditure in five years at $1,3 billion. In addition, the number of UN peacekeepers have also shown a marked decrease from 65 000 in 1995 to 25 600 at the end of 1996. The number of peacekeeping missions have decreased from 22 in 1994 to only 16. The UN's new Secretary-General, Kofi Annan, has suggested that "peacekeeping as a primary activity of the United Nations will not end." However, the negative trend in peacekeeping missions, deployment and spending suggests that a number of critical issues need to be reviewed before a new wave of hopefully more successful peacekeeping initiatives can be undertaken.

The cash crisis for the UN, with a budget deficit of $2,3 billion in unpaid dues, undermines the ability of the organisation to continue as the world's leading peacekeeper. Moreover, the

UN cannot settle the $1 billion debt owed to 81 member states which provided troops and equipment for operations during 1996. Understandably, member states are more and more reluctant to participate in UN operations because of the high costs involved. At the end of 1996, the UN owed Pakistan $67 million and India $58 million for their contributions to peacekeeping.

Former UN Secretary-General Boutros-Ghali confirmed that some member states refused to take part in future operations until they were paid. Boutros-Ghali summarised the problem before the UN Security Council in 1996 saying, "You give me a mandate for a peacekeeping mission. But you don't give me the troops and the money I need to implement that mandate."

The UN plan to establish a standby force intended to accelerate the deployment of forces to trouble spots, has only met with five positive responses from its 185 members. The standby agreement is designed to ensure the rapid deployment of a significant number of troops to fill the three to six-month gap between the UN authorisation of a peacekeeping mission and full deployment. The North Atlantic Treaty Organisation's (NATO) take-over of the UN's peacekeeping operation in Bosnia suggests that peacekeeping may move increasingly towards control by regional organisations which have the ability to finance such operations.

The most costly UN peacekeeping operation was that of Somalia which totalled $1,6 billion. The Somali experience has provided an important lesson for all potential African peacekeeping missions. Major operational challenges in Somalia were posed by problems relating to geography, transportation and the complex political system.

The colonial division of Africa has ensured that peacekeepers on the continent will always face major political complexities. Africa's artificial political borders, combined with decades of colonial manipulation and economic exploitation, guarantee that the continent's political jigsaw will provide serious and expensive challenges for peacekeepers. The lack of infrastructural development and the political intractability of most African conflicts confirm that the financial cost for peacekeeping on this continent will always be high.

The British experience in Bosnia supports the contention that peacekeeping operations tend to cost more than originally planned. The cost of the British contribution to NATO's Implementation Force (IFOR) in 1996 amounted to £300 million. This was above and beyond the cost of sustaining the deployed forces in home bases. During the 1995/96 financial year the cost of involvement was carried by the Ministry of Defence. Over the period 1992-1995 of the United Nations Protection Force's (UNPROFOR) deployment, the Ministry of Defence was reimbursed by the Foreign and Commonwealth Office (FCO). The FCO then began to lobby the UN to recover the costs of the British military participation. The Ministry of Defence expressed a concern that IFOR expenditures should not undermine defence expenditure as a whole. Moreover, it was pointed out that it was extremely difficult to predict how much would be spent on peacekeeping. The Ministry's suggested solution to the problem was to include a "substantial contingency element" within the defence budget earmarked for peacekeeping which would be returned to the Treasury if not used. The British deployment in Bosnia also highlighted the need for a substantial logistic operation. Planning for the mission assumed that participants would provide their own "national stove-pipes" to support their forces. The British supply operation makes extensive use of the port of Split in Croatia. The Royal Logistics Corps (RLC) has been under pressure to meet approximately 1000 daily requests for supplies. The logistics system is based on the concept of 'just in time' thus supplies have to be flown in daily. The costs of the operation are extremely high and require a complex transportation and communication system.

In March this year, the US Department of Defence indicated that a further $2,1 billion was required to pay for peacekeeping operations in Bosnia. Secretary of Defence William Cohen indicated that if the funds were not made available, the military would be forced to scale back on training and other programmes. Under rules set up by the Republican-controlled Congress, money for any emergency must be offset by cuts in existing defence programmes to avoid adding to the national debt. Funds earmarked for long term procurement and weapons purchasing programmes are likely to be used to pay for the Bosnia operation. In 1992, former Secretary of Defence Les Aspin proposed the establishment of a separate fund of $300 million (Contributions for International Peacekeeping and Peace Enforcement Activities fund) intended to assist other countries to participate in peacekeeping and to minimise budgetary problems for the US. The proposal was rejected as "yet another raid" on the Pentagon budget.

At the first meeting of the Chiefs of Staff of the Member States of the Central Organ of the OAU held in Addis Ababa during early June 1996, the issue of peacekeeping and methods to finance these operations were raised but not discussed in any detail. A wide range of other issues were dealt with and some excellent proposals were laid on the table, but funding received only minor coverage. The official report on the meeting indicated that financing peacekeeping operations was "of a policy nature and should, therefore, be left to the policy makers." Some participants suggested that the UN should be responsible for funding. It was concluded that this issue, as well as logistic problems, would be dealt with by the proposed group of experts to be called the Budget and Logistics Committee. At the same time, there was general acceptance that African states, individually or collectively, would have extreme difficulty in providing the necessary resources for any major peacekeeping operation.

Funding for peacekeeping is a critical issue for any government. The potential costs of such operations and the massive logistic commitment for long distance operations are key factors in any decision-making process. Developing countries, South Africa included, cannot rush into any peacekeeping venture without careful consideration of the financial implications. South African involvement in a Somalia type operation could consume between one third and one half of the nation's annual defence budget. The solution for the financial crisis with Africa's peacekeeping may lie in the establishment of a peacekeeping bank, set up by donors from the developed world, who could lend or grant money to peacekeeping participants. The peacekeeping bank would be advised by military experts as to the feasibility of any operation and would require reasonable guarantees of success before making loans or donations. The successful peacekeeper would be rewarded with lower interest rate payments or the conversion of loans into grants.

CASUALTY TOLERANCE

A clear estimate of the number of casualties which would be acceptable is essential for any military operation, peacekeeping included. The Vietnam war indicated the limits of public support in the face of mounting casualties. Between 1961 and 1973, 47 244 American troops were killed and over 300 000 wounded. The unacceptable losses had a major impact on decision-makers and popular support for the war in general. The US Government discovered that public and congressional support for any military operation was essential. Colonel Harry Summers addresses this issue in his recent book The New World Strategy, and concludes that, "[i]f the war in Vietnam proved nothing else, it proved the American people could not be excluded from the strategic equation." In 1984, US Secretary of Defence Caspar Weinberger outlined the Weinberger Doctrine, emphasising that "before the US commits combat forces abroad, there must be some reasonable assurance we will have the support of the American people and their elected representatives in the Congress." High casualties will erode public support and are therefore important in the decision-making process. This factor, the so-called 'sixth test' of the Weinberger Doctrine is applicable to any democratic country considering the deployment of military force for peacekeeping.

The number of casualties any government can tolerate in a peacekeeping operation is a key issue that has to be decided before any deployment commences. A negative public response to high casualties in a peacekeeping operation, not considered to be of major importance, could obviously have very serious ramifications. High casualties could have long term effects on a nation's willingness to participate in future operations. The UN experience in Somalia illustrates the importance of the casualty tolerance issue. The first announcement of US casualties in Somalia led to popular calls for an immediate withdrawal from UNOSOM II. Following the death of the first four US soldiers, Senator Robert Byrd suggested that the "operation was crumbling" and that it was "not worth American lives lost and injuries sustained."

The US public began to apply very strict limits on the number of casualties acceptable in a far-off peacekeeping operation which had no clear place on the national interest agenda. On 5 June 1993, twenty-four Pakistani soldiers were killed in an ambush set up by supporters of Mohammed Aideed. The following day the UN Security Council passed Resolution 837, demanding the immediate apprehension of those responsible for the attack. Consequently, US forces were mobilised in a manhunt for Aideed. A few weeks later, a major clash occurred with Aideed's forces, leaving 18 American troops dead and 75 wounded. This event clearly surpassed the US casualty tolerance level and President Clinton immediately announced the phased withdrawal of US troops. American forces in Somalia were confined to force protection missions until the completion of the phased withdrawal. By all accounts, the US' failure to capture Aideed was caused by "inaccurate and untimely intelligence."

With the rise in casualties sustained by UN peacekeeping forces world-wide, most countries have become increasingly reluctant to commit forces. For any democratic government it is extremely difficult to justify casualties in peacekeeping operations where clear and compelling national interests cannot be identified. Lack of public support will thus always be a limiting factor in peacekeeping operations.

The Somali experience turned into the US' "peacekeeping Vietnam"-the US remains extremely reluctant to become directly involved in any African peacekeeping operation. Instead, the emphasis has shifted to efforts to sell the idea of an 'African Crisis Response Force' (ACRF-subsequently renamed the African Crisis Response Initiative (ACRI)). The ACRI has been clearly designed to promote African peacekeeping without endangering the lives of US troops. The plan contains an emphasis on humanitarian support based on the US strategic airlift, in conjunction with extensive diplomatic initiatives involving the UN, OAU and regional stakeholders.

The solution to potentially unacceptable casualties in peacekeeping could possibly be found in the provision of high quality body armour for participating forces, combined with the necessary equipment and skills to do the job. In addition, the US experience in Haiti provides some guidelines for reducing peace operation casualties. Long before the US XVIII Airborne Corps landed in Haiti, the US Army's 4th Psychological Operations (PSYOPS) Group at Ft. Bragg had analysed and divided Haiti's population into twenty different target groups to be provided with appropriate information and warning of the impending US involvement. Thousands of leaflets were distributed, supported by extensive radio broadcasts. Prior to the US intervention, the Pentagon expected widespread conflict and unrest leading to unacceptably high casualties. However, only one US soldier was killed and the overall campaign was successful. According to the mission commander, "there (was) no question that PSYOPS helped save lives."

INFORMATION SUPPORT FOR PEACEKEEPING

Adequate preparation for a peacekeeping operation should include detailed and quality intelligence. This issue was emphasised in former UN Secretary-General Boutros-Ghali's An Agenda for Peace. Peacekeeping forces need what NATO calls the 'Commander's Critical Intelligence Requirements (CCIR)'-the minimum information required for operational success. Information systems which provide instant battlefield awareness are essential for combat supremacy in any military operation. This information should be provided by the UN, or by participating states. Without CCIR, peacekeeping operations are unlikely to succeed. The UN has acknowledged this point and have debated the launching of 'spy' satellites to support peacekeeping, but high costs have led to the idea being shelved.

The use of the word 'intelligence' immediately promotes a negative image. During the Cold War, opposing intelligence organisations became increasingly powerful and secretive. Intelligence became a key component in the ideological struggle between East and West. The elements of Cold War intelligence included collection; analysis (forecasting); counter-intelligence (protection); and covert action.

The fourth element of the Cold War intelligence menu raised the most concern and controversy. The use of covert action to eliminate opponents or overthrow foreign governments clearly brought into question the process and function of intelligence organisations. At the same time, the nature of the ideological struggle between East and West enhanced the role of intelligence organisations and promoted secretive covert action activities which in turn undermined the legitimacy of the organisations themselves.

Post-Cold War intelligence activities no longer resemble the programmes of the past. Collection is based more and more on the almost overwhelming supply of open sources. Traditionally, the majority of intelligence information was obtained from open sources in any event. Counter-intelligence relates increasingly to a very small area of activity.

The era of obsessive information protection has been replaced by a new culture of transparency, the Internet and a world-wide flow of information which clearly benefits mankind as a whole. Covert action is irrelevant in the more open, interdependent and democratic international system.

Modern intelligence activities thus focus on analysis, or strategic forecasting. Making use of mostly open sources, supplemented by advanced processing technology, the average intelligence officer joins together the relevant pieces of the intelligence puzzle and provides the intelligence product to the decision-maker. In one sense therefore, "intelligence [remains] fundamentally a service required by those who have to make decisions."

The quality of the intelligence product is of vital concern to the decision-maker. The ideal intelligence officer should thus be a highly qualified and skilled individual, capable of assembling, analysing and communicating information. In the post-Cold War world, intelligence is nothing more than processed information for use by decision-makers. The trained assassin, or disguised undercover agent, are no longer part of the modern intelligence agency and no longer relevant to the modern intelligence agenda.

The new intelligence process is guided by the broad definition of security. In 1968, former US Secretary of Defence Robert McNamara published a book entitled The Essence of Security in which he proposed a definition of security which included a wide range of non-military elements. McNamara stressed that "security is development and without development there can be no security."

Since then, other scholars have come to realise that security is a broad concept which cannot be limited only to military force and the identification of enemies, or potential enemies. In 1980, the UN's Independent Commission on Disarmament and Security Issues concluded that military strength alone could not ensure security in an ever-changing international system. More recently, the security 'definition debate' was highlighted by Buzan and Thomas, both of whom agreed that security had been too narrowly defined in the past.

The intensity of the Cold War and the danger of surprise nuclear attack, possibly resulting in planetary devastation, preoccupied security experts and led to a neglect of the broader and, in many ways, obvious security issues. With the end of the threat of nuclear war, or the threat of a limited regional war escalating to a nuclear exchange, broader security issues have come into focus.

The new agenda contains a vast array of different elements each requiring specialist attention and analysis. Ekins, for example, suggests that there are "four highly credible, but also totally avoidable threats to our existence on earth-war, hunger, repression and eco-disaster." Mankind no longer faces the prospect of a quick and devastating nuclear exchange, but rather needs to contend with what may be called broad-based, steadily increasing, threats to human survival. In response to new threats, intelligence organisations need to master international information networks as providers of relevant security information and recruit the services of specific field specialists able to add value to the intelligence product. The modern day intelligence officer is concerned with a completely open research and analysis agenda which represents the interests of society as a whole and not the particular interests of any ruling élite, party or ideology. Thus, in the post-Cold War context, national intelligence organisations are well suited to support peacekeeping and conflict resolution.

The UN has neglected to set up a comprehensive information gathering and processing system to support peacekeeping operations. Clearly, the implementation of an advanced information processing system by the UN would significantly benefit peacekeeping operations at both the planning and execution stages.

With regard to planning, intelligence could be used to accurately calculate troop requirements, the availability and utility of facilities (especially airfields), local infrastructure (roads) and logistic requirements. Quality planning would positively influence calculations with regard to the supply of troops and support personnel for peacekeeping, thereby minimising costs and maximising chances of success.

In addition, the potential for hostile action and the capabilities of potentially hostile forces need to be carefully evaluated to avoid tactical surprises, especially in the early stages of operational deployment. The use of air transport to deploy peacekeepers implies that information on possible belligerent anti-aircraft capabilities are crucial. Moreover, where a peace enforcement operation is envisaged, the identification of the hostile forces' centre of gravity becomes critical.

The UN process of ad hoc ground reconnaissance has resulted on a number of occasions in serious time delays in the deployment of troops, as well as the insufficient provision of supplies. The use of both aerial and ground-based surveillance, using sensors and imaging technology, would significantly improve any peacekeeping force's ability to monitor the theatre of operations. Lockheed Martin Corporation is presently developing a reconnaissance vehicle, known as 'DarkStar', which will provide near real time, continuous, all-weather, wide area surveillance to tactical commanders.

Moreover, it is specifically designed and constructed to operate in high threat environments. Technology of this kind would be ideal to provide intelligence support to peacekeeping operations. Intelligence specialists have identified unmanned aerial vehicles (UAVs) as potentially one of the greatest force multipliers. The Pioneer UAV was used extensively during the Gulf War (483 missions, totalling 1559 hours) with good results. The Predator UAV's multiple sensors provide an effective close-up picture of ground operations capable of revealing objects as small as 20 centimetres in diameter from an altitude of 4 000 metres.

The development of an aerial border patrol system similar to the US counter-narcotics Command and Management System (CMS) to monitor cease-fire agreements in support of peacekeeping operations would also be useful. Other options for the provision of quality intelligence includes the Hughes synthetic aperture radar system capable of providing 1,8 metre resolution images from an orbital distance of 110 kilometres.

The Sinai Support Mission, established by the US in 1974 at the request of both Israel and Egypt, used sensor technologies to successfully monitor military activity in the Sinai. In April 1982, the Multinational Force and Observers began to make effective use of ground sensors, aerial photography and on-site verification to ensure the implementation of the Camp David Agreement. Advances in the field of satellite imagery have provided tactical information support for peacekeeping forces. During Operation Restore Hope, the US' operation in Somalia, the US Army Space and Strategic Defence Command provided the 10th Mountain Division with a multi-spectral satellite imagery terminal capable of accessing civilian LANDSAT satellites. This ensured a quick response mapping capability for tactical use by unit commanders.

The US operation in Somalia confirmed Sun Tzu's two thousand five hundred year old thesis-good intelligence is vital for any military operation. In his book entitled Somalia Operations: Lessons Learned, Kenneth Allard points out that "while 'information' is the term of choice, operations in Somalia proved that, whatever it is called, intelligence has a crucial role to play at the lower end of the conflict spectrum." US forces in Somalia made use of a wide range of information gathering equipment, including night-vision devices, ground-surveillance radars, tactical air reconnaissance and unmanned aerial vehicles. An important source of intelligence proved to be soldiers in the field using eyes and ears to provide commanders with quality "situation awareness."

The UN operation in Somalia suggests that peacekeeping operations have created a new form of 'information warfare' within which the peacekeepers compete with those who oppose the peace process. Success in this new information environment however, requires a mindshift away from the traditional intelligence approach of identifying and assessing the 'enemy'. In peacekeeping operations there are no enemies, but there may be factions or groups which use force to undermine the peace process.

Nevertheless, the approach towards peacekeeping, as with any form of military deployment or conflict, should be based on the logic and science of war. In the case of Somalia, the forces of Mohammed Aideed became the central opponents of peace and were therefore identified as hostile. At the same time, it is clear that in every peacekeeping operation there is a possibility that the peacekeepers themselves will become the target of hostility. Good intelligence will be able to predict and prepare for this eventuality. In Somalia, despite the technological aids outlined above, the US did not have sufficient quality intelligence and thus paid the price. The issue of intelligence is therefore one of approach, more than technological barriers.

CONCLUSION

Preventive diplomacy is the best response to growing regional low intensity conflict, especially in Africa where the political, social and geographical complexities make peacekeeping unattractive. At the same time, preventive diplomacy requires adequate early warning and the speedy response to a crisis. Early warning should be provided by national governments and international information networks, supported by the developed countries until such time as the capacity of the UN and the OAU are further enhanced. Moreover, individual states should be encouraged to initiate preventive diplomacy, in consultation with regional neighbours and organisations, as well as the UN, in order to begin peace negotiations before conflicts escalate. When preventive diplomacy fails, peacekeeping may be the next best option. However, decision-makers require sufficient funding for successful peacekeeping. The funding problem will have to be solved before peacekeeping becomes a respected and successful element in global conflict resolution. Moreover, an accurate calculation of casualty tolerance and public support for a peacekeeping operation is critical, especially if a long term involvement is envisaged. High casualties will erode popular support for peacekeeping and make this activity more difficult to implement. Recent peacekeeping operations have confirmed that quality intelligence is essential for success. Without adequate UN or regional intelligence networks in place, states should allocate intelligence assets to assist peacekeeping operations in the interest of international peace and regional stability.

4

Multi-Track Diplomacy in the 21st Century

A freedom fighter, struggling against the military occupation in his land, is encouraged by a religious-based peace mission to try another approach. He puts down his weapons and opens a centre for conflict resolution, to mediate local disputes and promote dialogue and non-violence. A village elder, with modest financial help from an international agency, arranges a traditional ceremony of reconciliation to re-integrate child soldiers who committed atrocities, under duress, against their own families during a recent civil war.

Mid-level community and political leaders attend a series of facilitated discussions with their counterparts across the communal divide of their conflict. Several years later, many are in important government positions, and ideas generated in those conversations begin appearing in the political discourse. An influential journalist meets with his colleagues from 'the other side' of an ethnic conflict in an NGO-sponsored dialogue, and subsequently refuses to use stereotypical or derogatory language about 'them' in his news coverage. A rural affairs specialist working for a relief organization in the developing world, after attending a training program in conflict resolution, mediates a successful agreement to a chronic dispute between pastoralists and agriculturalists.

Multiply these stories many thousand times over, and a picture of multi-track diplomacy in the late 20th century begins to emerge. People from all walks of life and wielding influence over various sectors of their society, find myriad ways to promote peace in settings of violent conflict. Working at different levels of social organization, from the political to the institutional to the social, these individuals, and the organizations and institutions through which they operate, are the visible manifestation of the multi-track approach.

Many who step forward as local peacebuilders in their own communities are influenced by third party actors, a growing force of professionals and private citizens who design and implement programs of peace-building or conflict prevention, management, resolution and transformation in places of conflict around the world. In some cases, these individuals become so committed to the practice of peace-building that they themselves become professionals or para-professionals in the field, creating institutions of their own and operating as catalysts and third parties to others.

Only short while ago this body of peace-builders hardly existed. Now they are legion, operating out of university programs, mediation centres, democratization institutes or conflict resolution NGOs. They are associated with citizen diplomacy initiatives, with religious groups, with business or professional associations or with political parties. They come from humanitarian relief and development agencies, from human rights organizations, from grassroots women's networks or from prestigious think tanks.

They may be psychologists, lawyers, sociologists, activists, political scientists, journalists, public servants, artists, organizational consultants, government officials, academics or housewives. In short, the community of peacebuilders actively working throughout all levels of society, from the top down and the bottom up, in places of ethnic and civil conflicts around the world, has mushroomed, and multi-track diplomacy is flourishing.

Why this should be so is a topic that could reasonably be considered in an article by itself. Here, however, we will start from the present and look forward, identifying the challenges to global security in the 21st century, and the possible ways in which multi-track diplomacy might make a contribution in the world of the new millennium.

A LOOK AT THE WORLD OF THE 21ST CENTURY

Multi-track diplomacy, then, enters the 21st century as an established presence; a systems approach to peace-building that embraces a large network of organizations, disciplines, methodologies and venues for working toward the prevention and resolution of violent conflict around the world. It has its success stories, told elsewhere in this book, and its best practices; its challenges and edges for growth.

To understand how multi-track diplomacy might play a role in the world of the 21st century, it is necessary to examine some of the trends in world affairs that are looming on humanity's horizon as potential threats to global security in the coming era. Let us examine eight of these trends in some detail:

The Globalization of Violence

The benefits of globalization that have so affected our communications and economic systems have also been available to those forces in the world bent on destruction, greed and violence. With increased access to world-wide markets, the internet, cellular communication, international banking facilities and other tools for moving information and resources across great distances at high speed, those involved in such nefarious pursuits as drugs, the illegal arms trade, the sex trade, terrorism, gambling, money laundering, the black market, racketeering and other such nasty past times have been able to be more effective in their own endeavours, and to take advantage of the increase in power and reach that comes with working together. The illegitimate industries, like their legitimate counterparts, are cooperating, consolidating and diversifying their interests, forming a shadowy infrastructure that covers the globe, destabilizes vulnerable systems, and thrives on chaos.

Many of these actors are involved behind the scenes in conflict situations, benefitting from the continuation of the violence while having no direct interest in the particulars of that conflict. Though they will never come to the table as part of any formal peace talks, their power is great, especially in certain high political circles without whose connivance they could not operate.

The Breakdown of Systemic Integrity

All kinds of systems are losing the strength and certainty of their boundaries at the end of the 20th century. Cells cannot hold their integrity, as new viruses and diseases pose epidemic threats to large populations. Environmental systems cannot maintain their ability to function properly, as species necessary to the balance of nature die out and the natural world becomes polluted beyond its ability to either sustain or purify itself. Families fall apart; moral systems degenerate; educational systems in some places lose their capacity for operating as learning centres and become, instead, warehouses for the social control of desperate children. Economic systems that have sustained great prosperity over time dissolve in an instant, erasing the possibility of a decent standard of living for millions of people anytime in the near future. Political systems disintegrate, leaving thugs, ad hoc militias and greedy despots in charge of whatever patches of land they can hold by force and threat. Whole nations disappear into the chasm of chaos, or seem poised to do so momentarily.

The Rise of Rogues

Partly as a result of this disintegration of integrity, rogue individuals and nations are emerging in record numbers. People and institutions that function outside any traditional boundaries of law, persuasion or sense of the common good are establishing their capacity to operate across established boundaries at will. Narco-terrorism, nuclear terrorism, the threats of germ and biological terrorism, private armies under the control of warlords and profiteers, maverick states that respond not at all to international pressures or sanctions-these manifestations of uncontrollable, dangerous rogue forces pose untested threats to the world and its institutions of civilization.

The Depletion of Natural Resources

Both a cause and an effect of some of the phenomenon already described, the degradation and depletion of earth's natural resources are posing a major threat to the sustenance and stability of life on the planet. Water, oil, land, forests and breathable air are in increasingly short supply, and reserves of precious minerals necessary for the continuation of modern technology are dwindling. The imbalance of overpopulation with the means to sustain life has already contributed to some of the past decade's worst conflicts, such as in Rwanda. The hole in the ozone layer, global warming and the poisoning of the oceans, direct results of our industrial and economic systems, are, in turn, contributing to the very breakdown of systemic integrity we discussed earlier.

The Institutionalization of Polarization

While there have always been factions and differences in human society, the deepening of polarization as a norm of social, political and economic interaction has become apparent in the last decade. In the U.S., the two main political parties have descended into an entrenched adversarial relationship in which bipartisanship and cooperation are increasingly rare. The North and the South, the developed and the developing worlds, are still deeply divided over power and resources, and the distance between the economic 'haves' and 'have nots' in many countries is growing, and dangerously so. With intensified polarization comes extremism. Throughout the latter part of the 20th century, we have witnessed the threat to regional and global security posed by the rise of nationalistic and religious extremism. As these movements attain power, stature, and resources-such as in the case of the Taliban in Afghanistan, the far-right wing in Israeli politics or, the BJP/Hindu nationalist party in India-they become woven more thoroughly into the fabric of modern life. Less on the fringes, where they can be ignored, they have migrated to the centre of our world screen, where the threats they pose are highly visible-and highly volatile.

Challenges to the Nation State

As empires fall, political boundaries change, and ethnic groups gain access to arms and world attention for their causes, the familiar system of nation states which has ordered the global political and economic systems for so long is being tested from all sides. With between 5,000 and 10,000 different ethnic groups in the world, and only 185 member nations of a UN which affirms in its Charter the right of self-determination, the stage is set for potential conflicts. At both ends of the spectrum, from consolidation to disintegration, the nation state system is facing challenges. As Europe seeks its union, Quebec seeks dis-union. As the Czech Republic and the Republic of Slovakia find a relatively easy way to separate, the Kurds, the Chechens, and the East Timorese have not been so fortunate. The new millennium will require humanity to be creative in designing ways that peoples and national groups can experience the dignity and integrity of their identity while simultaneously maintaining the unity and viability of a world order based on law and mutual respect.

Changing Power Blocs

The fall of the Soviet Union and the rise of the United States as the single superpower in the world is not the end of the story. Far from it. Much is in play in Europe, with the evolution of the European Union and NATO, and in Asia, with the awakening of China to its potential for power in the world. Turkey, poised between East and West, could shift its sizable weight in one of several directions, not all of which bode well for security in Southeastern Europe. The disintegration of Russia could lead to any number of scenarios in which powerful entities might rise from the ashes of that state so recently a major player in world affairs. These are but a few examples of the shifts that are taking place-seismic shifts-in relative strength, alliances and relationships as old and new nations flex their muscles and take or lose advantage on the world stage due to some of the other phenomenon previously mentioned.

The Traumatization of the Human Family

Millions of people around the planet are suffering massive trauma from recent wars and associated famine, displacement and destruction. As civil wars increasingly target women and children, and group massacres, large scale atrocities and rape become common weapons of war, large populations are profoundly wounded, in body, mind and spirit. In some countries, whole generations are debilitated, especially in those places where child soldiers have formed the backbone of the fighting forces. In others, the psychological debilitation is already moving into the second, third and even fourth generations. Post Traumatic Stress Disease (PTSD) is probably the most widespread disease on the planet. This means that many places in conflict remain vulnerable to political manipulation and ongoing cycles of violence, as the people are lacking the personal strength and inner resources to resist the forces that call for retribution and revenge.

IMPLICATIONS FOR MULTI-TRACK DIPLOMACY

These trends present a sober picture indeed of the world of the 21st century. The realm of multi-track diplomacy, as one small player in the global drama, exists within this context, yet brings a perspective, a commitment and a set of methodologies that are at humanity's leading edge for dealing with these most difficult issues. In fact, I would go so far as to suggest that the work of peace-building is at the forefront of our planet's evolutionary journey in these times.

The very dangerous conditions described in the section above arise from, and thrive in, a worldview and set of assumptions about the world as a place of separation. Separative consciousness sees duality and difference as opportunity for superiority, dominance and control, and breeds materialism, greed and violence. For many centuries the dominant western world organized its political, social and economic systems on this basis. The general breakdown in the global (and environmental) environment we are seeing now can be understood as the natural ripening of the inherent seed of destruction in the separative worldview, for when only the parts are seen, without reference to the whole, duality will play itself out in struggle, contest and conflict indefinitely.

We live at a time when large numbers of people on the planet are discovering that there is another worldview, a holistic or unitive view, that acknowledges the parts as inherently inter-related and part of a larger innate wholeness. Beyond the duality we share a common human experience, a common spiritual source, and a common capacity for connecting through that source to ways of being that will honour both the diversity and the unity in the family of life. The world is living through a major period of transformation, as the bankruptcy of one worldview becomes apparent, while the new worldview is still in its infant stages. This produces both the potential for chaos and the potential for great creativity. The peacebuilders of the world, and the multi-track approach to peace in particular, because of its systems orientation, carries that creative potential and is, therefore, a vehicle for humanity's evolution into a new state of consciousness.

In addition to these obvious activities, multi-track diplomacy can face the unique challenges of this transformational period in seven quite specific ways:

Maintaining Flexibility in the Face of the Unknown

The state of world affairs is, as we have seen, in a period of great flux. Many events that we can reasonably anticipate may or may not occur. Others that we have not considered may happen tomorrow. A single event of biological terrorism, for instance, could easily change the face of life on this planet as we know it. A single expansive move by China, or new confrontation in the Balkans or the Middle East, could re-configure political relations for many years to come. The truth is, peacebuilders need to be prepared to move in several directions at once, both responding to whatever opportunities present themselves for positive and effective work for peace, and also being pro-active in turning challenges into opportunities. To maintain this flexibility as a whole field of endeavour requires greater reflexivity, discourse and coordination among theory builders and practitioners from all parts of the world.

Recognizing Healing as the Key to Transformation

Because of the profound human trauma discussed earlier, and the brokenness of many systems, healing and reconciliation are critical aspects of any multi-track diplomacy process. New and sustainable peace systems must take into account the mending process that comes with acknowledgement of the harm done, apology and forgiveness when possible, completion of mourning, and healing at the individual and group levels. One of the greatest challenges facing peacebuilders today is not just how to engage individuals in this type of healing, but how to engage whole systems, and especially the leadership, for unless humanity learns how to heal itself, the trauma will condemn us to repeat the same cycles of violence from generation to generation.

Building the Infrastructure for Peace

The forces of war have an existing infrastructure that enables them to mobilize and actualize their aims -they have armies and arms suppliers; transportation, commerce and communication systems; banking, taxing and other funding methods; media, education and propaganda systems; and government ministries, clans, villages, political parties and other entities capable of taking action.

The forces of peace have little of this. We have come a long way in recent years toward developing organizations and networks that can serve as vehicles for carrying and coordinating peace-building activities, with an accompanying research, education and media capability as well. Much more needs to be done to create both a human and an institutional infrastructure for peace-building, in order to concretize these methods and approaches in social, political and economic systems that can both stand on their own and work together toward a shared goal. In addition to such institutions, we need the capacity to move money, materials, people and technologies rapidly and efficiently to wherever needed on the planet. In this way the transformation of consciousness is assisted by building alternative structures so that as the old collapses, there is something in place to sustain that which is being birthed.

Taking the Holistic and Positive View

One of the hallmarks of a multi-track approach is the capacity to see the whole, and the inter-relationship of the various parts. We know that development and peace are mutually interdependent, for instance, and that democratization requires the capacity for conflict resolution and problem solving at a group level, so we see the natural interface of several disciplines. This kind of relational awareness is critical to building peace systems, for it encourages the kind of connections, bridges, alliances and networking that are essential to the ongoing support of the change process. Stepping back and seeing the whole picture, especially that of the evolutionary moment in which we stand, allows us to hold the gate open for a new range of possibilities. It also allows us to affirm the positive view that, despite all the problems in the way, peace is indeed possible. In this way we energize the potential rather than the despair, and keep hope, that precious and fragile flame, vibrant and alive.

Making Peace From the Inside Out

People whose life is given to peace-building, whether as outside third parties or actors within conflict systems, are generally motivated to service, and as servers, may be prone to work themselves beyond the point of balance. Certainly working in war zones, with wounded people and in tense and violent circumstances can produce symptoms of secondary trauma, compassion fatigue and burn-out.

Because multi-track diplomacy is a systems approach, in which even the intervenor is part of the system, and because it is a multi-level approach, in which the personal level is just as important as the inter-group level, those involved in this field have the opportunity to use our own technology with ourselves, becoming agents of peace in our being as well as in our doing. When we are taking the time to integrate what we teach about peace in the outer domain with our deep experience of peace within, we can be much more effective, at the individual and at the institutional levels, in two ways: we are clearer and stronger channels for the outer work when we take time to reconnect with our own inner source of peace, and we are better models for others, showing by our presence as much as by our actions that peace is a viable and dynamic state.

Creating New Pathways for Shifting Consciousness

A colleague, Robert Fuller, once spoke about finding 'a better game than war.' Peacebuilders taking a multi-track approach are engaged in this endeavour. We know that the 'war option' is a lose-lose game; we come offering a better way, a way that goes even beyond win-win toward the transformation of the consciousness that would allow us to build truly just and peace-able societies. Because the methods and pathways for this shift are inherent in the principles and practices of peace-building with a holistic view, we occupy a position in the world analogous to the early road or railway builders. We are opening the paths, setting the tracks in place, laying down the rails, making clear the direction that will shape the future of our planet.

Our tools-methods for cooperation, creative joint problem solving, reconciliation, prevention, dialogue, mediation, negotiation, and communication, among others-are the tracks that we are setting down, so people will be able to transport themselves across old territory in new and better ways. As with all road building, once we open a path, more and more travellers will use it, especially if it carries them to where they want to go. The ways of thinking and acting we are inviting people into is a different, and a better game than war, and our work makes it possible for people in large numbers to make that shift. Knowing this, we can be more intentional about it.

Empowering Peacebuilders for Local Action

Multi-track diplomacy invites everyone into the game of peace-building. It says that there is a place and way that people from any sector of society can make a contribution to peace. Those of us engaged in travelling to places of conflict to make interventions there realize that building peace is primarily a local task. What we can offer is to give people a view and a direct experience of what is possible, help them do what they want to do faster and better, and perhaps strengthen their capacity to use appropriate tools and skills. We can motivate, catalyze, inspire, instruct, facilitate, encourage, support, assist, demonstrate, and convene. We can present possibilities, open minds to new ways of thinking, and cheer people on as they take charge of changing the systems they live in. We can articulate theories and best practices, provide a safe space where people can meet 'the other', or elicit inner individual and cultural wisdom about peace and conflict resolution. What we can never do impose our solutions on others, or build their new systems for them.

Our power to empower is perhaps the most important role we can play in the 21st century. The more individuals who feel empowered to work in their own systems for peace and conflict transformation, the closer the world comes to that critical mass that will allow for a massive leap in consciousness, allowing new processes for peace that were previously unimaginable to become normative, and easy.

Exercising our power to empower means generating more stories like those shared elsewhere in this book, building a base of success from which we can all learn and draw. It means enabling people to have that critical understanding of what true power is, the very opposite of the power of domination and control that characterizes war systems. Ultimately, exercising our power to empower means that the next article written on the role of multi-track diplomacy will have infinitely more peacebuilders-like those mentioned in the very beginning of this article-to showcase as examples of those engaged in the courageous act of creating viable, sustainable peace systems on this precious planet we all call home.

CHANGING HISTORY-PEACE BUILDING IN NORTHERN IRELAND

On Good Friday, April the 10th, Northern Ireland politicians stumbled out from the portals of Stormont into the breaking daylight. Many of them were not far from tears. All were obviously exhausted by the roller coaster of adrenaline and the lack of sleep they had incurred during the last few days and nights of the talks, as deals were crafted, walk-outs were threatened and averted, and the apparently insuperable barriers on decommissioning and other issues were overcome. Both the British and Irish Prime Ministers had been called upon to provide support in the last few days and even President Clinton had assisted by encouraging telephone calls. The waiting populace held their breath alternating between despair and hope.

The hope was justified-the miracle happened, the Belfast Agreement was reached. After thirty years of a bloody civil war, Northern Ireland's political parties finally achieved consensus on the principles, and in some cases the practice, necessary to govern a society divided on constitutional, political, and cultural perspectives. Six weeks later, by a vote of over 71%, and despite the best efforts of fundamentalist nationalists and unionists, the deal was endorsed by the peoples of the island of Ireland, North and South. The road to peace appeared to have been secured.

What had brought Northern Ireland to this particular turning point? What had been the major developments in eventually securing the peace? While obviously the debates about such developments will continue for some decades, the following would appear to have been the most important in creating a positive context for a political solution.

A. Community Development/Community Relations work within and between communities which opened up new possibilities for dialogue and co-operation between them.

When civil violence broke out in 1969 in Northern Ireland and particularly in the aftermath of the riots in Belfast and Derry/Londonderry in August 1969, the British Labour Home Secretary, James Callaghan announced the establishment of a Ministry for Community Relations and a Community Relations Commission which was charged with the promotion of policies which would improve community relations2.

The Commission decided to adopt as its main strategy the initiation of local community development programmes across Northern Ireland, based on the belief that communities which lacked self-confidence were more likely to relate aggressively to one another. Furthermore, it believed that the problem, particularly for people in more socially marginalized communities, of relating to the structures of power, contributed to feelings of helplessness and resentment which in turn contributed to community tensions. (Hayes) The Commission survived until the Sunningdale Agreement in April 1974, which set up a new power sharing assembly for Northern Ireland. In one of its first actions, the power sharing assembly abolished the Community Relations Commission on the basis that henceforth the politicians themselves would be responsible for community development and community relations issues. Ironically, the new assembly itself only lasted five months due to disagreement among the politicians about the remit of cross-border bodies which had been set up as part of the Agreement, and a loyalist workers strike which paralysed Northern Ireland.

However, the process of community development remained an important method of facilitating communication within communities, and between government and communities, and this process continued to underpin many programmes subsequently initiated and funded in the last two decades.

Over a decade later, in 1985, the Standing Advisory Commission on Human Rights commissioned a report on the current state of community relations work, and its potential for future development. (Frazer & Fitzduff) This report on the under resourced, underdeveloped and unstrategic nature of much of the work, suggested a theoretical framework for its development, and suggested some practical structures that should be considered if the government intended to take the work seriously. It suggested the creation of a specialist community relations unit within government and the creation of an independent community relations body which would address issues of policy, training, and funding community relations work. In 1987, the Central Community Relations Unit (CCRU) was set up, which was located at the heart of government and in 1990, the independent body, the Community Relations Council (CRC) was established.

COMMUNITY RELATIONS 1990-98

In drawing up its initial strategic plan the CRC decided not to concentrate on developing more 'reconciliation' groups, but expanded its remit to include bodies who had not previously been working actively at peace-building e.g. business, church and sports groups, health and education boards, etc and many groups from the voluntary and community sector. It also worked closely with the Trade Unions who had, since the late 1980's, been developing anti-intimidation and anti-sectarian programmes for the workplace.

Subsequently there was a significant expansion of the number of groups working at peace-building much of which growth was facilitated by a hugely increased financial investment in such work 3 so that by 1998 the number of civic groups engaging in contact work, and developing programmes and training to address issues of human rights, cultural diversity, co-operation on social and economic issues single identity work, neutral venue work, anti sectarian work, anti-intimidation work as well as political dialogue and mediation work had increased significantly i.e. from 40 in 1986 to 140 in 1996 4.

As the theoretical framework for such a focus expanded the work also began to engage a much wider spectrum of people, including those who had previously been cynical of the 'peace and doves' stereotype attached to the work. (Fitzduff) It therefore became more possible to build a coalition of people and organisations addressing both the 'softer' issues such as understanding and co-operation, as well as the 'harder' issues of inequality, rights, policing and political and constitutional differences.

In addition, the programme begun in the 70's of more substantially resourcing community development began to pay significant political dividends. Such work, in the absence of local democracy, had provided for community participation in governmental consultation processes, about social, economic and political issues. By the 1990's, however, it had also helped to generate a new breed of 'community' politicians who developed loyalist, republican and feminist thinking in a way which significantly enriched the political mix of parties who were eventually able to sign the Belfast Agreement.

Parties such as the PUP, the NIWC and Sinn Fein all have considerable experience at community and social politics. 5 Such work also provided them with fruitful contacts gained from their collective experience in addressing local social issues together, and such experience should augur well for the social and economic tasks that face them as representatives in the new Assembly.

External assistance offered by the European Union was also of significance. When the ceasefires were declared in 1994, the EU decided to help to underpin the peace by allocating £250,000,000 to help build up the economy and establish peace.

Such funds have been useful, as their criteria for distribution included in many cases the need for communities to work together on funding decisions. Such processes ensure that communities can no longer continue to be unaware of each other's social and economic needs, and have in many cases provided very useful training for future collaborative government at both local and regional level.

Political Dialogue and Development work which focused on work with politicians and others on political divisions and political options.

Given the small size of Northern Ireland-less than 3 hours drive from end to end-it is hard to imagine just how difficult it is to facilitate and promote political dialogue. This is partly because of the culture of silence which is adhered to between the communities where raising any issues of cultural or political difference is seen to be either impolite or dangerous, depending upon the circumstances. For politicians, who exemplify community differences, being seen to have any meetings outside of the context of formal dialogue-which dialogue is usually characterised by hostility is almost impossible. And for much of the conflict, it was almost impossible for the government, and most political parties to have any dialogue at all with Sinn Fein, because of their perceived association with the IRA and paramilitary violence. 6

In such circumstances, much ingenuity was needed on the part of many groups to facilitate political dialogue and to eventually achieve sufficient consensus between the parties to move into inclusive dialogue.

Primary among these dialogues processes were those conducted by the Quakers and others with and between politicians, particularly during the early nineties and which kept open dialogue through processes of shuttle mediation. In addition, some academics were extremely useful in organising workshops for politicians and others, often outside of Ireland, in places like Washington or South Africa, where it was easier to meet than at home. Often such conferences gave the participants opportunities to address wider perspectives and possibilities for conflict resolution, as well as providing opportunities for relationships to form between the politicians-which relationships could never have formed in the socially and politically constricting circumstances of Northern Ireland.

Another particularly useful initiative was that by a small group of Protestant clergy who opened a confidential process of dialogue with Sinn Fein, at a time when such processes were viewed with deep opprobrium by most political parties, and who provided a useful context within which Sinn Fein could address the reality of their perceptions of the hopes and fears of the Protestant/Unionist community. Other groups such as the Glencree Centre for Reconciliation, just outside of Dublin, also involved itself in workshops with politicians, particularly following the ceasefires of 1994. And community workers themselves-some of whom were ex-republican and loyalist prisoners-eventually began to find many creative ways, despite the danger to them from their own and their opposing community, to involve themselves in processes of dialogue and relationship building through their common social and community concerns.

What was important about all of the above processes was that they were almost all conducted in confidence and thus provided a safer context within which politicians fears and hopes could be constructively addressed. Such dialogue processes-in addition to those eventually developed by the Government and between political parties-were to prove invaluable in accumulating the possibilities, and the beginning of enough understanding and trust on the part of at least some politicians, to enable the peace process to truly begin.

What was also useful was the eventual emergence of a party that was not dedicated to a particular political position-but to the dialogue process itself. This was the Northern Ireland Women's Coalition which was formed just six weeks before the election to the Northern Ireland Forum for Political Dialogue in 1996.

It was formed in response to the dismay felt by many women in Northern Ireland at the lack of response by existing political parties to the need to include women in Northern Ireland politics. The party included nationalists and unionists, and was jointly chaired by two women from both perspectives. Its members came from all classes of life e.g. community workers, professionals, academics, nuns, trade unionists, etc. and they fought the elections on a cross-community approach. They secured a place at the negotiating table, focusing on principles of equality and inclusion. Although originally treated with sexism and hostility by many parties, particularly the unionist parties, they were eventually able to play very useful part by facilitating discussions between the parties-often using a shuttle-mediation approach-on difficult issues like the release of prisoners and decommissioning.

Another newcomer to the peace process was the business community who began to develop their approach to the ending of violence in the early nineties. Whereas before they had been content to complain about the effect of the violence on business from the sidelines, they now began to coalesce with the Trade Unions to see if a more strategic approach could be put into place which would put pressure on both republican and loyalist paramilitaries to end their campaign, and to pressurise the politicians in getting down to the business of building an agreement. Groups like the Chamber of Commerce, the Institute of Directors, the Confederation of British Industry, and all the major trade unions joined together and began to make statements urging the need to end the war, and the need for serious political negotiation. In addition, they involved themselves in dialogue with all the political parties, including Sinn Fein, even before the ceasefires were announced in 1994. Their influence was very salutary, particularly on the Unionist political parties, who began to feel the need to respond to the pressure from them to enter into serious political dialogue.

During the nineties, the United States was also of substantial assistance in helping to develop and secure dialogue and peace. The US had gradually developed a perspective which was able to take account of the needs and fears of Unionists as well as nationalists, and-spurred by the interests of the huge Irish vote in the USA-they began to focus on ways of ending the violence. People like Congressman Bruce Morrison, and business men like Bill Flynn and Charles Feeney visited Ireland to persuade the IRA of the need to end the military campaign, and to engage with the unionist community.

Clinton granted a visa to Gerry Adams to enter the US in 1994 while the IRA was still bombing cities and killing people, in the hope that it would assist his alleged quest for a solution. Although such activities were initially viewed with suspicion by many within the British Government, many subsequently came to appreciate the assistance which such interventions were able to offer. Such assistance was particularly exemplified by the assistance of Senator George Mitchell who acted as Chair of the talks process for almost two years and whose efforts were invaluable to its success. Equality work which ensured equal access to power and resources for Catholics as well as Protestants and economic development to assist this.

The outbreak of civil violence in 1969 in Northern Ireland which cost over three and a half thousand lives was significantly attributable to the failure of policies of equity in Northern Ireland since its inception as a state in 1921. Although the newly formed region of the UK contained within its borders a substantial number of Catholics who were unhappy with their status within Northern Ireland, few efforts were made by the newly elected unionist government to sufficiently address their responsibilities involved in governing a divided society. Such a failure with its concomitant patterns of inequity, biased voting systems, unrepresentative policing, a maintenance of ghettoisation in education, housing, and workplaces, and a significantly alienated minority created the context for the eventual development of a civil war.

In 1972 the Unionist Northern Ireland government was dismissed by the British government, and direct political and security control for the region from London began, Such belated interest from London-which had previously shown little care for on-going inequities in the region-eventually helped to ensure the development of a more equitable and culturally representative society in Northern Ireland.

EQUALITY LEGISLATION

In August 1969 the British government declared that every citizen of Northern Ireland was entitled to the same equality of treatment and freedom from discrimination as obtains in the rest of the United Kingdom, and a series of legislative reforms to address existing inequalities was introduced, first by the Northern Ireland parliament and after it had been dissolved in 1972, by the Westminster parliament.

In 1969 legislation was introduced to investigate complaints of maladministration by government departments, and in 1972 a commission was established to promote fairness in staff recruitment in the local councils, which had been so noted for their discriminatory nature. In 1973 the Northern Ireland Constitution Act provided for a legislative assembly to address discrimination on the grounds of religious or political belief and the Act also established the Standing Advisory Commission on Human Rights to monitor the effectiveness of laws against discrimination.

As discrimination in housing had been a major grievance, control of all public housing allocation was transferred from local council authorities to a regional authority, and voting reforms were introduced i.e. house ownership was no longer deemed a prerequisite for voting rights, and the multiple vote given to business owners was abolished, as both of these had effectively discriminated against Catholics. Local council boundaries were redrawn more accurately to represent the reality of citizen distribution, and a proportional representation system of voting was introduced which increased nationalist chances of gaining power where their numbers were substantial enough, and increased the number of councils under nationalist control.

Employment Inequities

Following the civil rights disturbances of 1969, major disparities in employment levels in Northern Ireland had been confirmed. (Cameron 1969, Rose 1971) In 1971 it was estimated that 17.3 per cent of Catholic males were unemployed, compared to 6.6 per cent Protestant males. In 1976 the Fair Employment Act was passed, making discrimination in employment on religious or political grounds unlawful and a Fair Employment Agency (FEA) was established to receive complaints of discrimination in employment and to investigate the extent to which there was inequality. This agency was eventually replaced in 1989 by the Fair Employment Commission (FEC) which was given extra resources and powers by the government in pursuit of its task i.e. monitoring of the religious composition of workforce was introduced, and indirect discrimination was made illegal.

Targeting Social Need

However, by the early 1990's, after two decades of government attempts to address equity issues in Northern Ireland, the indicators still showed that the Catholic community in many areas remained seriously disadvantaged e.g. forty-five of the top fifty unemployment blackspots areas in Northern Ireland were almost exclusively Catholic. Faced with a major challenge of the continuance of marginalised ghetto areas (mainly Catholic, but also some Protestant areas) and the link between such areas and the use of paramilitary violence, the government decided that a major initiative was needed to address such alienation. (Poole) It set up Targeting Social Need (TSN) programme to tackle areas of social and economic differences by targeting government policies and programmes more directly to those areas or sections of the community suffering the highest levels of disadvantage and deprivation.

Extra attention was also given under the TSN programme to providing further opportunities for training, to increasing development work for indigenous industry creation, particularly in the most marginalised areas, and to ensuring that individual job creation agencies further biased their work towards those areas that were most seriously disadvantaged.

Policy and Fair Treatment

In 1994 the government introduced a new initiative called Policy Appraisal and Fair Treatment (PAFT) to ensure that issues of equality condition policy making and action in all spheres of government activity, and to ensure that considerations of equality, equity and non-discrimination (not just in relation to religious/political affiliation, but also in relation to other areas of inequality) are in-built from the outset to the preparation of policy proposals, including legislation and strategic plans for the implementation of policy and the delivery of services. These guidelines now apply to all Northern Ireland government departments and all government agencies

Two decades later, under the jurisdiction of direct rule from London, many inequities have been addressed. Complaints are no longer heard in Northern Ireland about rigged voting systems, unfair housing allocations, or unequal educational funding. Only primarily in unemployment-where levels of long-term unemployment among Catholic males is still twice as high as among Protestant males-does a significant problem remain, despite the various legal and social initiatives which have been undertaken to address the issue. Such advances mean that the anger and resentment many Catholics felt at being excluded under a Unionist regime is no longer as potent a factor in continuing the support for violence.

Education work which provided new possibilities for contact and mutual understanding between children and young people.

The educational systems-like most systems in Northern Ireland-is sectarian, with almost all children attending single identity schools. In 1981, the first integrated school for both Catholic and Protestant children was opened, and since then more than thirty have been established through the hard work of parents. 9 Although still only serving a small minority of children (3%) they have served as a vital initiative in transforming the existing education system. Under pressures from such schools, some of the existing schools are now willing to consider opening up participation to pupils from other communities.

Significant work has also been undertaken to ensure that, even within segregated schools, pupils have an opportunity to address existing cultural and political divisions.

By the early 1990's, through the dedication of academics and teachers determined to address cross-community misunderstanding and division, programmes within schools designed to increase understanding among children and young people e.g. Cultural Heritage, Mutual Understanding and Contact programmes were an obligatory part of every schoolchild's curriculum. And by 1990, a common history curriculum was being taught in all schools in Northern Ireland, whereas before 1990 Catholic and Protestant schools often taught completely different versions of history. By 1994, a common religious curriculum was inaugurated. Through such initiatives, the power of the schools as a purveyor of perspectives which often increased mistrust and prejudice between communities had been diminished.

District Council Community Relations programmes which established locally led initiatives to address issues of division between the communities.

Northern Ireland has twenty six local councils which have, with varying degrees, exemplified the hostility which has pervaded much of Northern Ireland public life. In many cases they were significantly responsible for the kind of discriminatory behaviour that led directly to the civil unrest of 1969. Their abuse of powers was so obvious that they were all stripped of most of their responsibilities in housing, health care, and social services which were all centralised. Even when using what limited powers were left to them their work was often characterised by acrimony, hostility and in some cases physical violence.

However, a decision was made by the Central Community Relations unit to involve these councils in community relations work and in 1990, a District Council community relations programme was developed which was eventually established within all Councils despite deep resistance by most of them. Each of the twenty six district council now has at least one full-time community relations worker addressing coexistence needs in its local area and as their programmes has had to ensure an overall commitment from what are often very divided councils, their very existence has marked a substantial sign of progress in the field.

Such programmes involved contact work, co-operative economic development programmes between the communities, cultural events such as concerts, drama etc which exemplified cultural diversity, mediation, problem solving and political discussion workshops. The evidence is that where such relationships have been active for at least two years, relationships between communities have significantly improved. (Knox and Hughes)

Cultural Traditions work which developed programmes to exemplify cultural differences as positive, rather than negative. This included Media work which validated cultural diversity and promoted discussion on issues of difference.

For the entire period of the existence of the state, expressions of cultural and political identity have been contentious. Flag flying, the use of the Irish language, language and unionist and nationalist parades, have all been seen as a threat to the political realities and aspirations of the other side. In a contested territory, such expressions have a significant potential to accrue into civil disorder. (Mc Cartney 1994)

Since 1921, many such expressions on the part of nationalists in Northern Ireland were deemed illegal. Several legislative Acts (1951 and 1954) outlawed the flying of the Irish flag, and laws were also passed forbidding the use of Irish language street signs (1949) or the use of any language other than English in court (1739). All transactions with the government had to be conducted in English. 10 Such laws contributed to significant community tension and defiance-e.g by 1992 over 550 Irish language street signs had been erected in nationalist areas in clear defiance of the law and many nationalists also began to use the Irish language and its lack of official support as a cultural weapon with which to challenge the authorities.

Much of this has now changed-mainly due to the work of the Cultural Traditions Group (CTG), a group of academics, practitioners and policy makers, drawn from both the nationalist and unionist communities, an operating under the auspices of the Community Relations Council. 11 Many within this group recognised that the negative government response to the Irish language had been both short-sighted and unnecessary. They established and achieved government funding for the Ultacht Trust, a group set up on a non-sectarian basis to develop and fund the Irish language. The government were also persuaded to fund those schools that taught through the medium of Irish on the same basis as other schools, and to assist with the funding of a daily newspaper in Irish.

Eventually, in 1992 the Secretary of State for Northern Ireland announced that where there was a local demand, street names in Irish could be erected alongside the English name. Correspondence in Irish is also now dealt with by the government, and although there is as yet no official policy on publishing official documents in Irish, this does happen when requested e.g. the Belfast Agreement was published in Irish.

In broadcasting, there were also many issues that were a source of considerable contention to the nationalist minority. There was an exclusion on the reporting of minority cultural issues, including sport, and the Irish language was banned from radio and television for almost the first fifty years of the Northern Ireland state.

Following the Civil Rights campaign, the new-found culturally assertive capacities of the nationalist community began to achieve some successes in the early 1970's when the British Broadcasting Corporation (BBC) was persuaded to introduce occasional radio programmes in the Irish language. Although there was considerable resistance from many unionists, the BBC persisted with the experiment, and were eventually persuaded to introduce a regular Irish-language programme in 1981, followed by some schools broadcasting in 1985. In 1991 the BBC broadcast its first television production in Irish. Although the total hours broadcast in Irish are still minimal, particularly when compared to those available in Gaelic in Scotland, or in Welsh in Wales, the barriers to the use of Irish in broadcasting have now substantially disappeared.

In addition to its work on the language, the Cultural Traditions Group also helped to further develop the work of the broadcasting companies by encouraging, and in some case funding, initiatives which exemplified cultural diversity programming and encouraged debate on political and cultural issues. Such work has assisted a context of diversity and challenge which has eventually led to a much healthier and open context for discussion on the many issues which were eventually pertinent to the Belfast Agreement and the setting up of the subsequent Assembly. The use of the Irish Language, and expressions of nationalist and Irish identity have now receded as a significant source of political tension. The community are now used to hearing regular Irish language programmes on radio and television, the tricolour usually flies freely, without official interference, and street names in Irish are now accepted as delivery addresses by the postal services. A constructive framework for valuing diversity has now at last been laid and has ensured a much more positive context for the agreements on cultural pluralism that were made in the Belfast Agreement.

The Need for Civic Society Involvement

In a situation like Northern Ireland where the state retains some coherent and credible levels of governance, it is of vital importance that the government itself should be engaged in processes of conflict management which can assist peace building through e.g. the development of policies that promote patterns of equity and inclusiveness through legislation, resource allocation and appropriate policies to ensure such principles.

However, even where the state appears to function in a cohesive fashion-as was the case for much of the Northern Ireland conflict-it will often not of itself be able to either start processes of equity, inclusiveness, and political dialogue and agreement without pressure-and support-from civil society.

Investing in a top-down, hierarchical approach to the management and transformation of an ethno-political conflict is unlikely to succeed for a variety of reasons. Governments themselves are often seen as part of the problem by minority groups because (as was the case in N.Ireland) they are often seen to have validated and resourced their particular groups and ignored or excluded the needs of other groups.

Governments also often lack the flexibility to develop creative processes for the management of diversity and indeed experience in places like Northern Ireland, South Africa and the Middle East has shown that training for such diversity is often in the first instance developed through the more independent processes of NGOs and others, where bureaucracy is often lighter, and independent funding sometimes ensures a more open approach to such issues.

Primarily, however, governments find it hard to deliver on political agreements because politicians are often the people who find it the hardest to develop policies of diversity in the face of the fears of their electorates. Thus there is often a need for a constituency for such validation to be developed by their electorate which can enable or permit them to move with energy on such policies, and here NGOs and others can play a crucial part. Such was the case in Northern Ireland where the work of the NGOs was crucial in developing processes of dialogue, models of training, and constituencies for political agreement both during the pre-agreement phase of the peace process, and the 'YES' campaign that followed to secure its endorsement.

The Need for a Variety of Approaches to Peace—Building

Unfortunately, fundamental disagreements between theorists and practitioners about priorities in approaches to conflict resolution work have often limited its development. This was certainly the case in Northern Ireland where throughout much of the seventies and eighties there was major dissension between those who see such work as primarily needing a structural approach to management and those who see the work as needing primarily a psychocultural approach. (Ross) Those focusing on structural work-who saw the problem as one of incompatible interests which arise from the structure of a community-concentrated on issues of justice and rights, equity and political issues.

Those approaching the work from a psychocultural perspective-which emphasises the need to develop relationships between conflicting groups-concentrated in the first instance on eliminating the fears, ignorance and hostility between communities through contact and co-operative possibilities which provided access to groups about each other's histories, religions, cultures, and fears.

Both approaches of course have their limitations, and tension between groups and institutions about prioritising such approaches was both limiting and unnecessary. 12 Eventually, groups focusing on relationship building began to energetically included dialogue on difficult issues of structural problems as part of relationship building, and those involved in such structural work began to avail of the skills of those who could provided the productive context within which such dialogues could take place.

Reframe the Problems where Possible

A major factor in trying to end the obstacles to dialogue and agreement has been attempts that have been made to circumscribe accustomed or declared stances on such issues as dialogue, and constitutional possibilities. These have included e.g. the use of 'unauthorised' and 'deniable' contacts to facilitate dialogue where such was deemed either useless, obnoxious or in some cases illegal; the presentation of a common social focus as an excuse for assisting talks between loyalist and republican community workers in Belfast; the use of parallel or proximity talks to ensure that all political parties could be include in discussions; and the use of shuttle mediation in such situations were examples of lateral thinking that was useful in difficult situations.

When very contentious issues arose in multi-party talks-such as decommissioning or policing-and began to slow down the talks processes, the use of independent commissions to discuss these issues with neutral facilitators was very helpful. Prime examples of these were the Independent Commission on Decommissioning and the newly formed Independent Commission on Policing. Such developments meant that these issues were not allowed to derail the various talks processes.

Perhaps the most major creative success is the Belfast Agreement itself, which has developed a unique constitutional framework which secures a system of overlapping and interlocking national and cultural loyalties, and which has effectively brought an end to the idea of any possible identity or loyalty hegemony in Northern Ireland.

All citizens can now legally avail of both British and/or Irish passports. People can choose to look to London or to Dublin-or to Northern Ireland-for their cultural identity and heritage. The agreement has broken the much out-dated notion-in this world of increasing ethnic mobility-that nationality, ethnicity and territory are necessarily legally or constitutionally overlapping.

The Future

It is a well established fact to those of us working in conflict that in fact conflicts do not end-they just change. Undoubtedly significant challenges remain to be addressed. 14 Among these can be numbered the possible further development of some of the splinter groups who have split from the main paramilitary movements, and the need for the existing Assembly parties to constructively and collectively deal with this challenge. The issue of contentious parades still remain unresolved and there is the continuing difficulty of the possible destabilisation of the Assembly through the growth of more 'anti-agreement' representatives who could coalesce around such issues as the failure to agree to a process of decommissioning and the difficulties in re-developing a police service that is more acceptable to nationalists.

However, thanks to the previous work undertaken, and to the nature of the Belfast Agreement itself, there is now in place a variety of very useful mechanisms which have been designed to deal with these and other inevitable difficulties that will arise over the coming years.

Effectively, the war is ended. For many, committee papers have been substituted for guns. Meetings with British civil servants-and even British Prime Ministers-have become part of daily life for erstwhile Sinn Fein/IRA and Loyalist activists many of whom are now full or part-time engaged in national and local politics and who are now having to depend upon the use of politics rather than force to address the myriad local and regional issues that are now their collective responsibility.

The road to such an agreement has been long, complex and often bloody. Almost thirty years and three and a half thousand dead have been the result of the fear, discrimination, intransigence, anger and violence with which communities and government have limited their much surer and swifter progress towards peace. The peace has been long in the coming, and hard in the making. It does, however, at last appear that the hard work and the courage of many, creative approaches to both dialogue and constitutional solutions have eventually yielded enough to take Northern Ireland to a future where politics and not violence will primarily prevail. If this proves to be the case-it will truly be a new beginning for Northern Ireland.

A JOINT EFFORT-THE SOUTH AFRICAN PEACE PROCESS

The tumultuous political transition that occurred in South Africa during the 1990s, variously described as the South African 'miracle', the 'negotiated revolution', or the peaceful change from apartheid to democracy, is a success story that should never be taken for granted. The determined actions and sacrifices of many individuals and organisations, as well as national and international developments, shaped this process. There was nothing inevitable about it-in fact at various stages of this process the prospects of peaceful progress or civil war were balanced on a knife-edge.

When, in February 1990, Nelson Mandela was released from 27 years in prison, and liberation movements such as the African National Congress (ANC) and the Pan Africanist Congress (PAC) were unbanned, South Africa had just gone through a debilitating year of political violence. With 1,403 people killed, 1989 had been the worst year of political violence in modern South African history. A political and strategic deadlock between the Apartheid State and the anti-apartheid forces had developed. The release of Mandela fuelled expectations of constitutional negotiations that would lead South Africa out of its political cul-de-sac. It was assumed that political violence would abate and that peace was at last within reach.

This optimism was largely misplaced. Violence did not abate. Fierce clashes between ANC supporters and supporters of the largely Zulu based Inkatha Freedom Party (IFP) took place. In many instances, the security forces were playing a sinister role of fuelling such conflicts. In fact 1990, the year that many thought would be the precursor to liberation, democracy and stability, became a year of unprecedented political strife and killings. 3,699 people were killed through political violence, a 163 percent increase over 1989. Hopes for a peaceful change dimmed as the increased political violence prevented constitutional negotiations from commencing. It became clear that if South Africa was to break out of the growing spiral of violence and polarisation, political leaders would have to manage the coming transition more effectively, and rules of conduct would have to be agreed upon in order to minimise the political violence and intolerance.

In the face of these developments, an embarrassed South African political leadership began realising that they were incapable of stemming the violence on their own. Bilateral meetings between Nelson Mandela, then deputy president of the ANC, and Chief Minister Buthelezi, leader of the IFP, took place. One day after Mandela and Buthelezi had announced a 'watershed agreement effectively outlawing violence, intimidation and political intolerance among their followers' a fierce battle between more than 2,000 supporters of the ANC and the IFP took place in the province of Natal. At least 8 people were killed, 60 injured, and about 56 houses burned to the ground. The calls for peace by political leaders had no effect.

President de Klerk and his ruling National Party were embarrassed by their apparent inability to contain the violence that weakened their negotiating power. Growing allegations of 'third force' involvement and of the active participation and fuelling of the violence by de Klerk's security forces were strongly denied by him.

The impression therefore gained ground that violence was out of control and that neither South Africa's political leadership or De Klerk's security forces were able to address it effectively. Interventions from national role players other than the government and political leaders seemed to present the only hope to stem the worsening political violence and instability.

The church was the institution that first attempted a national intervention at the beginning of 1991. This was one year after the release of Mandela. The South African Council of Churches (SACC), an umbrella body for many churches, including the Methodist and Anglican Churches, called for an urgent national meeting of all leaders of strife-torn communities. The SACC, which had over many years been a strong critic of apartheid, did not represent Afrikaner churches and was distrusted by some of the political opponents of the ANC, including Chief Minister Buthelezi of the IFP. It was therefore not surprising that Buthelezi was sceptical about an SACC sponsored meeting. This was one of the main reasons why it never got off the ground.

South Africa's business community, primarily white, was also experiencing anxious times. The initial optimism that the release of Mandela would lead to political stability and the lifting of international economic sanctions, and therefore an economic upswing, had proved to be groundless. One interest group within the business community, namely the Consultative Business Movement (CBM), decided to take up the challenge. It was a voluntary organisation of senior and more progressive South African business leaders who acknowledged and supported the need for fundamental transformation in the country. In a low-key manner, the Consultative Business Movement met with the ANC, the South African Communist Party, Chief Minister Buthelezi and the Central Executive Committee of the IFP, a delegation of cabinet ministers from the National Party and with the leaders of the largest labour federation in the country, the Congress of South African Trade Unions. At all these meetings, the violence in the country was discussed. Nothing concrete emerged, but the CBM had placed itself on the map as an organisation with a potential facilitating role.

Whilst political violence was escalating to alarming levels, President de Klerk organised a 'Peace Summit' to which he invited all political groupings in the country. Some of the major political forces, for example, the ANC, declined to participate. They saw him as part of the problem of violence and not as the one who could provide a solution. His inability to deal with the violence through his government's security forces highlighted his impotence. It had become clear that without the involvement of the ANC, his Summit would not achieve much.

The frustration and helplessness being experienced by South Africans in general contributed to a gloomy future scenario of ongoing violence, growing instability and even prospects of a low intensity civil war. Commentators, both locally and abroad, predicted a bloody future. All efforts at bringing political violence under control had failed: the political leaders had been unsuccessful in stamping their authority on their followers. The churches were not trusted by all. De Klerk himself and his government had no credibility among the majority of black South Africans and big business was too close to the government to be trusted by the ANC.

The success in turning this critical and depressing situation into one of hope, lay in attempts to find more creative multi-track approaches towards achieving peace. No bilaterals or single organisations had succeeded in bringing South Africa's main political leaders together to talk peace.

The various initiatives that followed, and that contributed to the eventual peaceful political change in 1994, involved a whole range of interest groups and role players. Leaders of the South African Council of Churches and the CBM took the step of jointly exploring what role civil society could play to halt the slide towards growing polarisation of South African society. They expanded their discussions to include the leadership of the Congress of South African Trade Unions and also made contact with de Klerk's office. In further discussions (these were all informal and low-key), key figures from the Dutch Reformed Church, such as its former moderator, were invited. The Dutch Reformed Church was regarded as an Afrikaner church with influence over the Afrikaner establishment. The church and business leaders from the SACC and CBM then met with Buthelezi as well as with President de Klerk.

What they were seeking was an understanding for the need to call a peace meeting through the joint offices of the churches and business. The initial responses by Buthelezi and de Klerk were sceptical. De Klerk stressed that the government did not need the help of facilitators because it was in direct communication with all relevant parties. He did, however give a mandate to a trusted senior figure in the Afrikaner establishment who had attended De Klerk's failed peace summit, to meet with church and business leaders to explore the possibilities for a more representative peace meeting.

These informal discussions gathered momentum. Participants soon conceptualised the process that would have to be followed if violence was to be reduced. A meeting, referred to as a 'think tank for peace', to which all relevant political groups and others would be invited, was planned for 22 June 1991 in Johannesburg.

The response to the invitations was very encouraging. Never before in South Africa's history had so many diverse political groupings agreed to meet on one platform to talk peace. During the daylong meeting, which was held in the sumptuous offices of a large business concern, Archbishop Tutu played a crucial role in steering the ship through some dangerous rapids. Behind closed doors, different perspectives of the political violence and the political intolerance were considered.

South Africans at large received the outcome with a sigh of relief. It was agreed to establish a new preparatory committee, this time consisting mainly of representatives of various political parties but chaired by a prominent non-partisan businessman. The committee decided to establish five working groups that would look at the following issues:

Group 1: Code of conduct for political parties

Group 2: Code of conduct for Security Forces

Group 3: Socio-economic development

Group 4: Implementation and monitoring

Group 5: Process, secretariat, and media

Each Working Group was to consist of three nominees from the government/National Party, three nominees from the IFP, three nominees from the ANC/South African Communist Party/ Congress of South African Trade Unions alliance, one religious leader, and one business representative from the preparatory committee. September 14, 1991 was set as the target date by which the reports from the five working groups had to be completed and on which a National Peace Convention would be held to ratify and sign the agreements. South Africa's political, church, trade union and business leaders would be invited to attend.

Whilst the political leadership backed the work of the five Working Groups, there was no let-up in the violence and killings between their supporters and the security forces on the ground.

To an increasing extent, South Africans realised that, unless the planned National Peace Convention was successful, the chances of commencing constitutional negotiation were slim and so were the chances of peace and stability. The Convention therefore had to be successful. And so it was.

The National Peace Convention was a remarkable occasion. The written reports from the working groups had been collated to form what was from then on referred to as the National Peace Accord. With the exception of three white right-wing parties, the national leaders of all South Africa's political groups attended. This had never happened before. For the first time Mandela, de Klerk, and Buthelezi were together and actually sitting next to each other. Add to that the leaders of the South African Communist Party, the Pan Africanist Congress and a number of smaller parties, and it becomes clear why the National Peace Convention represented a breakthrough for South Africa. It showed that the deep-seated differences that existed would, in future, not prevent the various parties from speaking to each other about common interests.

Leaders from various religious denominations were there. So were trade unions, the business community, the diplomatic corps, Zulu king Goodwill Zwelithini, traditional chiefs and newspaper editors. The symbolic significance of such a gathering was powerful, something that the media conveyed with full fanfare.

Witnessed by all those present, the political leaders signed the National Peace Accord and undertook to make it work. This was to be a daring experiment in conflict resolution on a national scale. The Accord provided for the establishment of a network of representative peace committees at national, regional, and local levels. Basic democratic norms would have to be abided by, political intolerance would not be allowed, dispute resolution mechanisms were built in, a code of conduct was provided for both political parties and the police, and a programme of socio-economic development was to be initiated.

The first broad outlines of the new South Africa were established. As an evaluation mission from International Alert concluded, 'Its [the accord's] significant success lies in developing a 'peace culture', in securing an ideological commitment from the principal political actors to 'political tolerance', and in being able to establish procedures and mechanisms for crisis management.' This approach towards achieving peace, in which the elite as well as ordinary communities had a role to play, and in which labour unions, churches, business, traditional leaders, other civil society structures as well as political parties were involved, meant that people from across South Africa became part of a peace process with a common objective in mind. By April 1994, when the first democratic election was held, one national peace committee, eleven regional, and 250 local peace committees had been established throughout the country.

After the signing of the National Peace Accord, political leaders soon turned their attention to the next major challenge that required urgent attention, the proposed multi-party conference to negotiate a new democratic constitution for the country. Political expectations were high; something the Peace Accord was unable to address. It was not geared to transform the country from apartheid to a democracy. It was also not geared to deal with the danger presented by the multiplicity of military forces in the country. Nor was it capable of defusing the threats of sabotaging of the negotiated change by armed white right-wing groups. A number of simultaneous and multi-track approaches to deal with these threats were initiated.

By the end of 1991, the Conference for a Democratic South Africa, CODESA, had constituted itself as the multi-party forum through which constitutional negotiations would take place. The country's political leadership participated in these often tension-ridden discussions, week after week, for many months, while their supporters were attempting to make the Peace Accord work on the ground. All the Peace Committees could achieve was to help contain political violence to levels that would otherwise have been even worse.

After a particularly brutal massacre in June 1992, in which 48 people, mainly women and children were killed, local and international outrage followed and the constitutional negotiations came to a grinding halt. After an appeal to the

United Nations by Nelson Mandela, the General Assembly decided in August 1992 to deploy UN observers to South Africa. Within the next few months they were joined by monitors from the Commonwealth, the Organisation for African Unity and the European Community. In terms of the UN resolution, they attached themselves to peace committees in various parts of the country where they made a significant impact. With their distinct uniform or flags, they were seen by friend and foe as 'the ears and eyes' of the international community. This enabled international monitors to have a restraining impact on potentially violent situations such as huge political rallies or protest marches. Their contribution to the eventual successful political change should not be underestimated.

In order to assist in preparing citizens and institutions for a totally different political and social future, many civil society structures were busy facilitating contact and interaction between erstwhile enemies or with state and other institutions that faced fundamental transformation.

These were crucial initiatives: communication and joint planning for the future was facilitated between the South African Defence Force and the military wing of the ANC. Afrikaner establishment figures from sports, the arts, business and the media were introduced to leading politicians and others from exile in a systematic way.

Low-key contacts with white right-wing groups were established with the hope of staving off any serious attempts to derail the coming election and to secure their participation in the elections. Some non-governmental organisations focused on research and policy changes that would soon become necessary. Many other examples could be mentioned. All these efforts constituted a productive and multi-faceted approach by civil society structures towards achieving a peaceful transition from apartheid to a democracy.

During the entire pre-election period, international economic and financial sanctions remained in place and were used to apply pressure for change on de Klerk's governing National Party and on the business community. Even sanctions played their part in the eventual successful outcome of this process.

A peaceful political transition was therefore pursued through a multi-track approach involving all sectors of South African society as well as the international community. The peace process resulting from the National Peace Accord was merely one of the tracks that brought South Africa to its first democratic election. Coming soon after the Peace Accord, CODESA was the track on which the actual new dispensation was brokered, and for almost two years, these two processes worked in tandem. Other tracks involved civil society structures, the international monitors, and informal interactions by non governmental organisations and a variety of groups.

All these initiatives went through testing times. Although deaths as a result of political violence had peaked in July 1993, shortly before the elections, in March and April 1994, a serious escalation of political violence suddenly occurred. During March alone, 552 persons had died. A state of emergency was declared in the province of KwaZulu-Natal and security forces were placed on the alert.

An inexplicable change occurred during the last week before the election was due on 26 April 1994. Violence subsided. An almost eerie absence of political violence and death during the four voting days occurred. The co-operation and goodwill that was exhibited between South Africans from across the spectrum created a new sense of national unity and optimism for the future. It had a major influence on the national mood for a year or two.

As was to be expected, however, the post election honeymoon has since lost a lot of its sparkle. Despite the miraculous transition in South Africa, enormous challenges and problems face the country. The successful peace process over the past ten years will, however, always provide justification to South Africans for the belief that should national crises occur, they have it within themselves to pull together and overcome such crises.

ISRAELI-PALESTINIAN PEACE-BUILDING

We would like to share our thoughts on the relevance of Israeli-Palestinian case to work conducted worldwide from coexistence to peace-building and reconciliation. While ours is a particular case-and we often think that our conflicts present unique features when explaining the difficulties in resolving them-we should be also aware that it shares similarities and differences with other ethnopolitical disputes. In fact it belongs with many others to the category of protracted communal conflicts, the prevailing category of violent disputes in the post-Cold War period. From this perspective, the Israeli/Palestinian conflict perhaps shares less attributes with the Syrian/Israeli border dispute (over territorial claims on the sparsely populated Golan Heights) than with other identity-driven confrontations in former Yugoslavia, Cyprus, Sri Lanka or Indonesia.

We will centre our comments on the last decade of joint work conducted on the part of non-governmental organizations, academics, and other professional groups interested in a historic compromise based on the search for common ground. Our wish is to present a critical introspect, although it may be difficult to retain objectivity when we are both so centrally involved in the process itself. In the next pages we would like to present a brief background followed by a diagnosis of the obstacles, as well as the achievements, of the groups presented in the book in different sectors. The article concludes with some prescriptive comments applicable to others.

Framing the Issue

After over a century of discord, marked both by intermittent acts of violence and officially declared wars (about one a decade), the Israeli-Palestinian conflict has eventually resulted in a lengthy peace process. The current process was inaugurated at Madrid in October 1991 as a regional enterprise and took shape as a bilateral understanding through the 'Oslo channel', which was endorsed by both sides in the famous signing of the resultant accords on the White House lawn in September 1993.

Israel's first agreement with Egypt in 1978 failed to lead to a subsequent reconciliation with its other Arab neighbours, leaving the core dispute with the Palestinians active for another two decades. The 1988 recognition by the Palestine Liberation Organization (PLO) of a 'two-state solution' did not meet with the approval of the then Likud government in Israel, and it was only in the aftermath of the 1991 Gulf War that negotiations were able to progress. The process launched in Madrid that same year came at first to a diplomatic impasse in Washington, but this was followed by a complex, but effective, track two process in Oslo.

The rise to power of Prime Minister Netanyahu's hard-line government in 1996 slowed down the implementation of the interim agreements and totally disrupted the timetable established for completing an agreement of final status issues (including borders and security, Jerusalem, Jewish settlements, Palestinian refugees and other issues such as management of water resources). The parties were expected to reach an agreement on these important issues by 1999, but by now it seems that the situation will remain an open challenge at the dawn of the 21st century.

We would like to focus on the interaction of Arabs and Jews across the Green Line that has separated the 'small' Israel from the territories of the West Bank and Gaza that were occupied in the June 1967/Six Days War. These areas have seen only partial re-deployment in areas now under the control of the Palestinian National authority, while the rest of the occupied lands remain under shared rule but total Israeli military control. The larger part of the West Bank and a smaller portion of Gaza are still in Israeli hands and this territory includes not less than 130 new Jewish settlements.

This delimitation of scope is important since within the 'small' Israel there has been a longer history of rapprochement between Jews (80% of the population) and Arabs (20%), efforts often described as a drive towards 'coexistence'. This last term is not popular amongst Palestinians, and to a lesser extent amongst Israelis, who are involved in 'peace-building' as a complement to the efforts at 'peacemaking' among their leaders. The issue at stake is found within the former term, since a Palestinian state has not yet come into existence and any efforts towards any other solution are considered to be insufficient for eventually ensuring a 'real peace' that can cement the post-negotiation stage of 'reconciliation'. Hence, 'coexistence' across the yet undefined borders is often perceived as a false 'normalization.' The term for this in Arabic (tatbyeh) connotes unilateral acceptance of the Jewish state without first securing the full recognition of the individual and collective rights of the Palestinian people.

Meanwhile, the Jewish side achieved its political independence fifty years ago and has since worked to secure it through military superiority over coalitions of Arab states, and surely over the Palestinians. It has also worked to consolidate its presence in the Middle East through peace accords with Egypt (the most important and strongest Arab country) and the Hashemite Kingdom of Jordan (with which Israel shares its longest current border). The State of Israel has also developed a vibrant economy stimulated by generous foreign aid and consolidated democratic institutions.

What makes this conflict even more difficult to resolve is the fact that the people of both nations have historically claimed the full possession of the entire land of Greater Israel or Palestine, and that throughout history there have been few moments of convergence of objectives between their respective leaderships.

Yet, from within the context of these constraints, there has been a growing recognition by each party of the rights of the other to self-determination and support of the Oslo peace process has reached a high of 75% in both societies. Still, only a small segment of this population actively strives towards the fulfilment of this goal either separately or together with their counterparts.

At the other end of the spectrum we find a militant extremist minority often driven by 'divine inspiration' to commit acts opposed not only to the particularities of the Oslo Peace Process, but to any reconciliation.

This contingent perceives the conflict in terms of a zero-sum game and claims that its side (these sorts exist on both sides of the conflict) has absolute rights and that there is no room for compromise. Their use of various acts of violence and terror, as well as civil disobedience, provides them with a relative advantage as compared with the mostly reactive and law-abiding protesters from the 'peace camp'. The Israeli silent majority seems to have been more affected by the zealots' opposition to the peace process than by the support it receives from pragmatics and moderates.

Obstacles and Opportunities

To what extent can we establish the success or failure of such endeavours made in support of peace? No clear methodology has been found yet. One could argue that the situation could always have been worse. For instance, the conflict is now considered to be of a 'low intensity level' compared with its past stages or the current situation with similar conflicts elsewhere around the globe. It could be argued that without the sustained efforts of NGOs on both sides there would not have been a sense of hope for the resolution of the conflict; that without peace demonstrations and human rights monitors, the suffering of the Palestinian side would have been greater.

At the same time, it is quite depressing to realize that only a small fragment of the population of both societies has been involved in peace-building activities, and that the fragility of such undertakings have often declined as a result of terror by committed fundamentalist extremists from both sides. Even the most insignificant minorities when driven by 'God's will' can effectively disrupt the peace process. A serious impediment to face-to-face contacts results from the closures of the Palestinian areas that often follow incidents of terror. Still, there is a need to recognize the presence not only of physical barriers, but also of psychological barriers that are no less difficult to overcome while neither side is still unable to display significant levels of reciprocal compassion.

The facts on the ground have placed Israel in the position of relative strength, generating an asymmetric relationship with the Palestinians that makes joint efforts towards peace-building more difficult.

The Palestinians will not assent to claims of a 'lasting' peace before the Israeli power and the international community both recognize some basic aspects of 'justice'. Thus we find the first gap between the goals of the Israeli side-with a noticeable and at times very active 'peace movement'-Peace Now in its best moments could gather more than 200,000 in Tel Aviv-and a much smaller constituency led by a significant number of skeleton NGOs that make up the 'human rights community.'

One the one hand, for many Israelis the search for a 'lasting peace' is an act of enlightened self-interest. On the other hand, many Israelis find it difficult to express solidarity with the demands to refrain from human rights violations of the 'other' when this means identifying with members of a nation from which a small minority of the population is still perpetuating horrendous acts of terror towards them.

After the June 1967 war, the first Palestinian NGOs were established to prevent human rights violations and, during the Intifada, they grew into a self-reliant driving force working in the absence of an elected authority. After the Oslo accords, more NGOs were established to raise awareness among the public on women's rights, democracy, and transparency. Only lately, several NGOs were established in support of the Peace Process. What makes the relationship between the two parties more difficult is that among the Palestinians there has been a widespread disillusionment with their Jewish counterparts who have not made their struggle for peace a top priority in their lives. The occasional participation in a demonstration or signing of a petition falls significantly below their level of expectation. Indeed, few Israelis have joined those involved as paid staff or volunteer board members of human rights NGOs. Yet, it is important to recall that those few are strongly committed Israeli activists that have been fighting against administrative detention, housing demolition, the use of 'moderate physical pressure' (that amounts to torture) in interrogations, and other violations.

We detect a certain level of tension around these issues. It has been difficult to generate an atmosphere of cooperation when the asymmetry on the ground is so clear. The practical limitations on the freedom of movement and the effect of humiliation by Israeli security forces combine to generate a mood amongst Palestinians that is adverse to voluntary participation in cooperative endeavours with Israeli partners. Furthermore, the unequal number of Israelis (five million Jews and one million non-Jews) and Palestinians (two and a quarter million), the gaps in the educational, technological, and socio-economic levels, and years of consolidation as a democratic entity-all of these factors increase the disparities. One of the consequences is that we often find more Israelis seeking Palestinian partnership than vice versa-a problematic situation when planning activities based on equality which also means numeric parity.

Lastly, we need to recall that in the not remote past, and for a long period of time, the Palestinian leadership first and then the Israeli leadership later forbade any contacts amongst our peoples-although there has been direct contact since 1967. Palestinian dialogue pioneers have been killed by extremist groups and-no doubt a more moderate level of limitation-Israeli peaceniks have been jailed, or politically ostracized, for talking to PLO representatives. While academic and intellectual projects and encounters have been developed since the Intifada (the Palestinian uprising in the West Bank and Gaza that started in November 1987), most of the dialogue and cooperation programs started after 1993 through the support of 'People-to-People' initiatives of friendly governments, with Norway in the lead.

This structural weakness in 'peace-building' has marked the cooperation within this area, where people of goodwill tend to act separately, or at best in short-term projects of bilateral cooperation between NGOs, and even less so among professionals under the umbrella of public institutions such as universities. The official Palestinian policy is still to reject such 'normalization' in the face of existing inequalities. Yet, there have been not a few NGOs ready for cooperation and some of them have even utilized such contacts in their defense of Palestinian rights, both in relation to the Israeli and Palestinian authorities.

Another concern lies in the ability to understand the culture and tradition of the 'other'-from how to share the grief when facing acts of terror and violence to the differences in group dynamics in the conduction of meetings. Though many Palestinians know Hebrew, few Israelis understand Arabic, and as a result most of the peacebuidling activities are conducted among those who speak English, thus omitting the real grassroots people, who are often more emotionally antagonistic to each other. Furthermore, there are only a handful of joint Israeli-Palestinian NGOs, and most of these are more radical than liberal in their political orientation, and therefore unattractive to the majority of activists on either side.

This marks a major difference from the Arab-Jewish coexistence activity within Israel, where the tendency has been prevailingly to work together in common institutions. In peace-building across the divide, the majority of interactions are conducted by separate Israeli and Palestinian NGOs acting together for a specific period of time. While this mode may more appropriate for what eventually is heading into two distinct but intertwined states, there is still a long way to go for each side to reach out to other similar organizations in its own civil society. For instance, the possibility for a joint Israeli/Palestinian peace education project that would have a multiplying effort in involving or getting interested other NGOs in each side interested in education.

Paradoxically, even if progress in coexistence work can be noticed, we cannot expect a high level of success for Arab/ Jewish cooperation efforts in Israel without reaching an effective peace-building among Israelis and Palestinians. The remaining level of conflict in the latter relation makes it impossible to reach the attainment of equal rights in the first. This is not meant to belittle the importance of a pluralistic commitment to work simultaneously in seeking the fulfilment of both goals. Rather it is intended to simply stress the need to prioritize and understand that real reconciliation will not occur unless we put more energy in producing changes of leadership conducive not only to the reactivation but also towards the 'humanization' of the Peace Process. Implicit in this is the necessity to fight simultaneously both for the respect of human rights and conflict resolution.

Although the scale of cooperation remains limited by the above mentioned obstacles, we need to stress that the diverse projects of schoolchildren, youth, artists, professional groups, women, and political movements of both sides have shown a high level of creativity. In many ways the Israeli/Palestinian laboratory is an exemplary reservoir of ideas to be emulated elsewhere. Needless to say, we also acknowledge that there is a lot to learn from peace-builders elsewhere. The numbers and qualities of joint projects have increased over time, and it is true that they have done so with the help of generous funding from abroad. In most cases, they have managed to endure the downs of the Peace Process, and that in itself can be seen as an achievement. We do not have space to systematically point out to the many success stories, some are described elsewhere in this volume, and we will confine ourselves to relate briefly to the categories analyzed in this book, with a few illustrations.

Track Two Diplomacy

While the national leadership received the international recognition for the historic signing of the Oslo accords on the White House lawn, these agreements would never have been produced if not for the initiative of non-official second track diplomats. The Israelis and Palestinians who worked through the secret channel in Oslo to produce the framework for the current peace process stand as the most prominent example of the potential of second track diplomacy to make real and lasting advancements in the building of peace.

Media

While the media has perhaps the greatest potential for reaching the masses in whose opinions the fate of the peace process may ultimately lay, the existence of joint endeavours in this sector is really quite limited. Elsewhere we advocate co-authored newspaper editorials as a means for affecting public opinion. While we maintain that such work is important it is relevant that we point out that there is no structural cooperation between Israeli and Palestinian media. Two examples of genuine, ongoing cooperative media projects may be cited, and commended; but it must be stressed that by the nature of their target audiences they have no real effect on the mass population. First is the Israeli-Palestinian Sesame Street television program that may foster in the next generation a culture of peace but cannot have an impact on the politics of the day. Second are the publications of the Alternative Information Centre, a radical left-oriented organization of Israelis and Palestinians critical of the two leaderships and of the Oslo process, but little resonance in both societies.

Religion

Christian, Jewish, and Muslim moderates have met in various different initiatives aimed at using religious leadership to foster support for peace, finding more common ground than expected. The response of those involved in such projects tends to be initially quite positive. But in the long run little inroads have been produced on their respective clerical establishments. No doubt, given that the main dimension of our national conflict is now related to religion, the need to continue to invest on this area needs to be more recognized

Education

It is possible to point out numerous joint projects in the field of education, yet almost without exception these projects are conducted between Israeli Arabs and Israeli Jews. As noted elsewhere, such constructs, confined to the bounds of 'small' Israeli, tend to draw attention away from the greater picture of the Israeli-Palestinian situation. The barriers to cooperation between academic institutions imposed from above on both sides are also existent for the large public school sectors. On the part of the Israelis, the tremendous influence of the orthodox religious in the educational leadership must be weighed. For the Palestinians there is a refusal on the part of the leadership to engage in cooperative endeavours with Israeli institutions until it is possible for schools in the West Bank and Gaza to enjoy free exchange of students.

Women's Issues

Women are among the most prominent individuals working for peace and are involved in large numbers on the Israeli side. This seems not be the case on the Palestinian side where most women leaders seem to devote more energy in the struggle for equality and to show a tougher stand towards normalization with their peers. Few organizations exist and one of the most active over a sustained time has been 'The Jerusalem Link', a coalition of two Israeli and Palestinian feminist peace organizations in East and West Jerusalem, active in promoting both peace and human rights through a two-state solution. It is often responsible for organizing protests against housing demolitions, and other acts by officials that endanger the progress of peace.

Private Sector

Israeli and Palestinian individual businesses have been inclined to trade and seek join ventures or deals, making this cooperation more attractive perhaps than any other. Yet in the motivation for their compulsion to work side by side can be found the very factor that yields private enterprise cooperation ineffective in directly affecting peace-building. That is, the private sector tend to be apolitical, and businesses are inclined to foster only good will and obviously the individual interests of the beneficiaries.

Individual/Community-Based Initiatives

Given the constant tension, the animosity resulting from individual violent acts and collective reprisals, the reduction of the resulting hatred is a top priority in setting the atmosphere for peace-building activities. Unfortunately, only a few initiatives have been undertaken in this field. Dialogue groups have been in existence for a while, such as the Rapprochement Centre in Beit Sahour. but in the long run the effect of talk that does not lead into action has been detrimental to its continuity as a whole. One of the most recent projects is the Parents' Circle, a group formed by a religious Jewish Israeli man who lost his son through an act of Hammas terror.

He refuses to join in the ranks of the families of victims of terror organized in Israel to actively oppose the peace process on the basis of the persistence of such acts. Instead, he has been bringing together Israeli and Palestinian bereaved parents who have lost a member of the family through politically motivated or military violence. They work together to convince the leaderships on both sides that only through establishing a genuine peace will the two peoples be able to put an end to the terror.

These observations can be put within a larger context to affirm that the lack of progress in the peace process has negatively affected democracy in Israel and the process of democratization in the Palestinian Territories. There have been many indications that the quality of life, not only in economic terms, but also in terms of basic freedoms and political/civil rights is increasingly restricted by the procrastination in the advancement of peace. This message has not been successfully communicated to large sectors of the population on both sides, and it still remains a task for those involved in coexistence and peace-building work to undertake as part of their efforts to make the connection between democracy and peace. To get out of this vicious cycle there is a need for the liberal civil society to realize that fragmented efforts need to be understood within a wider picture. On the positive side, there is a connection between democracy and peace (the popular formulation is that democracies tend not to fight wars with one another), and, on the negative side, the first of these deteriorates as a result of paralysis in securing the latter.

In retrospect, we should convey our concern that the dedicated efforts of a small but active part of both Israeli and Palestinian civil societies do not seem to have been effective in positively redressing the adverse trends in the peace process. Extremist groups using violence, civil disobedience, and insubordination on both sides have bypassed the cumulative impact of the many activists involved in 'people-to-people' activities. This despite the fact that the former group constitutes a smaller portion of activists. It may well have to do with the enormous impact of the use of violence, terror, and collective punishment, and the peace forces may revise again the inventory available for effective engagement in civil disobedience and other non-violent methods. The enthusiasm for cooperation has decreased with the decline and eventual halt of the Peace Process. Paradoxically, at times when peace-building is more necessary than ever, the level of motivation of the civil societies to work hand in hand is lower.

For Israeli NGOs it is necessary to fight simultaneously for the end of occupation while at the same time minimizing the day-to-day suffering of the Palestinian population. For Palestinian NGOs it is crucial to transcend their sense of frustration with the lack of 'peace dividends' by still showing public concern and rejection of the use of terror against Israeli civilians. During this last electoral campaign in Israel, the impact of such acts by rejectionist groups is feared; but so far no strong peace message has been coming from the Palestinian civil society as a preventive measure to project another image of the Arab hostility in the Israeli public eye.

Since there is a high level of consensus among Israelis and Palestinians around the plausibility of a 'two-state solution,' the main area of concern remains the fear of terror and reprisals. In this context of lack of personal security to the individuals of both sides, the advocacy of non-violence in the Palestinian struggle for independence, even if not accompanied by support to the Oslo process, could be a tremendous contribution to setting up the conditions for more positive interactions.

Separately, we have analyzed the limitation of the 'people-to-people' work mostly as positive, but introverted, activities that lack clear political objectives, and therefore remain at best a constructive tool for interactions amongst a part of civil society. Such activities indeed build trust, affect attitudes, and reduce stereotypes among the participants in hundreds of programs. Yet there are two additional elements that have not been developed. One of the two missing dimensions is a deliberate attempt to affect the attitudes of policy makers. Sporadic interactions between peace-oriented Palestinians and pro-government Israeli parliamentarians have shown that there is a powerful tool for moderating the views of some. This has not been pursued by the Israelis in 'people-to-people' networks. Sometimes this kind of action can be conducted diagonally from one civil society to the leadership of the other or by jointly trying to affect the leadership of both. Wide publicity about such activities can also affect public attitudes.

The second dimension precisely focuses on efforts to address public opinion and grassroots attitudes. Little has been done to utilize the mass media, such as television, radio talk shows, and daily newspapers. Again, joint appearances (if possible the

Israeli/Palestinian team speaking the language of each audience), co-authored op-eds, successful coverage of 'people-to-people' programs, documenting emotional movements are all appropriate methods. Needless to say, the multiplying effect of a deliberate effort to stimulate a better atmosphere is one of the most powerful tools-particularly at the time of electoral campaigns. It can also contribute to the adoption of confidence building measures such as the decrease of human rights violations, and amnesties for released political prisoners.

One would hope that a realistic and charismatic leadership could radiate confidence not only to its own people but also to the other nation. If such an atmosphere would simultaneously exist on both sides, then we could bring the Peace Process to completion. Even then we would submit that a handshake is not enough, and the human fragility of such equation has been seen in the tragic assassinations of President Sadat and Prime Minister Rabin. Such processes need to be accompanied by an active involvement of the peace forces at all stages of negotiation.

Surely, when the time of reconciliation comes after the agreements, the public dimension of the process will require the groups and prominent individuals within civil society to play an exemplary role. What makes it more troublesome is that we do not find such statesmen available, even from one of the two governments. At this time the challenges of peace-building are formidable and the odds against the extremist forces-now backed also by one government-are not good. This has characterized the late period in our Process and only a more creative, professional, interactive and devoted peace movement on both sides can generate the dynamics that will trigger a real change of minds and hearts among their brethren.

REFLECTIONS ON PEACE BUILDING

The following section of this book tells 35 inspiring stories describing peace-building initiatives from around the world. Here we focus on some of the lessons that can be learned from these and other examples. Naturally, these lessons draw on the work of the many experts who have reflected on this subject on earlier occasions.

Uundoubtedly one of the most important documents relating to these issues is the outline of guidelines and principles based on the accumulated experience and wisdom of the Institute for MultiTrack Diplomacy. Also included are elements of the 'Agenda for Peace and Justice for the 21st century' currently being drafted by the Hague Appeal for Peace, as well as the Strategic Plan developed by the Coexistence Initiative of State of the World Forum (see annexes).

Involve as Many People and Sectors as Possible in Peace-building

It is an obvious point but one which is, nevertheless, frequently overlooked: it is essential that as many sectors of society as possible be included in any peace-building process. Many of the following stories illustrate how individuals and groups take responsibility for the society they live in, and how they can make a real difference.

Strengthen Local Capacities for Peace

If efforts to prevent, resolve and transform violent conflict are to be effective in the long-term, they must be based on the active participation of local civil groups committed to building peace.

Strengthening such 'local capacities for peace' may take many forms, including education and training, nurturing the volunteer spirit in society and highlighting the work of local peacemakers in the media. Granting basic human rights such as freedom of speech and press and freedom to organise oneself are prerequisites for including the different civil organisations in the peace process.

Conceive Peace Building and Reconciliation as a Process

Peace is not an abstract goal but a process; it must be built-up over a long period of time. Building peace must be an organic process, growing at all levels of society. Peace cannot be built just through exclusive conclaves of the leaders of the conflicting parties. The idea of 'historic agreements as a stepping stone to peace' has proven to be wrong on too many occasions. Longterm strategic relationships should be built which reach across the dividing lines of conflict in society.

Change and Transform the Conflict Pattern: Create Hope

A common feature of many of the following examples is that they succeeded in breaking the logic of war. Successful initiatives create hope and stimulate people to disengage themselves from war, as is shown by the peace zones in Columbia and the struggle to preserve the multicultural character of the city of Tuzla in Bosnia. Although people could not prevent an escalation of the surrounding violence, they succeeded in creating local alternatives. By inspiring others these initiatives have an extremely important spin-off effect.

Create Dialogue

Stimulate a feeling of interdependence, emphasise common identities and help people to understand the other side's position. Private peacemaking should focus on 'humanising the enemy'. The most effective dialogue often occurs when each side forcefully advocates its position and then listens to its opponent. It should be recognised that people can communicate with each other, but may not be ready for a dialogue. Much creativity is needed to bring the parties together for a first round of talks. In many situations-like in Somalia, Mali, Northern Ireland, Guatemala, and Sri Lanka-the importance of such an approach has been proven.

Promote Education and Enhance Professionalisation

Educational programmes should stimulate the universal awareness of coexistence, tolerance and reconciliation. Those involved in the peace-building process must be thoroughly prepared and trained. Professionalisation of peace building can enhance its effectiveness.

Exchange Experiences

Promote international exchanges between peacemakers from conflict regions. Learning from each other's experiences inspires innovative approaches as the examples of Sri Lanka, South Africa and Northern Ireland clearly show.

Include Local Authorities

The decentralised approach of grassroots and community-based organisations has resulted in many successes. Examples of these successes include the EU Peace Fund in Northern Ireland, the city approach of the World Council of Churches, as well as the creation of the over 200 local peace commissions in Kenya.

Strengthen Coalition Building between Civil Organisations

The effectiveness of civil activity is often hampered by a lack of coordination between groups operating in similar fields. As a result, scarce resources are wasted through duplication of tasks and failure to achieve synergy. There is a great need to create civil networks and/or platforms that promote coalition and constituency building. Global networks are needed to further strengthen individuals' and communities' capacity for peace building. Many of the following case-studies are an illustration of this need. Through networking they succeeded in multiplying their strength.

Institution-building

To sustain peace-building and reconciliation, institution-building should be stimulated at all levels of society and at the international level. In an increasingly globalized international system, the need to work at global institutions, actors and processes to create the climate for conflict resolution, prevention, peace-building and reconciliation, should be emphasised.

Make 'Conflict Impact Assessment' a Requirement

In order to maximise the benefits of development aid, dispensing bodies-governmental, intergovernmental and private-should be required to assess and report on the likely impact of their development-aid policies in terms of whether they will heighten or reduce the risks of violent conflicts.

Role of the Corporate Sector

The potential role of the corporate sector in peace-building is still not widely recognised. However, just as business can exacerbate tensions and fuel conflict, so it can contribute to building peace and security, as the examples of South Africa and Northern Ireland, described later in this publication, have shown.

Role of Donors

As the Abraham Fund and the EU Peace Fund for Northern Ireland illustrate, the role of donors can extend beyond the simple provision of financial support for projects. Donors can provide an extra impulse in the peace-building process by stimulating conferences, agenda setting, and developing directories such as The Abraham Fund's 'Handbook of Interethnic Coexistence'.

Prioritise Early Warning and Early Response

That prevention is better than cure is a truth which needs to be better observed in practice. Civil society organisations, governments and intergovernmental bodies should dedicate much more attention and resources to prevention, as opposed to reacting to violent conflict. In particular, mere political should be generated for early responses to potential conflict situations, both present and future.

Promote an Integrative Approach to Peace Building and Reconciliation by using a Combination of Approaches

In her contribution on Northern Ireland to this volume, Mari Fitzduff stresses the need for a variety of approaches to peace building. The experience of Mali provides a clear example of the importance of her message. The construction of a stable peace in the northern part of the country was not the result of any single action. It followed from a complex of efforts to rebuild trust, to address legitimate grievances, to reward combatants who chose to give up the fight, and to build incentives into the peace process that would assure the continued commitment of people on both sides of the conflict.

An integrated framework towards peace building should include:

- o a coherent and comprehensive approach by all actors;
- o partnerships between, and the coordination of, the various members of the international community and the national government;
- o a broad consensus on a strategy and related set of interventions;

- o careful balancing of macro-economic and political objectives, and
- o the necessary financial resources.

Twelve Principles of Multi-Track Diplomacy

1. Relationship-building strong interpersonal and inter-group relations throughout the fabric of society.
2. Longterm commitment-making an ongoing commitment to people and to processes that may take years to come to fruition.
3. Cultural synergy-respecting the cultural wisdom of all parties and welcoming the creative interaction of different cultural views.
4. Partnership-modelling a collaborative process by forming partnerships with local parties and with other institutions and coalitions.
5. Multiple technologies-utilising a variety of technologies, as appropriate, and creating new methods, as needed, to meet the unique requirements of each situation.
6. Facilitation-assisting parties to take responsibility for their own dreams and destiny.
7. Empowerment-helping people to become empowered agents of change and transformation within their societies.
8. Action research-learning from all that we do and sharing that learning with others.
9. Invitation-entering the system where invited or offered an open door.
10. Trust-building relationships of mutual trust and caring within the system.
11. Engagement-acknowledge that once we enter a system, we become a unique part of it, an engaged, caring, and accountable partner.
12. Transformation-catalysing changes at the deepest level of beliefs, assumptions, and values, as well as behaviours and structures.

Mainstream Multi-Track Diplomacy

Peace processes should combine Track One and Track Two approaches. Track Two diplomacy is usually most effective when it is linked to official processes and channels. For this, contacts as well as the exchange of information and experiences between both approaches should be frequent and structural. The history of the peace process in Cyprus provides one among many examples of the importance of linking both tracks. In making these links, the strengths, resources, and limitations of each approach should be taken into account.

POWER FOR PEACE

Track One diplomacy is about men in suits posing before squads of photographers before they disappear behind closed doors for discrete talks. It is also about encoded telexes and email-messages sent back and forth between embassies and government headquarters, evoking a world ruled by formal gentlemen-like codes, imperturbably exposed at press conferences and cocktail parties.

Track One diplomacy is the realm of traditional international politics as practised by foreign offices, ambassadors, special envoys and other officials representing governments. More than any other track, traditional diplomacy can play a decisive role in matters of war and peace.

The culture of Track One diplomacy, the traditional form of international politics, is clearly alien to the world of most Non Governmental Organisations and adherents of alternative political ways. However, proponents of unconventional diplomacy do not consider Track One to be inimical to less conventional approaches. All tracks that can lead to peace should be valued, they say, and the world of traditional diplomacy is no exception.

This point of view fits well with the non governmental peace builders' penchant for harmony and togetherness. It is also born out of pragmatic reasoning. Non-official actors in international politics are as aware as anyone else that the world of Track One diplomacy can exert enormous influence because, generally speaking, it has armies, guns and money at its disposal. Track One, in this sense, is synonymous with power.

Track One diplomacy is indeed suspiciously closely connected to warfare, because, as history books tell us, the same politicians who carry out delicate diplomatic manoeuvres can decide to use force should they prefer to pursue their political goals by other means. But its weight and resources can, of course, also make a difference if used on the side of promoting peace and reconciliation. It is exactly its ability to mobilize vast material resources that constitutes the major potential of Track One diplomacy over other tracks when it comes to going the difficult but rewarding path of conflict prevention, peace building and reconciliation. If politicians of conflicting camps are sincere in their determination to make peace, there will be peace.

The surplus value of Track One over Track Two diplomacy, therefore, is its ability to coerce on the parties in a conflict by directly or indirectly threatening to mobilize its military and financial-economic means. Track One can build up enormous pressure on conflicting parties to pursue a process of negotiation. A prerequisite for this scenario is that Track One actors are willing to intervene as a third party in a foreign conflict in the first place. There are signs that the world of Track One is increasingly receptive to unconventional approaches and collaboration with NGOs, as will be discussed later.

Another advantage of Track One over other tracks is that its actors have direct access to the most important players in a conflict when it comes to forging political agreements. A telling example of what Track One actors can contribute to reconciliation and peace building is the initiative of the Norwegian diplomat Johan Jorgen Holst. Holst discretely contacted Israeli and Palestinian diplomats and hosted secret negotiations in Oslo leading to a breakthrough in the Israeli-Palestinian conflict and the signing of the Oslo agreements in 1996.

The impact of Track One diplomacy can be enhanced enormously when its efforts coincide with complementary initiatives taken by Track Two or other non-official tracks of diplomacy. The signing of the ban on landmines in 1998, for instance, is the result of a successful campaign by international NGOs, but the involvement of Track One was obviously indispensable to anchor the agreement and supervise its implementation.

Scope of Action

A major difference between Track One and Track Two diplomacy is that the former, although more powerful and affluent, is in many ways more restricted in the scope of its actions than the latter. This is because a conciliatory move by an official governmental actor is intrinsically connected to other national interests. For instance, if a mediatory intervention in a foreign conflict is interpreted as being partisan by one of the relevant parties in a conflict, this could lead to economic boycotts or lack of support in international fora for the intervening country concerned. NGOs could also suffer a backlash as a result of intervening in a conflict, but generally speaking they can damage nothing but themselves on the mediating side. An official diplomat or institution, on the other hand, represents an entire nation and its interests and is putting these interests at stake in any intervention.

In democracies, Track One Diplomacy's scope of action may be further limited due considerations of accountability and restrictive regulations of the legislature. Actors in other tracks usually have more freedom to act swiftly and try new approaches.

Track One diplomacy does have its weaknesses. The world of diplomats is said to have insufficient awareness of relevant expertise about international relations, peace and conflict resolution that resides outside the diplomatic community. Another peculiar characteristic of Track One is that commitment to a process of negotiation is often seen as a sign of weakness by political leaders.

One of the most striking flaws of the official diplomatic world, however, is its lack of professional negotiation skills. In many countries, most formal negotiators are known to be still operating without training other than their own experience and intuition. As negotiations are becoming increasingly complex, in an increasingly interdependent and multipolar world, professional negotiation training would be a sensible attribute for all diplomats, McDonald and other advocates of multi-track diplomacy say.

In spite of its weaknesses, Track One actors have become more receptive to peace building, conflict prevention, early warning and similar concepts. In a remarkable move for actors who tend to base their behaviour on the traditional considerations of power politics, an increasing number of national governments has become susceptible to the ideas of conflict prevention and peace building. Belief in the feasibility of alternative approaches is also gaining ground among international organisations and local governments, two other categories that are classified in the Track One category.

In this respect Canada is at the forefront among national governments. Ottawa declared in 1996 that it wanted to set an example to the leadership of the international community by increasing its investment in peace building. It announced a comprehensive peace building strategy, consisting of support to non governmental peace organisations and plans to prepare government agencies, including the armed forces, for tasks in the field of peace building, conflict management, mediation and the like. In September 1997 the Canadian Peace building Program was set up within the Department of Foreign Affairs, giving the new approach a solid place in Canada's Track One diplomacy.

Great Britain's Conservative government decided in 1996 to embrace alternatives to traditional diplomacy, including conflict prevention. London sent its entire foreign aid staff to conflict awareness courses and allocated 1 million pounds to pilot projects in conflict resolution. The present Labour government is continuing on this road.

The left-leaning social democrat administration in Germany, which took office in 1998, has also expressed its commitment to conflict prevention and peace building. Other countries that have already begun to invest significantly in peace building include The Netherlands, Sweden and Norway.

National governments' commitment to peace building is often implemented indirectly, through support to organisations specializing in Track Two approaches. This form of collaboration and coordination between official foreign affairs and non governmental actors is warmly welcomed by most 'alternative' negotiators and peace builders. Complementarity comes into play here. Mutual additionality of Track One and Track Two diplomacy is considered to be of crucial importance to create synergy between the two.

In some cases of Track One contributions to peace making, governments can build on domestic conciliatory traditions. For instance, the initiatives taken by the government of Mali to defuse the deep rooted tension between nomads and sedentary groups in the 1990s-a case which is discussed later in this volume-is in many ways an example of such an approach. On March 27, 1996, President Konaré, Ghanaian President Jerry Rawlings, and leaders of the Mali rebel movements and a large delegation of international observers gathered in Timbuktu for the highly symbolic destruction of all the surrendered armaments in what was called a 'Flame of Peace', to celebrate a peace process initiated by Konaré and hailed as 'visionary'. Here, the Mali government succeeded in motivating local leaders and communities to get a national peace process going.

The growing consensus on the feasibility of peace building and conflict prevention is also visible in multinational organisations. The United Nations, for whom peacemaking is its major mandate, has spent most of the 1990s redefining its mission to include coping with internal conflicts. The Agenda for Peace, published in 1992, was the starting point for this adjustment and notwithstanding its numerous failures to stem violence, the UN is still working to improve its peacemaking abilities. Its early warning capacity, a prerequisite for any timely action to control an upcoming conflict, is said to have definitively improved. In theory, the UN has huge peace building capacities because it has the potential to bundle the resources and expertise of powerful member states. In practice, the organisation's abilities are, sometimes fatally, limited by disagreement or the member states' lack of political will of member states, especially the permanent members of the Security Council.

Regional Organisations

In Africa, the consensus about conflict management since the early 1990s was captured in the institutional framework of the OAU's Mechanism on Conflict Prevention Management Resolution. This Mechanism is mandated to develop an approach to peace building for both internal and intrastate crises. So far, however, the OAU's new Mechanism has played a limited role. The OAU was still overtaken by violent events in the 1990s, a failure that can be attributed to its limited resources and staffing. But the OAU did send special envoys to several hotbeds to make attempts at mediation. In Congo-Brazzaville, this helped bring about an accord that temporarily stopped the use of violence in that country. In Burundi the UN representative forged a political agreement in 1994, which at that time defused tensions in the country. The OAU also deployed a monitory mission in Burundi, but this intervention is widely regarded as being of limited effect.

The Organisation of American States (OAS) has shown a much more modest commitment to the field of peace building and conflict management. It declared a form of interest in the field however with the establishment of the so-called 'Santiago Mechanism', an agreement on taking swift collective action in case of coup-attempts in any of of the member countries.

The Organisation for Security and Cooperation in Europe (OSCE) has developed one of the most effective structures of conflict management. A large portion of its early warning, early action and mediation capacity has been put in the hands of one individual, the High Commissioner on National Minorities. This official, whose function is to detect of ethnic tension in Eastern Europe, has been allowed a large amount of personal initiative. The silent but persistent interventions of the first OSCE High Commissioner, Max van der Stoel, a soft spoken Dutch diplomat, are highlighted in this section of this volume. He scored several successes in defusing upcoming ethnic conflict in countries such as Estonia and Rumania.

The personal peace-making qualities of Van der Stoel are matched outside Europe by former US president Jimmy Carter. Formally working as a non-official mediator, Carter's intervention on government level could be dubbed One-and-a-half Track Diplomacy. He managed to get peace processes going on a governmental level on several occasions. The Carter Center's intervention in Korea, described later in this book, taught the former president once again that Track One's confrontational tendency in dealing with political crises is often counter productive. Carter observed that the tendency towards imposing sanctions in international crises cuts off openings to communication. 'Nations rarely achieve their goals this way,' he commented flatly. Meanwhile, Carter's ability to change politicians' attitude also illustrates that Track One diplomacy is susceptible to arguments from outside of its own realm.

Openness to innovation and unconventional approaches are also breaking ground in the most modest section of Track One diplomacy: local government. New forms of international cooperation between local governments are emerging. These activities, especially those sustained by long-term ties between cities in different parts of the world, can also contribute to enhancing peace and reconciliation. While the flaws of local governments' actions are being taken into consideration (amateurs in the international realm could do a lot of damage), the potential of local authorities in the quest for peace increasingly gain recognition. The peace process in Tuzla furnishes some compelling examples of what local governments can accomplish. Personal commitment and colleague-to-colleague contacts are key factors in the success of peace building and municipal international cooperation has extensive experience with this strategy.

Some of the cases that are presented below may not fit in the Track One category in every detail. Given that, reality can never be completely made to conform with a schematic straitjacket, the editors took the freedom to take a pragmatic approach. Jimmy Carter is not a government official, but his reconciliatory efforts are exclusively aimed at the highest governmental circles and his stature as a mediator is to a large part derived from his personal experience as president of the United States, the world's top Track One position. The Mali peace process has been an undiluted governmental initiative, despite the fact that its implementation unfolded partly through actions by local communities. The Tuzla peace initiative also shows the sign of a mixture of actors but is nevertheless interpreted as having its centre of gravity in local governmental circles. The OSCE and UNESCO reconciliation activities are Track One in its purest form.

THE EARLY WARNINGS OF THE OSCE'S HIGH COMMISSIONER ON NATIONAL MINORITIES

Europe's Trip-Wire

Throughout most of the nineties, Mr. Max van der Stoel has ploughed with sustained vigour through the minorities minefield that is Central and Eastern Europe and the former Soviet Union. Nearly once a week, unmindful of the vagaries of the weather, undaunted by scepticism and even mistrust, the OSCE's High Commissioner on National Minorities has moved from Kyrgyzstan to Kazakhstan, into Albania, through Romania and Macedonia, listening with care to the various sides, asking questions, making suggestions, offering assistance.

The High Commissioner's office, established in 1992 by the CSCE, precursor to the OSCE-Organization for Security and Co-operation in Europe-is akin to a trip-wire. His job is to alert the OSCE before tensions develop into fullblown crises. So the former Dutch Minister of Foreign Affairs, who has worked out of the Hague with an 11-person staff since January 1993, functions as an Early Warning and Conflict Prevention mechanism for the international community. Or, in the appropriate official jargon, he's 'an instrument of conflict prevention at the earliest possible stage'.

Ethnic conflict is recognised as one of the main sources of large-scale violence in today's Europe. Minority issues simmer or have exploded in many OSCE participating states-Albania, Croatia, Estonia, Hungary, Kazakhstan, Kyrgysztan, Latvia, Romania, Slovakia, the Former Yugoslav Republic of Macedonia and Ukraine.

There is no general agreement on what constitutes a (national) minority, either in the OSCE or elsewhere. Van der Stoel himself is not definitive. 'The existence of a minority is a question of fact and not of definition,' he says, quoting the Copenhagen Document of 1990: 'To belong to a national minority is a matter of a person's individual choice.'

He adds: 'I know a minority when I see one. First of all, a minority is a group with linguistic, ethnic or cultural characteristics, which distinguish it from the majority. Secondly, a minority is a group which usually not only seeks to maintain its identity but also tries to give stronger expression to that identity.'

Europe has no shortage of such groups. And the High Commissioner has accumulated a considerable portfolio based on interventions in a wide range of disputes between them and their governments.

His approach-conducting on-site missions, using preventive diplomacy at early stages of tensions, encouraging dialogue, and ensuring confidence and co-operation among parties-is possible because the position of High Commissioner is a comparatively independent one, the holder being free to decide when to intervene in a crisis, and the degree of such intervention.

Van der Stoel goes beyond the minorities' general complaints and the majorities' general justifications. His focus is on down-to-earth facts-the dull details that make all the difference. This approach is used as much in Albania (Greek minority concentrated in the southern region) as well as Croatia (displaced persons and refugees belonging to national minorities). It is used in the Baltic states of Estonia and Latvia where a great number of the population was not recognised as normal citizens when the countries regained their independence in 1991. If Russians have to pass an exam on Estonian or Latvian language, Van der Stoel wants to know, what sorts of questions are asked? (Extremely difficult ones.) If the governments insists on the non-Estonian residents being able to speak the language fluently, does it offer courses? If it takes so long to attend to a request for citizenship, why is that?

Intervening on behalf of ethnic Serb citizens of Croatia, who want to return home, he argues with care about definitions. Should they be called 'internal migrants' or 'displaced persons'? Then Van der Stoel reminds the government of Croatia of its pledge 'to create conditions for the voluntary, safe, dignified and speedy return of all displaced persons and refugees, regardless of their nationality and ethnic origin'. The Croatian constitution is also invoked. Article 15 states inter alia that 'Members of all nations and minorities have equal rights in the Republic of Croatia'.

That is the diplomat's hallmark-patience, reminding governments of their obligations to the rule of law, and holding them to their commitments.

When a row developed in the former Yugoslav Republic of Macedonia over the use of the Albanian flag by people of Albanian origin, he adopted a similar approach. (Twenty-three percent of the population of Macedonia is of Albanian origin.) Two people had died during disturbances related to the continued raising of the Albanian flags next to the flag of the Macedonia over two town halls run by Albanian mayors. After a visit (one of many to this country) and discussions, Van der Stoel urged 'all nationalities within the State to strive to find solutions for inter-ethnic problems by rejecting ethnic hatred and intolerance and by seeking constructive and continuous dialogue, with equal rights for all ethnic groups as the guiding principle.'

Intervening on behalf of the Slovak minority in Hungary, Van der Stoel focuses on the need for direct representation of the various national minorities in Hungary in the Hungarian parliament. And he takes a dim view of plans to cancel regional radio programmes in the Slovak language-lasting 90 minutes a day-on days that the Hungarian Parliament is in session, and replacing these reports with broadcasts of parliamentary debates.

Likewise, he seeks to ascertain that the Hungarian minority in Slovakia and Romania is treated in accordance with the international standards.

Ukraine's Crimean Tartars view themselves as indigenous peoples. After hearing there case, Van der Stoel suggests a legal framework within which this could be considered. While acknowledging that Ukraine is under no international obligation in this regard, the High Commissioner points to the general assumption that 'the right of persons belonging to national minorities as laid down in various international instruments also accrue to indigenous peoples.'

And he invokes Article 11 of the Constitution of Ukraine, which lays down some important principles regarding both indigenous peoples and national minorities by stating that the state will assist in the development of their ethnic, cultural, linguistic and religious identity.

So while the job of High Commissioner on National Minorities is framed by a set of good intentions reinforced by an exalted mandate, in reality its success has to be measured in terms of actual practice.

Van der Stoel himself says about his work: 'You should not expect miracles from this sort of work. You have to arm yourself against disappointments and against what you perceive as perfectly unreasonable criticism. I think I have to realize that I have achieved something when a situation does not destabilize any further or when a small step towards a solution is being made.'

No miracle worker, but a juggler perhaps. The varying interests and contending positions and perspectives held by minorities and political rulers of the states they occupy, must be balanced. Despite the impression conveyed by the name, this is not an Ombudsman for National Minorities, nor is Van der Stoel required to investigate individual human rights violations. This is the reason the job title is 'on National Minorities', rather than 'for National Minorities'.

Apathy is a big impediment. Van der Stoel, a diplomat experienced in today's harsh world realities, but patient and caring in his approach, is expected to cry wolf whenever a potential conflict looms. But what if no-one listens?

That was the case in Kosovo, where Van der Stoel acted until February 1998 as Personal Representative of the OSCE Presidency. In January 1999, while the international media focused on the 'crisis' there, Van der Stoel lamented another case of opportunity lost. 'I do not pretend that I have the magic formula,' he told a Dutch newspaper. 'But probably far too little has been done. I have the feeling that the international community has begun taking action too late.'

The assumption in the framework that established the post of High Commissioner is that protecting the rights of persons belonging to national minorities will contribute towards a country's ability to reduce the tensions that create a context for wider conflict.

The office has limited political clout, however. A fair amount of 'indirect' means can be used to press for recommendations, including a gentle reminder that an unfavourable report can have implications for the much-coveted relationships some of these nations seek with western nations and organisations.

'However, the role of these means should not be overestimated,' notes Stefan Vassilev, adviser to the OSCE High Commissioner on National Minorities. 'The events in Kosovo showed that international diplomatic pressure and dependence on foreign aid could not always serve the "carrot and stick" role.'

Further, the High Commissioner cannot handle individual cases concerning persons belonging to national minorities. His mandate does not permit the consideration of national minority issues in situations involving organized acts of terrorism or to communicate with or acknowledge communications from any person or organization that practices or publicly condones terrorism or violence.

'Early warning' must be followed by early action on the part of the world community. In that way, highly tense situations can be prevented from becoming full-blown conflicts.

To Van der Stoel's chagrin, in Kosovo such 'early warning' was unheeded until a point of no return was reached in that province of former Yugoslavia wrecked by fighting between secessionists and the Serbian national army.

Sometimes a softly approach is required-watching a case from the earliest stage possible, monitoring it carefully to see what changes occur. SICLOMON is the acronym used for this by the High Commissioner's staff-'Situations to be closely monitored'. This is applicable when there are-still weak-signals of unfolding prerequisites for a trouble but it is too early for a full scale of international activities. Often too much international involvement could contribute to the development of the pre-conflict situation. To turn blind eyes or just wait and see is also not the proper response.

In this respect the High Commissioner can choose a 'passive' approach involving mere collection of data (as a follow-up to a signal obtained throughout the general routine monitoring process) through different means including sporadic contacts with some of the actors on the ground, contracts with other international organisations, and visit to a country. That can move to 'active' involvement, which entails visits, dialogue with the actors involved, the issuing of recommendations and taking some action.

'Inevitably, there is a "grey area" between the two categories,' notes Vassilev. 'There are also cases when development of a situation requires change of the High Commissioner's involvement from passive to active or the other way round. SICLOMON are also in this grey area.'

An important element of the High Commissioner's job is to build credibility and good working relationship with the various parties. 'The position of a close confidant with international leverage to all sides is the best option,' says Vassilev. 'Demonstrated preparedness to listen to and to understand each side's position and willingness to help each party in the process of finding mutually beneficial solutions is extremely helpful.'

The role must be carefully explained to all parties involved- the High Commissioner is not an international policeman but a facilitator or mediator. For example, normally none of the actors, is willing to make the first move in the form of inviting the other side to 'come to talk', which would be seen as a concession. The other side is also not willing to 'knock at the door of the adversary' or to 'come by foot' to it. Thus, establishing a mechanism or forum for dialogue through various types of round tables, consultations, seminars, and the like is of utmost importance, Vassilev suggests. An initiative by the High Commissioner, offering his auspices or hosting the event in a neutral site can sometimes be a face-saver. Finding accord among the leaders is one thing; finding one that can be sold to the respective constituencies is another story.

'In other words, each party has to gain from the final deal more than it would lose in the eyes of the respective supporters. Very often this requires extra efforts by the High Commissioner to organize a package of "accompanying measures" (sweeteners) to the main agreement which make it attractive to both sides,' says Vassilev.

Sometimes reaching a partial solution is preferable to further escalation. After accord has been reached comes the hard part-implementation. In fact, 'effective implementation of the reached agreements is the most important part of the High Commissioner's involvement. Failure to carry the implementation through undermines not only the results of the whole process in question, but would also significantly reduce... trust.'

The OSCE High Commissioner on National Minorities encourages and tries to facilitate larger and more active participation of minorities in the public and political life of the countries in which they live. He also adheres to the principle of integration vs. assimilation, in which efforts are made to overcome the fear (real or imaginary) that the majority of the population is seeking ways to assimilate a given minority, thus making it difficult to have real cooperation between them. Minorities are also encouraged to avoid self-isolation.

PEACEMAKING BY CONSENSUS IN MALI

'Let me repeat again today the pride that I feel to be at the head of a nation which has made tolerance and dialogue its cardinal virtues. As a modern state, Mali needs to add to its ancestral heritage of dialogue, a modern institutional infrastructure which demonstrates there is a real democratic process taking place.' (...) 'With this in mind, I shall ask my government to organize a series of regional Concertations in which every current of opinion will be able to express its views. Each participant will be invited to contribute to the debate, seeking to define solutions for tomorrow's problems. Our purpose will exclude systematic opposition to the ideas of others; nor will there be room for narrow sectoral demands. The government will bring to the discussion both its point of view and its proposals for change and together we shall seek the necessary consensus to achieve the transformations which we have started.' (President Alpha Oumar Konaré on 8th June 1994, the second anniversary of his inauguration as Mali's first democratic elected President)

The West African Republic of Mali ranks among the world's least developed and poorest countries, and in this vast and impoverished land, its northern regions are by far the least developed. With the exception of the 'interior delta' area of the Niger River and a few oases and mountainous areas, the entire zone is an infertile desert covering an area greater than France. Education, health care, water, communications, and transportation infrastructure are almost totally non-existent. In this area lives a ethnically diverse population numbering something less than one million inhabitants, of which the Songhoys and the Touaregs are the most numerous.

Like many of the nations of Africa, Mali has been governed for extended periods of its post-colonial history by non-democratic regimes. From 1968 until 1991, President Moussa Traoré presided over a repressive, corrupt, and incompetent one-party regime. Throughout the Traoré period, very little economic development took place, and that which did was largely restricted to the Bamako region and other regions of the south. The poverty of northern Mali was further aggravated by repeated periods of drought.

Traditionally, the Touaregs and Arabs have looked more to the north for trade relations than to the southern areas around Bamako, the capital of modern Mali. In the late fifties, northern peoples had pushed for the establishment of an independent central Saharan state, and in 1963, a revolt by Touareg supporters of this state was brutally suppressed. During the drought years, many young Touareg refugees ended up in Libya, where Libyan leader Muammar Gaddafy was both able and willing to exploit their alienation from Bamako. The Mouvement Populaire de Libération de l'Azawad (MPLA) was founded in Libya in 1988, by exiled Malian Touaregs who were serving as mercenaries in Libya's Arab Legion. When its leaders returned to Mali in 1990, they launched the rebellion of Mali's northern peoples against 28 years of repressive central government.

General-President Moussa Traoré reinforced his army in the north and launched a brutal and violent campaign to crush this rebellion. Many of the victims of the military's efforts to put down the rebellion were innocent civilians. The inevitable result of the military heavy-handedness was to turn previously uninvolved Touareg youths into rebels, and to antagonise other ethnic groups.

As the violence continued, the Touareg fighters issued a 21-point declaration which included various demands for improved economic development, better social conditions, reduced military presence, multi-party democracy, a greater political role, and amnesty for their rebel activities. The northern rebellion coincided with increasing civil unrest in Bamako and the south, as demands for multi-party democracy and an end to the Traoré regime grew louder. Traoré needed to bring troops back to the capital to prop up his tottering regime, and so, in January 1991, the government of Mali signed a peace agreement with the rebels.

It made little difference. In March, 1991, Traoré was arrested, and Mali began a transition process to multi-party democracy under the leadership of General Amadou Toumani Touré (known as A.T.T.) And in the north, despite the agreement, which was, in any case, viewed by many in the south as a 'capitulation', the violence continued. The MPLA, which had already split into separate Touareg and Arab factions, splintered further, and fighting among the factions was often as intense as battles between rebels and government forces. Military units carried out summary justice, in one case killing a group of rebel leaders who had been imprisoned in Timbuktu. Government officials could no longer safely travel outside of the northern towns. Traditional leaders, who were viewed by the rebel leaders as too closely allied with Bamako, were also perceived as enemies. Anarchy and banditry prevailed throughout the north.

There were continued efforts to put an end to the violence. Algeria, in particular, played a crucial role in promoting efforts to reach a negotiated settlement. The new regime also attempted to bring more northerners into the government. A Peace Agreement was signed in April 1992, a 'National Pact' which accorded a 'special status' to the north. The Pact also provided for the demobilisation of armed rebels and their integration into the Malian military or police forces or into civilian life, an exchange of prisoners, the return of refugees, economic development for the north (and commitments to seek international funding for that development), local responsibility for law enforcement, and, significantly, the establishment of a commissioner for northern Mali, reporting directly to the President. This pact provided a framework for an end to the violence, but real peace would still prove elusive.

Conditions improved for short periods, but would then deteriorate. More than two hundred thousand people fled the fighting and banditry, taking refuge in neighbouring countries, or moving southwards.

Acts of ethnically motivated violence were also reported in some of the larger cities and towns. As the elected civilian administration headed by President Alpha Oumar Konaré took office, the economy came under severe pressure from the combined effects of years of mismanagement and war. In May 1994, a new element was added to the already highly explosive mix-an armed movement known as Ganda Koy (Masters of the Land) was launched by sedentary peoples who were fed up with the violence and banditry.

Mali was on the Verge of Civil War

That this did not occur is to the credit of President Konaré and his new Prime Minister, Ibrahim Boubacar Keita, who both understood that they could never impose a military solution on the rebels, as well as a large supporting cast of local and international actors who persisted in working with the warring parties to find a way to re-establish the rule of law.

The construction of a stable peace in Northern Mali did not come about as the result of any one single action, but as the result of a complex of efforts to rebuild trust, to address legitimate grievances, and to reward combatants who chose to give up the fight. Building incentives into the peace process that would assure the continued commitment of people on both sides of the conflict to peace.

Six essential aspects of the Malian peace process:

(1) Building civilian-military relations

(2) Discreet mediation by national and international figures

(3) Decentralisation of governance

(4) Promotion of reconciliation through civil society

(5) A process of disarmament and demobilisation

(6) Investment in the re-integration of former rebel combatants

Even while the violence continued, the government convened a series of meetings at the local level beginning in 1994. In convening these meetings, the government was embracing the African tradition (and following the pattern it had already used to effect the transition to democracy following the 1991 popular revolution) which goes beyond the traditional western democratic process where elections are the determining factor in shaping government. In the African tradition, decisions are taken at the village council, where elders preside over a discussion involving the entire community. Participants at the hundreds of meetings that took place from 1994 through 1996 included political parties, the administration, trade unions, religious groups, and NGOs, but subsequently, and more importantly, the local leaders, women's organisations, social organisations, economic co-operatives and associations, and other institutional representatives of civil society. All these meetings stressed the inseparable relationship between security and peace.

The administration also undertook to reform the military, improving conditions and training for soldiers, and improving communications both within the military and between the military and civil society. While both security and development were considered to be crucial to achieve stability in the north, the approach adopted by those involved in peacemaking efforts has been described as 'security first'. This followed from the logic that the armed civilian population would only give up its weapons if they believed that the security forces were capable of defending their families.

Also the kind of development required to build trust and improve living standards in the north could only be achieved if donors felt confident that hostilities would not break out again and that development professionals could safely work in the former areas of conflict. Interestingly, one element of the overall peace plan was an attempt (with only limited success) to persuade development agencies to make modest contributions to the implementation of security projects.

Beyond Symbols: Weapons for Development

In 'The Weapon Heritage of Mali', authors Van der Graaf and Poulton argue for a programme tying weapons collection to community development assistance. Instead of providing cash payments to individuals who hand in their weapons, development assistance is provided to communities for programmes like improved water systems, health care, and education.

While a 'Flame of Peace' is in and of itself both practically and symbolically valuable, a development for weapons programme helps not only to reduce the number of weapons in circulation, but it also to bring communities together to provide for both security and development, and quite possibly to prevent those who hand in a weapon from simply going out and acquiring a new one.

As discussed above, Mali's northern peoples felt little connection to Bamako. Part of the wisdom of the reconciliation process pursued by the Konaré administration was to accept this reality and to work with it, by offering to extend more power to local authorities. Decentralisation has been a central plank of Konaré's vision of society. During the many meetings of civil society, one goal was to convince people to support locally elected authorities, consistent with one of the points agreed to in the National Pact, and this is now moving ahead with the establishment of a nearly 700 locally elected 'communes' throughout Mali.

Robin-Edward Poulton, Senior Research Fellow at the United Nations Institute for Disarmament Research, who has worked on conflict resolution for many years in West Africa, describes the Konaré approach as 'ambitious' and 'visionary'. He observes that 'most of Africa's states will flourish in the 21st century only if they are able to reconcile the need for broader economic or monetary unions with the pressure from local groups to assume their cultural identities.' Poulton concludes that 'decentralisation is the new framework which will make people responsible for their own lives, for mobilising national resources and using them locally for productive investment.'

These activities certainly contributed to reduced tensions between the government, the northern non-combatants, and the rebel fighters. But peace could only be truly secured by a process of demobilisation and re-integration of the rebels into the fabric of Malian society. This was largely accomplished by setting up a programme which provided for the cantonment of former combatants, the turning in of weapons, the closing down of rebel bases, and the integration of some of the former fighters into either the armed forces or the civilian sector. Participants in the programme were paid $200 pocket money, free food and training, uniform and a small monthly payment during the duration of cantonment. Those who came in without a weapon received $100 and were accepted into a UNDP credit programme to help them establish themselves in civilian life. While fewer than 2000 of the ex-combatants were actually integrated into the police, the military, or civilian administration, between November 1995 and January 1996, another 9000 individuals benefitted from the civilian integration programme and nearly 3000 weapons were collected. The cycle of violence had been definitively broken.

On March 27, 1996, President Konaré, Ghanaian President Jerry Rawlings (chairman of the Ecowas at that time), leaders of the Mouvements et Fronts Unifiés de l'Azaouad (the MFUA, uniting the various rebel factions), Ganda Koy, and a large delegation of international observers gathered in Timbuktu for the highly symbolic destruction of all collected weapons in what was called a 'Flame of Peace'. The weapons were stacked into a giant pyramid, doused with fuel, and then ignited by the presidents of Mali and Ghana. The rival movements issued a joint declaration in which they affirmed the indivisibility of Mali, pledged their support to the Malian constitution, renounced the use of violence, exhorted their fellow African fighters across the continent to 'celebrate their own Flame of Peace', and finally, proclaimed the irrevocable dissolution of their respective organisations.

Citizen Carter: The Statesman

What happens to Presidents after their term in office ends? Once voluntarily departed, or shoved out the door, do they spend long leisurely days by the leafy pond? Play endless rounds of golf? Covet high-profile memberships of corporate boards? Not so for former American president Jimmy Carter.

In June 1994 Carter could be found in Pyongyang holding intensive talks with Kim Il Sung, the North Korean dictator over a way out of a nuclear crisis with the United States. A few months later, Carter's name was back in the news. This time he was part of a three-member delegation trying to mediate the departure from office of Haiti's military rulers. By the end of the year, the former US president was trying to negotiate peace in Bosnia. As one American columnist described Carter, 'He goes everywhere, doing good.'

The visit to North Korea was made under a cloud of scepticism, and even some opposition, back in Carter's homeland. But there was more than grudging applause when the ex-President announced in a television interview a credible agreement with North Korea to 'freeze' the illegal nuclear programme, which President Bill Clinton had said publicly North Korea could not be allowed to pursue.

That deal effectively aborted a US campaign to press for international sanctions against North Korea. It also eased military tension between South and North Korea. In the same way-by talking, and attempting to find common threads for agreement-'Citizen Carter, the statesman', as he has been described by the newspaper USA TODAY, pulled another rabbit out of the hat by brokering a deal that led to the United States calling off a planned invasion of Haiti. The dramatic events in which Carter became involved in 1994 marked the culmination of an activist post-White House role the former President has carved out for himself since leaving office in 1981. Working through The Carter Center, a non-profit, privately run body based in Atlanta, which he set up with his wife, Rosalynn, in 1982, Carter has used the considerable weight of his office as former president to become one of the world's most effective peacemakers. In sometimes last-minute visits to disparate parts of the globe, the trademark charm and a reputation for caring, have opened doors closed to others.

Carter was president of the United States from 1976 to 1980. He was succeeded by Ronald Reagan. During his time in office, he was a central figure in the historic 1978 Camp David peace accords between Egypt and Israel. But the popular perception in the United States is that his presidency was marked by the Iran hostage crisis, an oil embargo, high inflation, and the like.

Run in partnership with Emory University, The Carter Center has set lofty goals which underpin some of the very ideals that were hallmarks of a Presidency which pursued a foreign policy based on human rights considerations. Already, the Center's work has erased some of the bitter memories of its founder's presidential years. Its Mission Statement include promoting peace and human rights, resolving conflict, fostering democracy and development, fighting poverty, hunger, and disease throughout the world.

Carter Center programmes are wide-ranging: eradication of Guinea worm disease in Africa, India, Pakistan and Yemen; working to promote democracy and human rights; increase farm yields in the developing world; child immunisation; the prevention of river blindness. In the United States, the Center runs projects to erase the stigma of mental illness and improve access to and quality of services and treatment for Americans who experience mental disorders. It runs various youth projects as well as in preventive health care programmes.

In addition, Carter Center monitoring teams have overseen multiparty elections in Haiti, Ghana, Panama, Paraguay,

Guyana, Suriname, Zambia, Nicaragua and the Dominican Republic. The Atlanta-based centre has assisted the strengthening of the economic and institutional foundations of emerging democracies.

Carter personally, and members of the Center's International Negotiation Network (INN)-a 25-member conflict resolution body comprising Nobel Peace laureates, former heads of state, conflict resolution practitioners, representatives of international organisations, governments, and non-governmental organisations-have mediated many of the 30 major armed conflicts taking place somewhere in the world at any one time.

Described as an informal network of eminent persons, the INN is chaired by Carter, whose high personal profile tends to make less pronounced the contributions made by other INN members to activities undertaken by the Center's Conflict Resolution Program (CRP) in Sudan, Bosnia, the Great Lakes region, Liberia, Ethiopia, the Korean Peninsula and elsewhere. INN also ran a successful project in the Baltics which brought together Estonians, Russians living in Estonia and Russians from Moscow, to discuss integration of the Russian-speaking community into Estonian society.

In the words of The Carter Center, 'The CRP regularly monitors many of the world's armed conflicts in an attempt to better understand their histories, the primary actors involved, disputed issues, and efforts being made to resolve them. When a situation arises where President Carter has a unique role to play and specific conditions have been met, the CRP directly supports his intervention.'

INN member Kumar Rupesinghe says non-governmental organisations (NGOs) such as The Carter Center, being 'unofficial organisations', have the advantage of building trust and confidence between two sides and using their resources to work toward negotiation. 'With no strategic or political motivations, NGOs have greater flexibility... in responding to the needs of people,' says Rupesinghe.

But such is the profile given to The Carter Center by the man who founded it and who remains its driving force, that it is not likely to be perceived as just another NGO. In fact, at times the Atlanta-based body could be criticised for conducting a milder version of the Clinton administration foreign policy in North Korea and Haiti-supporting Washington's policy doves over the more hawkish elements. Before visiting North Korea, Carter obtained President Clinton's nod, although some officials in the State Department opposed to the trip. And while his initiatives in Haiti were undertaken in an unofficial capacity, the former President was thoroughly briefed beforehand and in turn reported on the outcome of his missions to Washington.

Others say by holding negotiations with Somalia's Mohamed Farah Aideed, North Korea's Kim Il Sung, Haitian military ruler Raoul Cedras, and Bosnian Serb leader Radovan Karadzic, the former President merely enhanced the reputations of despots. The more cynical view of Carter is that the ex-President is driven by a determination to erase the memory of a failed presidency, and restore his place in history, possibly by receiving the Nobel Prize for Peace.

Not that such considerations matter to beneficiaries of the Center's varied programmes, who will no doubt argue that the ends are justified by Carter's high-profile and high-octane energy means. For it is the case that Carter's status and reputation-the sheer weight of the name-have opened doors and forced parties at loggerheads to explore the possibilities of reconciliation. Gritty diplomacy and refusal to take 'no' for an answer, have been Carter's hallmarks. And his approach have become so much an embodiment of the Center, there will doubtless be a big gap when he leaves.

'He's quite unusual,' notes Erwin Hargrove, a political scientist at Vanderbilt University. 'Most ex-presidents write their memoirs and retire. But Carter has a tremendous amount of energy and a desire to do good.'

Away from the fanfare, Carter and his team, including wife Rosalynn, used various other devices to bring warring parties around the negotiating table, or at least to consider that as a course. One year after that sequence of headline-generating ventures in North Korea, Bosnia and Haiti, Carter sponsored a major drive among Central African nations to secure the return of two million refugees displaced by the ethnic bloodletting in Rwanda. Meeting in Cairo, leaders of Zaire, Rwanda, Burundi, Tanzania and Uganda, agreed on various confidence-building and security measures in this regard. In the following year, the five leaders met again in Tunis, Tunisia to follow up their African initiative to promote peace, justice, reconciliation, stability and development in the Great Lakes region. In the Tunis Declaration on the Great Lakes Region, issued on March 18, 1996, the parties agreed on additional measures to meet commitments approved the previous year in Cairo.

Implementation of that initiative was subsequently overtaken by the pace of political events, including the overthrow of Zairian leader, Mobutu Sese Sekou, but focused world attention on the region, and galvanised involvement in efforts to deal with one of the major causes of instability. And the meetings secured, at the very least, a blueprint of commitments-pledges even-by Heads of State regarding improvement in the refugee situation, and reducing military conflict.

How does Jimmy Carter do it?

Writing in the New York Times in May 1995, Carter described the complexity of issues involved in the various conflicts raging across the globe and said they required 'innovative and varied approaches.' Carter always recognised that there are usually cases in which one party-or both-want peace.

'However, most ruling parties resist any official intervention in their civil disputes. Without their approval, it is inappropriate for a foreign ambassador or the United Nations even to communicate with revolutionaries who are attempting to change or overthrow the government.'

All too frequently, Carter noted, the tendency was to impose sanctions rather than encourage communication. 'Nations rarely achieve their goals this way and either give trade advantages to their competitors or alienate their allies who advocate different approaches.' Preparing for the 1995 Cairo summit, Carter visited Uganda, Zaire, Rwanda and Burundi for consultations with presidents, other political and military officers, diplomats, church officials and representatives of international organisations and NGOs. 'After some extremely difficult negotiations with sceptical leaders in Kigali and Bujumbura, they finally agreed to detailed agendas for our proposed conference,' Carter said in a report on the trip.

Interesting about the Cairo meeting was that it was closed to leaders from outside the region. An unpopular decision, but this resulted in what Carter described as 'totally unrestrained discussions of the most sensitive issues, old wounds were opened and mostly healed, and we all decided that a follow-up conference will be necessary, perhaps early in 1996, to include those who were excluded this time.'

They pledged in Cairo to prevent cross-border raids, remove intimidators from refugee camps detect and destroy the illicit and inflammatory radio transmitters; deliver persons indicated for genocide to the International Tribunal and urge others to do so.

Carter says he tries to convince participants in a conflict that he's not taking sides, keep goals in sight, and not allow himself to be side-tracked. 'I don't have a portfolio...' he told Washington Post while contemplating approaches to the Bosnian conflict in 1994.

That approach has led to Carter being branded an 'innocent abroad' disrupting efforts to toughen sanctions against countries considered hostile to the United States. But as the Atlanta Constitution notes, 'Carter's efforts seem to have contributed to easing some of the world's most difficult and intractable problems'.

PARTNERS AT WORK

At a time when 'ethnic cleansing' was normal practice elsewhere in Bosnia, in the city of Tuzla residents and local government succeeded in preserving much of their community's multicultural character. In explaining this extraordinary achievement Tuzla's mayor, Selim Beslagic, points to the city's tradition of mutual tolerance: 'We have always been a melting pot and have had the possibility to stay like that during the terrible war. That's why the nationalist forces could not manifest themselves here, though they have tried it.'

Another prominent inhabitant of Tuzla, Vehid Sehic (President of the Forum of Tuzla Citizens) complements: 'During the ages Tuzla has always been an open city with a strong solidarity among its people. Being an industrial city Tuzla harboured some 27 nationalities.'

'Tuzla has always been different. It was the city that started first to resist the Ottoman occupation. Then Tuzla resisted the Austrian-Hungarian forces. After the first World War it started the first big labour protests and during Second World War it fought against the nazi's.'

Tuzla, the forth biggest city in Bosnia Herzegovina and the economic and cultural centre of north-east Bosnia, initially was spared during the war. But when the Yugoslavian People's Army withdrew from the city in 1992 Tuzla was shelled every day by the Serbs. On the 25th of May 1995 a grenade hit the central square killing 71 civilians and wounding more than hundred.

The Forum of Tuzla Citizen was founded in 1993 by a group of people that wanted to fight the 'nationalistic forces'. Despite threats thousands of people joined the organisation. Now it has members from many political and religious movements. The Forum backed Mayor Selim Beslagic in his striving for maintaining a multi-ethnic society.

Six years later, Forum-President Vehid Sehic looks at the effects of war: 'In Bosnia nothing is the same as before. Also in Tuzla nothing is the same any more. Tuzla is less multi-cultural as a result of the war. That's logical. But it is the city that succeeded best in preserving its character. Also Tuzla is the city that is most dedicated to the return of refugees and displaced persons.' It was the hopeful conditions in Tuzla that inspired Dutch organisations and municipalities to create the Assistance to Bosnian Communities Foundation (ABC) in order to support the social and physical reconstruction of the region.

Ralph Pans, former ABC-chair and mayor of the Dutch city of Almere, underlines the positive aspects of Tuzla. 'In Tuzla there still are mosques, Catholic churches and Serbian-orthodox churches. It is the only city that did not choose for one religion and one nationality while destroying the other.' At present it is the only municipality in Bosnia ruled by a coalition of non-nationalist political parties.

To support this 'struggle against nationalism and to give a chance to the processes of democratisation and reconciliation' two Dutch NGOs-the Network for Municipal Peace Policy (PGV) and the Inter Church Peace Council (IKV)-decided to set up the ABC-programme, which started in June 1996 in Tuzla. On the Dutch side, some 30 NGOs and schools, and nearly 20 municipalities are active in ABC. They cooperate with 25 partner-organisations in Tuzla.

ABC is unique because the partnership is formed by citizens organisations. The Dutch ABC-headquarters stresses that the programme 'is not a classical humanitarian aid-programme'. Along with the supply of the necessary aid goods and the transfer of knowledge, it is trying to create lasting relations between organisations and communities in Bosnia and the Netherlands. 'It is a real exchange of ideas among citizens,' comments Sehic.

The Dutch and Bosnian organisations work together in formulating, preparing, implementing and evaluating projects. Before activities can go ahead the mayor of Tuzla and local leaders of the 'sounding board' are consulted. According to Igor Rajner, formerly the local ABC-director, external assistance to local problems can only be effective if 'the decision making involves the community. And this is easier through decentralised cooperation, which, by its very nature, is closer to local power structures and civil society.'

Nevertheless the partnership does not imply complete equality between the teams. 'This is normal,' explains Sehic, 'Bosnia just came out of the war. That legacy is also reflected in the partnership. The Dutch have a stronger democracy and economy and have more knowledge, ideas and money.'

The ABC-programme covers a patchwork of small projects ranging from infrastructure, education, culture, child care, work with youth and the elderly, trauma treatment, medical support and help for displaced persons. In 1998 nearly US$ 1.5 million were invested. (The programme was made possible through a Dutch Government donation). Sehic: 'I think at the moment these smaller projects at the citizen level are better than economic aid or large projects. With smaller projects there is a larger trickle-down effect and they are easier to control, preventing mishandling of funds.'

One of the larger ABC-projects was the renovation of apartment buildings. About sixty percent of the inhabitants of Tuzla live in high-rise apartment blocks with 14 to 17 floors. Because of the war, water pipes, electricity, cables and elevators no longer functioned. Many inhabitants had to carry buckets of water upstairs. Sometimes rain water would trickle down the walls rendering those apartments which still had electricity extremely dangerous.

A Change in Ethnic Composition

Whereas Tuzla had a population of 130,000 before the war, by the time the war was over the number of inhabitants had dropped to 105,000. Some 25,000 people had fled abroad while 900 soldiers and 300 civilians from Tuzla had died in the fighting. In the meantime many refugees had sought safety in the shelter of the city. In 1998 it was home to 41,000 displaced people who had fled from other parts of the country, while another 4,000 refugees were living in camps in the vicinity.

Despite the efforts to preserve the 'multi-cultural character' of Tuzla the war has changed the ethnic composition of the city. Before the conflict 48 percent of the population were Bosnian, 16 percent Serb, 15 percent Croat and 21 percent were described as 'others'. In 1998 the Bosnians made up 63 percent of the population, Serbs 9 percent, 'others' 14 percent while only the percentage of Croats had remained the same.

Three Dutch construction companies decided to contribute to the renovation of five buildings in Krecanska street, which had been selected for the project. The job was carried out mainly by the municipality of Tuzla and local constructors. During the renovation the elevators in the buildings were repaired, electricity was installed and new hydrofor pumps ensured that the water supply reached even the uppermost floors. The project not only provided comfortable apartments for 1,400 people, it also offered badly needed job opportunities to experienced construction workers. After the war, unemployment in Tuzla-which had previously been relatively affluent-reached eighty percent.

The ABC-programme also targeted other aspects of social life by addressing the tangible reminders of the war at the street level. In Simin Han, a village on the outskirts of Tuzla, many street lights were not functioning. In the morning and evening people had to rush to and from school and work in darkness. Bad visibility had already resulted in a number of accidents. With a donation of some US$ 4,000, electricity and streetlamps were provided. The community of Simin Han supplied the wooden poles.

'It's a small example of how collaboration can achieve quick results,' concluded United Nations agencies in the Atlas of Decentralised Cooperation for Human Development report. 'It is a project that literally 'sheds light' on the real meaning of cooperation.' ABC-coordinator Martin Aalders explained: 'We are involved in a partnership. And this doesn't mean importing ready-made solutions from abroad but stimulating the direct involvement of the institutions and the civil society of Tuzla.'

With the help of the Dutch partners other streets in Tuzla itself, such as Oktobarska street, were also illuminated, which not only helped prevent sprained ankles but also created a greater feeling of safety. Garbage collection became another priority. During the war garbage collecting vehicles broke down and refuse was often simply left on the streets. The Dutch municipality of Delft decided to donate a few hundreds of containers and some garbage collecting vehicles to Tuzla. This donation meant that large areas of the city could be cleaned-up.

The problems of Tuzla's thousands of refugees are also high on the list of priorities. Many of these refugees who had fled Srebrenica were housed in the nearby Mihatovici settlement. Here, a number of Dutch municipalities provided support for the construction of a day care centre for children. The

Netherlands has a special relationship with the enclave that was supposed to have been protected by Dutch soldiers against Serbian aggression.

That the programme went beyond providing 'hardware' is illustrated by the cultural exchanges. When actress Baisa Baki from Tuzla visited the Netherlands she noticed: "Theatre has another meaning for us. It is not a luxury any more, but a necessity. During the war it was the only way to give shape to our thoughts, our pain, the nightmare. That doesn't mean we only played tragedies. On the contrary, there was a great need for comedies. To be free from suffering for a moment. Now we are trying to reconstruct our identity by looking for plays by Bosnian dramatists. We will fill the holes in our culture.'

FROM 'DIVIDE AND CONQUER' TOWARDS 'COMMUNICATE AND RECONCILE'

A world without wars? Cynics may find the idea unrealistic, even comical. But it is central to a programme launched in February 1994 by UNESCO and since adopted by other sections of the international community. The Culture of Peace seeks to take advantage of what the specialised agency of the United Nations terms 'a growing belief that the culture of war, which has characterised the dominant civilisations of the past, can now be replaced by a culture of peace.'

Although a cursory glance at the world map may give a different impression-ethnic tensions and conflicts in the Balkans, internecine wars in Africa, civil wars of varying intensity in Asia-UNESCO says the culture of peace concept is, in fact, taking hold. The idea underpinning it is likely to be boosted and more widely exposed in the year 2000, which has been designated by the United Nations as International Year for a Culture of Peace and Non-violence. 2001-2010 will be the International Decade for a Culture of Peace and Non-violence.

Further, it is hoped to collect up to 100 million signatures by September 2000 on a Manifesto for a Culture of Peace and Non-violence drawn up by Nobel Peace Laureates that puts the obligation for peace on the individual as well as on the state.

UNESCO says the world has moved towards an order in which 'it is possible for the rule of international law and justice to replace reliance on military power.' In other words, a culture of peace can slip neatly into the vacuum left by the end of the Cold War.

At the conference in Yamoussoukro, Côte d'Ivoire, in July 1989, where the concept was articulated, participants urged a peace culture 'based on the universal values of respect for life, liberty, justice, solidarity, tolerance, human rights and equality between women and men.'

Three years later, the UNESCO executive Board and the body's general conference endorsed the Culture of Peace as part of the organisation's mandate to contribute to international peace and security. A fairly comprehensive set of objectives has since been developed.

UNESCO's director-general Federico Mayor says peace itself is being redefined. 'Instead of the absence of war, it is increasingly seen as a dynamic, participative, long-term process, based on universal values and everyday practice at all levels-the family, the school, the community, as well as the nation.'

That notion of peace is shared by the International Fellowship of Reconciliation (IFOR). Based in Alkmaar, the Netherlands, IFOR comprised people who have committed themselves to active non-violence as a way of life and means of achieving social, personal, economic and political transformation. IFOR secretary general Anke Kooke, and Interim Program Officer Jan Schaake, have linked the concept of A Culture of Non-violence to that of A Culture of Peace, with the latter embracing communication, democratic decision making and non-violent conflict resolution. 'It is the basis of freedom, security and equitable relationships and it encourages individual and group action for societal and structural change,' they state. 'A Culture of Non-violence embraces the non-violent understanding present in all spiritual practices.'

For there to be a transformation from a Root Causes of War toward a Culture of Peace and Non-violence, conflict resolution and societal changes should no longer be realised by violent means based on the isolation and destruction of the opponent, but by non-violent means, communication and democratic decision making. Courage and heroism are not based on the ability to use violence but on having the creativity to reach one's goal by non-violent means.

The overall transformation from a Root Causes of War towards a Culture of Peace and Non-violence is 'the transformation from exclusiveness and egocentredness towards sharing and community spirit; from 'divide and conquer' towards 'communicate and reconcile'. Just sharing not only involves other people dependent on the resources, but also future generations, animals and plants and taking the intrinsic value of natural resources into account.'

UNESCO considers itself well placed to carry the weight. The Paris-based body emerged from the shadow of war: formed just after the end of the Second World War, its constitution has echoes of the conflict. 'Since wars begin in the minds of men, it is in the minds of men that the defences of peace must be constructed,' states the section of the document frequently recited to underline the basis for the organisation's passionate endorsement of the Culture of Peace drive.

An intersectoral committee chaired by the director-general works with various other sectors and units of the organisation and has liaison with the United Nations in New York on the programme. In various countries, UNESCO National Culture of Peace Programmes keep the flame alight. Culture of Peace is integral to other UNESCO activities, including directly complementary ones like education.

The body's Associated Schools Project (ASP) has inaugurated an interregional pilot project called 'No to violence' in Brazil, Estonia, Haiti, Sri Lanka and Zaire. In 1995, Culture of Peace and ASP jointly sponsored several subregional peace festivals involving children between the ages of 11 and 13 in Cook Islands, Costa Rica, Greece, Grenada, Jordan, Thailand and Zimbabwe.

Joint approaches have been made on urban violence, attempting to link networks of schools in cities plagued by conflict. At various universities, UNESCO chairs have been established specifically devoted to the teaching of human rights and peace studies. UNESCO funds support independent media outlets in conflict-ridden nations like Rwanda, where the propaganda of Mille Collines radio station helped to foment the 1994 genocide.

Across the border, in Burundi, which has its own ethnic tensions, the organisation has helped sensitise journalists on the need for non-partisan and pluralistic information. Similarly in the republics of former Yugoslavia support given to independent media seeking to bridge ethnic divisions, have contributed to building up trust.

In various parts of the world, UNESCO field offices have been used as culture of peace dissemination points. Special projects have been undertaken in Africa, Latin America and the Caribbean; in Beijing, China, the UNESCO office has organised meetings with diplomats posted in the city to examine the implementation of peace programmes in multicultural contexts.

UNESCO clubs, some 4,800 of which are in existence, in over 100 countries, are also utilised to spread the idea. The fourth World Congress of the World Federation of UNESCO Clubs held in Romania in June 1995, decided to plan future activities around the theme 'Towards a World Charter of UNESCO Clubs for a Culture of Peace'.

El Salvador, Mozambique and Burundi have pioneered the application on a national scale of the Culture for Peace philosophy. Steps have also been taken towards setting up parallel programmes in Honduras, Nicaragua and Somalia. In El Salvador, the national Culture of Peace programmes coincided with the process of national reconciliation in 1993, based on the 1992 Chapultepec Peace Accords. Brokered by the United Nations, these agreements ended a long running armed conflict between the government and a guerrilla movement. So the UNESCO initiative was undertaken amid a broad programme to build peace after the conflict.

Following a Forum for Education and Culture of Peace held in San Salvador, in April 1993, under the co-sponsorship of UNESCO and the El Salvador Ministry of Education, the organisation helped mediate the process by which the government and civil society worked together in designing the strategic guidelines of the programme as well as its constituent projects.

In Burundi, the national programme was launched in December 1994, with the opening of a House of a Culture of Peace in the capital, Bujumbura. Staffed by a multi-ethnic team, the house provides both a symbolic expression of the national desire for peace and a material structure with the means and institutional power to put it into practice. 'It has become a centre for many individuals and groups working for peace,' says UNESCO. 'Despite the violence that has afflicted the city, work has continued on peace seminars for journalists, government administrators, educators and representatives from NGOs and the United Nations.'

One aspect of the Culture of Peace programme is a battle against on-screen violence. Here self-regulation is advocated, with the guidelines used by the British Broadcasting Corporation (BBC) considered appropriate. These require the consideration of questions such as whether the violence contained in a programme-be it fiction or non-fiction-is essential to the story. Can the violence be implied rather than shown? Are the brutal consequences of violence also apparent? Is violence being glorified?

'Faced with such questions,' says UNESCO, 'it is hoped that the media will begin to pay more attention to peaceful conflict resolution than it now does to violence.'

It's because of the momentum given the programme by such projects that director-general Mayor describes the culture of peace is 'a movement of movements in which everyone who is working for human rights, non-violence, democracy, social justice, sustainable development, women's equality, join together in a 'grand alliance' of social transformation.'

But how can Violent Conflict be Ended?

In 'UNESCO and a Culture of Peace: Promoting a Global Movement', the organisation says there is no magic wand approach. The concept of creating a culture of peace will evolve and grow only through practice. 'As a movement, it is like a great river, fed from diverse streams from every tradition, culture, language, religion and political perspective.'

For UNESCO, the essence of the culture of peace idea is that it cannot be defined as the absence of conflict. 'In a diverse and complex world,' says the agency, 'conflict will always be part of life. Instead of fearing it, we must learn to appreciate and cultivate its positive non-violent aspects, which include creativity and the redress of injustice.'

What the programme's advocates seek to do is transform violent competition into co-operation for shared goods. Thus groups engaged in conflict would work together in the development process itself.

In managing these Culture of Peace programmes, UNESCO is entering new territory: there are few historical precedents.

Funding is also a problem. Although the Cold War is over, governments still spend large amounts on the military. Resources devoted to military expenditure are equivalent to the total income of half the world's population. As UNESCO itself acknowledges, 'the Culture of Peace is still not high on the list of global funding priorities'. Yet, it remains an obligation to support the process that ensues once combatants have ended their mistrust and committed themselves to building a new society.

'If we are to achieve a Culture of Peace, we must pay the price for it,' says the organisation. 'We cannot be successful without a global reordering of priorities in which the present emphasis on military peace-keeping is matched by a commitment at least as great to non-violent peace-building.'

The United Nations' initial emphasis (after the end of the Cold War) on peace-keeping operations, based on keeping peace between states, is increasingly being extended with a focus on peace-building, conflict prevention and the construction of a culture of peace. For peace-building is important not only for getting countries out of conflict, but as a device to shift them onto the path of sustainable development. 'Action for a culture of peace correspond more closely to the concept of peace-building than to peace-keeping,' says UNESCO. Only time will tell if what UNESCO identifies as an 'emerging culture of peace' will eventually bring an end to the many conflicts that continue to take lives all across the globe.

INSPIRING STORIES OF PEACE-BUILDING

'This conference could augur well for the coming century. It would unite into one mighty whole the efforts of all States sincerely striving to make the great idea of universal peace triumph over strife and discord.' Count Mikhail Nikolayevich Muravyov, Russia's Foreign Minister, expressed the hopes of many when he spoke of the prospects for peace at the First Hague International Peace Conference in 1899.

One hundred years later we know these hopes to have been in vain. The first international gathering to promote world peace-the event brought together representatives of 26 countries-proved incapable of stopping Europe and the world from marching toward the general war that was the opening event of what British historian Eric Hobsbawm has called 'the age of extremes.' The 20th century was to become the most violent of all ages in history, unprecedented in the scale and intensity of killing and destruction. 1

One of the considerations that played a part in the birth of this book was the fact that, exactly one hundred years after the First Hague International Peace Conference, a large scale global conference will be organised by The Hague Appeal for Peace in The Hague (the Netherlands, May 1116). A few days earlier, an international gathering will take place in Belfast, Northern Ireland, organised by the Coexistence Initiative of the State of the World Forum. The conference (Diversity and Community in a Global Context: Learning from Europe) will deal with creating a greater understanding of the issues of coexistence and community building.

With 'People Building Peace', due to be presented at the conferences in Belfast and in The Hague, we aim to promote these issues which are crucial global challenges for the 21st century. The initiative for this publication was taken by the European Centre for Conflict Prevention, together with IFOR

(International Fellowship of Reconciliation) and the Coexistence Initiative of the State of the World Forum.

One could argue, however, that the need to organise these events makes clear that not much has changed. At the end of the century, the world seems to be more insecure than ever before. Deadly conflict has become a prominent feature of the transition period from the Cold War to the 21st century. With over 30 active internal conflicts and scores more potential trouble spots within and between states, the international community is anxiously asking itself whether and how such deadly conflicts can be prevented.

Searching for an answer to these questions, the group of prominent people who produced the Carnegie Commission's 'Preventing Deadly Conflict' report2 came to this conclusion: 'First, deadly conflict is not inevitable. Second, the need to prevent deadly conflict is increasingly urgent. Third, preventing deadly conflict is possible.'

The prevention of deadly conflict, the report argues, 'is over the long term, too hard intellectually, technically, and politically to be the responsibility of any single institution or government, no matter how powerful. Strengths must be pooled, burdens shared, and labour divided among actors.'

The time was not ripe for this kind of approach at the first Hague conference. But it is now! Modern foreign policy is no longer the monopoly of very small groups of statesmen and diplomats. Gone are the days when diplomats could conduct policies of which the citizens were unaware.

In the past decade the number of peacebuilders working at all levels of society in places of ethnic and civil conflicts around the world, has mushroomed. The contribution of civilians, whether working from the bottom up or the top down, to resolving the conflicts of our time can no longer be ignored. Churches, women's organisations, the media, and business have all demonstrated their potential for building peace. So too the role of education, the arts and sports is gaining increasing recognition. 'Multitrack diplomacy', as it is called, is flourishing, and provides a major reason for hope of a more peaceful world.

This hope is rooted, as one of the great thinkers on peace-building and reconciliation, John Paul Lederach, writes in this book, 'in the resiliency of people (...) who, in spite of decades of obstacles and violence, keep taking steps toward peaceful coexistence with their enemies.' Hope is also rooted in the fact that the second half of the 20th Century, though rife with violent conflict, 'engendered the most prolific advancement of non-violent conflict transformation activities systematically known in human history, setting the stage for a potential singularity of peace-building in the 21st Century.'

In this book the reader will find many excellent examples of the valuable and frequently successful, initiatives taken by citizens of many countries, to resolve conflict, to prevent violence, and to reconcile parties that have been at war. Apart from introductory chapters written by experts in their particular fields, the book also presents a global overview of the most important organisations.

Aiming at a broad audience, we have chosen to employ a journalistic approach. Almost all of these casestudies have been written by journalists, on the basis of their independent research and documents from the organisations involved. We hope to have given credit to all actors involved, especially in projects initiated by Northern organisations in Southern countries where information was sometimes hard to find. People from all around the world have contributed to this publication. That cultural diversity is reflected in both the content and the style of the articles you will find collected in this book.

It has not been our aim to promote certain projects or programmes at the expense of others. What we were looking for were 'real-life stories', which give a true account of the possibilities of peace-building by small groups or even individuals, without down-playing the many difficulties involved. We hope the readers will gain more insight into the potential as well as the possibilities of the several tracks involved. We aim to inspire people and local communities working for peace and to support the work of educators, policy makers and international networks. Our intention is to raise the profile of the subject, provide links to organisations dealing with conflict resolution, citizenship, democracy and the longterm promotion of coexistence, peace-building and reconciliation.

Of course, one could argue that despite all efforts for peace in countries like Israel/Palestine, Bosnia or Angola peace is still a very distant dream. We should however realise that peace is a process, to which many of the initiatives described here have given an impetus, relatively small sometimes, but still meaningful. The building of peace is a multiparty effort, including setbacks as well as inspiring steps in the right direction. We should try to learn from both of these! One of the lessons which can be learned from the inspiring developments in countries like South Africa and Northern Ireland to mention two peace processes which are extensively covered in this publication, is the importance of a coherent and integrated effort involving as many tracks as possible. The multiplier effect which is created this way greatly enhances the chances for sustainable peace. The People to People Programme in Israel is another example of the importance of building peace at the governmental level as well as within the community at the same time.

The potential contribution to conflict resolution, peace-building and reconciliation of some of the sectors described here, is still relatively unknown. Arts and cultural activities as well as sports are tracks that offer many possibilities, amongst other reasons, because of the wide public they are able to reach. Also relatively unknown is the peace-building potential of a powerful segment of society, the corporate sector. Peace is profitable. A fact that has come to be realised by the business communities in South Africa and Northern Ireland. We can only hope that the management of many more companies, Chambers of Commerce, etc. will come to the conclusion that they too can play an important role in the transition from violence to peace and democracy.

Another thing we can learn from the stories presented here is that 'ordinary people' as well as minority groups can make a difference. By means of their creative approaches, their perseverance and compassion, many individuals around the world have succeeded in transforming apparently hopeless situations. We are able to achieve much more than we are sometimes inclined to think! We feel that, apart from anything else, these case-studies clearly illustrate the potential of multitrack diplomacy. A substantial additional investment in these kinds of initiatives-which in many cases are relatively inexpensive would greatly enhance the chances for peace in many places around the world. To stimulate this, more publicity is a prerequisite. We aim to contribute to the making of video documentaries of several of these cases for television broadcast as we believe this is the way to really reach and inspire large audiences. We should also mention here the decision to produce a Swedish-language edition of this publication. We hope more translations will follow and contribute to the aim of reaching as many people as possible.

The response to our initiative in publishing this collection of inspiring stories, has been overwhelming. At the same time, we have noticed how hard it was in many cases to collect the necessary information. Some of the cases presented here have never previously been described! That is why we have already decided to further pursue this initiative by publishing another collection of peace-building stories in the near future. All suggestions of cases which could be included in this second edition are welcome (preferably before the end of this year). We are especially interested in examples of peace-building in sectors which are not included in this edition, like youth organisations, exchange programmes, trade unions, the academic world, the military, etc.

The two international events previously mentioned provided the direct impetus for this publication. however, we hope the influence of this publication extends beyond the immediate context of its birth. Recently the UN launched the International Year for a Culture of Peace in 2000 and the International Decade for a Culture of Peace and Nonviolence in 2001-2010. We feel that these occasions should be used by people and organisations worldwide to invest in this 'culture of peace'. We sincerely hope this publication will inspire many people to invest in peace-building and create a true culture of peace as we enter the next century. In a way, we owe this to our predecessors.

5

POVERTY: PRIME ENEMY OF PEACE AND DEMOCRACY

TOWARDS A NEW CULTURE OF PEACE AND NON-VIOLENCE

On the eve of a new century and millennium, the world is challenged, more than at any time in the past, to transform human history from its domination by war and violence to a new culture of peace and non-violence. What is so unique about this historical moment that the challenge only arises at this time? It is a moment foreseen in the correspondence between Albert Einstein and Sigmund Freud in 1932. Freud speculated that for the first time, the abolition of warfare seemed possible, because of 'these two factors-man's cultural disposition and a well-founded fear of the form that future wars will take.' The form of war has changed over the past century and has indeed become universally intolerable. For war now endangers the very existence of our planet. The victims of war have also changed. No longer are the vast majority of the casualties the combatants themselves. Instead, it is now civilians who suffer most: children, women, the elderly and infirm.

It is at this significant point in time that the United Nations General Assembly has taken a series of decisions:

1. proclaiming the Year 2000, the International Year for the Culture of Peace;
2. proclaiming the Decade 2001-2010 the International Decade for a Culture of Peace and Non-violence for the Children of the World;

3. requesting a Declaration and a Programme of Action for a Culture of Peace.

There are many factors in contemporary societies which favour this move towards decisive, concerted action. Humanity's 'cultural disposition' and capacity for common action has been greatly enhanced by modern technology.

By pressing a computer key, a person can make instant contact with others on every continent. This enables people-and, most importantly, the young-to learn about each other, exchange views and begin to coordinate their actions. Unfortunately, extremes of wealth and poverty increasingly divide the world into 'haves' and 'have nots', and many are still excluded from these cyber links. Indeed, we are challenged to ensure the fruits of technology are used to increase human solidarity rather than to divide people further from each other.

The 'peace movements' of yesterday have come of age. No longer confined to a single issue, they have diversified into the full range of issues contributing to a culture of peace: human rights, democracy, social justice, protection of the environment, international solidarity, gender equality. No longer restricted to protest against government policy, they are creating new forms of solidarity and positive action, promoting reconciliation, building bridges, cultivating peace.

Peace itself is being redefined. Instead of the absence of war, it is increasingly seen as a dynamic, participative, long-term process, based on universal values and everyday practice at all levels-the family, the school, the community, as well as the nation. Of course, there have been important forerunners of this process. There have been movements for non-violent social change such as those identified with Mahatma Gandhi and Martin Luther King Jr, and organizations such as the International Fellowship of Reconciliation, showing us the way towards a dynamic, active, positive vision of peace.

With the end of the Cold War, and the renewed capacity of the United Nations Security Council to take unanimous action for peace, UNESCO joined in the post-conflict peace-building initiatives of the UN by launching its Culture of Peace Programme. For us at UNESCO, peace has always been our core mission. UNESCO's Constitution, drafted at the end of World War II and dedicated to the permanent abolition of war, says 'wars begin in the minds of men,' and adds that therefore, 'it is in the minds of men that the defences of peace must be constructed.' Its words are as pertinent today as the day they were written: 'a peace based exclusively upon the political and economic arrangements of governments would not be a peace which could secure the unanimous, lasting and sincere support of the peoples of the world, and that the peace must therefore be founded, if it is not to fail, upon the intellectual and moral solidarity of mankind.'

In this spirit, UNESCO's Culture of Peace activities work to weave a web of cooperation and understanding in previously divided communities. In programmes such as those in El Salvador and Mozambique, reconciliation was achieved by bringing together those previously shooting at each other and engaging them in jointly designing and implementing human development proposals. In El Salvador, NGOs associated with the former guerilla movement worked together with government ministries to broadcast a radio series providing information on women's rights and giving a voice to poor rural women. The broadcasts were heard throughout the country and were accompanied by a grass-roots educational campaign involving voluntary community peace promoters.

The process of the project was as important as the results-the former enemies were gradually transformed into partners through their participation in a shared initiative. In Mozambique, parliamentarians representing parties on both sides of the former conflict visited their parliamentary counterparts in neighbouring countries to learn how violent conflict can be transformed into constructive parliamentary debate. The experiences in El Salvador and Mozambique-and in many other countries from the Philippines to South Africa, Burundi and Mali-have shown that reconciliation is possible through acknowledgment of the past and working together for a common future.

The United Nations initiatives for a culture of peace mark a new stage: instead of focusing exclusively on rebuilding societies after they have been torn apart by violence, the emphasis is placed on preventing violence by fostering a culture where conflicts are transformed into cooperation before they can degenerate into war and destruction.

The key to the prevention of violence is education for non-violence. This requires the mobilisation of education in its broadest sense-education throughout life and involving the mass media as much as traditional educational institutions. Just as violence is a learned behaviour, so, too, is the process of active non-violence. It must be learned and perfected through practice. The skills are many: active listening, dialogue, mediation, cooperative learning, conflict transformation. It may be said that, as we enter a new century, the 'second literacy' of 'learning to live together' has become as important as the first literacy of reading, writing and arithmetic.

The importance of learning cannot be stressed too much. We must all learn the skills and attitudes needed for a culture of peace. It is important, in this regard, to reassure young people that our behaviour is not pre-determined by genes or brain mechanisms. The consensus of leading scientists, expressed in the 1986 Seville Statement on Violence, is that 'biology does not condemn humanity to war.... the same species that invented war is capable of inventing peace. The responsibility lies with each of us.'

While the state, as always, has a leading role in the prevention of violence, it is not alone in this responsibility. The culture of peace is the responsibility of each citizen in his or her daily life, and can be translated into numerous forms of action. One initiative is the Manifesto for a Culture of Peace and Non-violence, written and signed by Nobel Peace Laureates. Individuals are signing the manifesto and their signatures are being collected throughout the world-with a goal of 100 million for the UN Millennium Assembly in September 2000.

The Manifesto commits each individual to cultivate a culture of peace 'in my daily life-in my family, my work, my community, my country and my region.' It makes the individual, rather than the state, the central actor in creating a world of peace.

The culture of peace is becoming a global movement-a movement of movements-in which everyone who is working for human rights, non-violence, democracy, social justice, sustainable development, women's equality, join together in a 'grand alliance' of social transformation. The action of nongovernmental organizations working for these varied goals is a particularly powerful motor of social change.

This book is a milestone in the movement towards a culture of peace. It documents how, throughout the world, people are making progress on the various issues that-taken together-contribute to the coming culture of peace and non-violence. I invite the reader to take up this book and learn from the rich experiences and visions documented in its pages. I also invite readers to take up the challenge and emulate these actions in their own communities. It is by joining together that we can make the global transformation from a culture of war and violence to a culture of peace and non-violence.

THE CHALLENGE OF THE 21ST CENTURY

Justpeace

We were seated in a small room, about fourteen of us. Some were under the bunks that lined three walls, some on the top beds with their feet dangling. It was our second, maybe third visit to the room. I remembered our first visit for the defining question that faced our little envoy of mediators and peaceniks. 'Before you start,' they had said, 'we just want to know one thing. What makes you think that violence doesn't work?'

Before we could answer they went on to recount a recent conflict where negotiations had failed, mediation was rejected, but violence brought change. The story served to reinforce a message driven deep into their psyche and experience from childhood up and that had brought them eventually to this room: Only the strong survive. But on this visit it was our turn. We asked what they thought about the just signed peace agreements.

The words of the leader, taking a deep breath, still seem to resonate in my head. 'I fear peace,' he said, 'cause at the end of the day I know I'll be back in this prison visitn' me children's children.' Honest; heartfelt words from the Maze Prison in Northern Ireland.

We were standing on a dirt playground outside an old school building where a tense meeting had taken place. It had been nearly six years since the end of the Nicaraguan war that raged during much of the 1980's. The gathering had brought together former enemies, foot soldiers and their families who had fought for either the Counterrevolution or the Sandinista Government. Driven mostly by their immediate survival needs these former fighters from both sides were engaged in a process of reconciliation and had formed a national network of veterans who were receiving training in mediation, peace-building and micro-enterprise development. At the end of the meeting one of the vets approached the lead facilitator and I overheard him say, 'I need $10.'

'Why,' she asked. 'My sister, she runs around at night screaming like a monkey. She tears at her stomach and says she wants the monkey out.' He fell silent for a moment. 'We went to the Doctors but they say there is nothing to stop the monkey. But, there is a brujo' he stopped in mid-sentence. 'You think the witchdoctor will help?' she went on. I can still remember him looking at his hands, rough from daily work in the fields. These powerful hands carried guns in the war that created the monkey in his sister's belly. But now six years after the war they were empty. 'It's all we know to do,' he said.

As a mediator and teacher many of my tools rely on words. Sometimes, as I found in these two real-life moments and conversations, it only takes a few words in a story to summarize complex aspects of Truth. Both the stories relate to the theme of this book: Peacebuilding and Reconciliation. Both raise questions about the nature and meaning of peace. These questions are not raised as insights from sophisticated observers or theoreticians, nor from the rhetoric of politicians or even the most dedicated nonviolent strategist. No, the questions emerge from the lives of common people, protagonists in the swirl of war and the effects of violence. Their questions are simple. What change will peace bring us? What is to be expected from this peace?

As I look back across 20 years of working for nonviolence, conflict transformation, and reconciliation and as I reflect on the recent decades of peace accords two things stand out. First, objective assessment suggests there are significant gaps in our capacity to build and sustain peace initiatives. Second, direct interaction with these processes provokes contagious hope.

The hope is rooted in the resiliency of people like the two mentioned above, who, in spite of decades of obstacles and violence, keep taking steps toward peaceful coexistence with their enemies. Hope is rooted in the fact that the second half of the 20th Century, though rife with violent conflict, engendered the most prolific advancement of nonviolent conflict transformation activities systematically known in human history setting the stage for a potential singularity of peace-building in the 21st Century. The gaps emerge from a reductionism focused on techniques driven by a need to find quick fixes and solutions to complex, long term problems rather than a systemic understanding of peace-building as a process-structure. In this short chapter I will suggest that we must do two things to address this challenge. We must identify several key gaps that emerge from recent peace-building experiences and we must develop an adequate language appropriate to the hopes we hold.

Three Gaps in Peacebuilding

As a starting point I find the most significant challenges to peace-building in the 21st Century emerge from three gaps. By gap I mean an inability or insufficiency in our conceptual and practice frameworks that weaken our capacity to sustain a desired process. The three I will explore are the interdependence, the justice and the process-structure gaps. Given the brevity of this chapter I will limit myself to summary observations about each aspect and the needs that they suggest.

THE INTERDEPENDENCE GAP

The Observation

Interdependence is built on relationships and relationships are the heart and bloodlines of peace-building. In peace-building there are many forms of interdependence. Most recognized is the idea that we build new or rebuild broken relationships across the lines of divisions created through and by the conflict. Using a pyramid to describe a setting affected by violent conflict I refer to this as horizontal capacity.

The effort to work with counterparts, enemies, across the lines of division. Most peace-building work, particularly in the sub-field of conflict resolution, has been aimed at improving aspects of relationships through negotiation, dialogue, and mediation by getting counterparts to meet with each other. However, if we ask the question 'who meets each other to develop relationships?' we find this answer: people who are at a relative equal status within the context of the conflict. Community people meet community people, mid-range leaders encounter each other, and of course, top level political leaders in the limelight sit across negotiation tables. In other words, the emphasis of dialogue has fostered horizontal relationships.

The most significant gap of interdependence we face is rooted in the lack of responsive and coordinated relationships up and down the levels of leadership in a society affected by protracted violent conflict. This is what I have referred to as the vertical capacity: the ability to develop relationships of respect and understanding between higher levels of leadership with community and grassroots levels of leadership, and vice versa.

To put it simply, high, middle-range and grassroots levels of leadership rarely see themselves as interdependent with the other levels in reference to peace-building until they discover they need them, usually when the process is under enormous stress and time constraints. If pursued the resulting relationship suffers manipulation or instrumentalist superficiality.

Correspondingly, we are hampered in our ability to create and sustain vertical and horizontal integration strategically necessary for implementing the kind of long-term peace-building we hope to put in place.

The challenge of horizontal capacity is how to foster constructive understanding and dialogue across the lines of division in a society. The challenge of the vertical capacity is how to develop genuine recognition that peace-building involves multiple activities at different levels of leadership, taking place simultaneously, each level distinct in its needs and interdependent in effects. Strategic change in a system requires that horizontal and vertical relationships move in tandem on an equal basis.

In far too many places and times vertical capacity has been weak. What one level of peace-building undertook was rarely understood by, much less conceived and conducted in a way that significantly involved other levels of the affected society. Yet all levels, at one time or another, are affected by and must coordinate their activities with each other.

In sum, the interdependence gap suggests that sustainability of peace-building require both horizontal and vertical relationship building and coordination. In conceptual and practical terms, the field of peace-building has concentrated more of its resources and capacity-building on the horizontal ignoring the vertical axis, leaving significant insufficiencies in the structure of the peace process to be sustained.

The Need

To address the interdependence gap we must find ways to:

- o Increase the recognition that peace-building is an organic system that requires relationships and coordination of multiple activities, multiple roles, at multiple levels. No one activity and no one level will be able to deliver and sustain peace on its own.
- o Increase the mutual understanding by each level of the particular approaches and activities required at the others. The orientation is toward awareness of the unique contribution each brings in order to build relationships of respect, provide greater points of coordination, and decrease the competitiveness of activity and control structures devised to protect turf but which ultimately limit the capacity of change and integration in the system.
- o Build relationships before, during and after formal Accords reach ink, between people who are not like-minded, like-focused, and like-situated within the

structure of the society. We need to bring an equal emphasis on vertical relationship building as we do to horizontal relationship building.

The Justice Gap

The Observation

Most people involved in protracted conflicts expect peace processes will provide changes both in stopping the direct violence and in addressing the structural issues they feel gave rise to the conflict in the first place. Particularly for settings of internal violent conflict, the latter will almost always require a systemic transformation of relationships in the affected society's political, economic and social policies and ethos. In the past fifteen years peace processes have delivered a reduction of direct violence but have rarely attained the aspirations of desired structural change. Thus, there persists a deep felt perception in many peoples' minds that to reduce violence peace compromises social justice. Let us explore this a bit more.

An expansive time view of any one of the most significant internal wars and their peace accord processes in the past couple of decades suggest an interesting paradox. It starts by the overall progression of conflict and its escalation to war, then negotiations and peace accords.

First, situations move from latent status into open conflict and direct violence when people feel there is a significant issue of justice and human or group rights that must change and in which there exist few if any other avenues for achieving due recourse.

People who take up direct violence are trying to address the perceived injustice or what Galtung called 'structural violence,' that is, they are trying to achieve systemic changes in the underlying economic, cultural, social, and political structures as those are perceived to detrimentally affect their lives.

As the conflict escalates there comes a time where the choice of means, war and socially sanctioned violence, for pursuing or defending against particular changes reaches a saturation point, or an exhaustion level. Mary Anderson suggests it is when people realize the 'system of violence' has become more oppressive than the initial injustice. In other words direct violence added onto the existing latent structural violence creates a situation in which everyone perceives themselves as oppressed and worst off than they were before. People then begin the process of re-evaluating their goals and methodologies, and they move toward negotiation and redefining their relationship. In the graph I depicted this as two separate lines, direct and structural violence which criss-cross each other over time.

In the past fifteen years these negotiations have resulted in a series of peace accords. A peace accord means that the direct violence line drops significantly, that is, the fighting stops. However, people expect the accords to address the fundamental issues that gave rise to the fighting, the structural violence, and that solutions will be produced on the same timeline as the diminishing curve of direct violence.

This rarely, if ever has been the case. It results in what I call the 'justice gap.' The war is over, formal negotiations concluded, and changes have come usually in terms of increased space for political participation. However the expectations for social, economic, religious, and cultural change are rarely achieved, creating a gap between the expectations for peace and what it delivered.

The significance of the justice gap in the context of the challenges we face in the 21st Century is to ask ourselves the question where has most peace-building practice, theory, and funding been invested in reference to the overall progression described above? My observation: Much greater investment has been expended in the study and development of methodologies and practice for reducing direct violence than in transforming structural violence. We have focused our lenses more on negotiation and peace accord fashioning between groups and their representatives than in understanding the processes of structural change. The justice gap emerges in part because we have not adequately developed a peace-building framework that reduces direct violence and produces social and economic justice.

The Need

To address the justice gap we must find ways to:

- o Increase the capacity of peace-building practitioners, both governmental and nongovernmental to integrate social justice building with direct violence reducing processes, two highly interdependent energies and foci, that are rarely held together at the same time.
- o Broaden the understanding of peace-building to integrate the fields of conflict transformation, restorative justice, and socio-economic development. In most post-Accord settings these have shown themselves to be highly interdependent perspectives, practices and skills yet are rarely conceptualized or practised together.
- o Reorient our investment (funding, research, and practice) such that we are not negotiation-centric at the expense of developing practices and frameworks for understanding how to create and sustain collaborative, nonviolent processes of structural change.

The Process-Structure Gap

The Observation

Peace Accords are often seen as a culminating point of a peace process. In the language of governments and the military the Accords are referred to as an end-game scenario. We fall prey to this thinking when we see the Accords as the way the war ended. In reality the Accords are nothing more than opening a door into a whole new labyrinth of rooms that invite us to continue in the process of redefining our relationships.

This is one reason I have preferred the words conflict transformation over conflict resolution. Resolution lends itself to a metaphor that suggests our goal is to end something not desired. Transformation insinuates that something not desired is changing, taking new form. When we add conflict transformation to peace-building we push the metaphor further. We embrace the challenge to change that which torn us apart and building something we desire. This focus on language pushes us to reconsider the idea of a 'peace process.' Process paints the image that peace is dynamic and ongoing. On the other hand I often hear people ask the question, 'How will the peace be sustained?' This question assumes a metaphor of peace as a product. In both instances our language fails us.

In recent years I have turned to theoreticians in what is sometimes called the New Science and found they encountered similar challenges. This approach includes quantum physics, chaos theory, self-organizing systems theory among others. For me two things stand out in their development. First, they had to shift out of old modalities of thinking in order to enter into totally new ways of looking at old realities. As Einstein was supposed to have said, no problem can be solved with the same consciousness that created it. Second, they had to develop new, or as the case demanded, retool old language to adequately describe the realities. One of their terms was a process-structure, a concept used to describe phenomena in nature that are, at the same time, process and structure. I have found this notion especially relevant to peace-building.

When we think of peace as a process we inevitably fall prey to critique that it is an endless dynamic that leads to no substantive outcome. When we envision peace as a result we fall into the trap that it is an end-state, only to discover that is neither an 'end' nor a 'state' and that if we treat it as such our desire to preserve or control it destroy its very essence. I believe that our language has limited our capacity to adequately describe the phenomenon we wish to understand and to the degree possible encourage. It has created a paradoxical hiatus reflected both in our theory and practice, the process-structure gap. Peace is neither a process nor a structure. It is both. Peacebuilding requires us to work at constructing an infrastructure to support a process of desired change, and change is permanent.

I use the metaphor of a river to illustrate this. A river is one of the phenomena the New Science calls a process-structure. When you stand up to your knees in a river what you see, feel and hear is the dynamic flow of water. It rushes around your legs with force and power, changing like the essence of water itself to get around any obstacle put in its way. On the other hand if you stand high on a mountain, or position yourself at a window of an airplane and look down at the river from a long distance what you see is the shape and form it has carved in the land. From a distance it looks static. You see it as a structure not a dynamic process. This is a process-structure. A river is dynamic, adaptive and changing while at the same time carving a structure with direction and purpose.

This is the challenge we face with peace-building. We must engender an adaptive, dynamic and responsive change process. At the same time the very process of change must have purpose and infrastructure to support its flow. In practice we have tended to think about peace as a process up to the point of the Accords, then suddenly, things should translate into structure, too often in purely bureaucratic terms. To conceptualize peace as process-structure moves us away from a myopic focus on agreements and events and toward a commitment of embracing the permanency of relationship building. Relationships are both dynamic and adaptive, yet they also take social, political forms that require accountability, vigilance, and willingness to change. We know this is inherently true of intimate personal relationships. We have been woefully insufficient in conceptualizing social, organizational, political and economic structures as responsive to relational needs and changing environments. When relationship becomes the centre what remains permanent is not a given form but the capacity to encounter and adapt, both of which are processes learned and relearned through conflict addressed constructively.

The Need

To address the process-structure gap we must find ways to:

- o Understand peace as a change process based on relationship building.
- o Reorient our peace-building framework toward the development of support infrastructures that enhance our capacity to adapt and respond to relational needs rather than being defined and driven by events and agreements.
- o Reconceive long-term peace structures such that they reflect the inherent responsiveness often present in periods of active negotiation and avoid the trappings of

isolating 'peace' functions in bureaucracies implementing time-bound mandates with little capacity to adapt and change to on-the-ground real-life needs.

CONCLUSION

The above discussion suggests we should adapt systemic and paradox-based lenses for understanding, responding to and developing the change processes for we wish to put in motion. I believe this must be reflected in our language. As a conclusion let me put forward a modest proposal and challenge that require a shift in practice and language.

At the writing of this chapter I find myself halfway through my fifth decade. If given the grace I may live to see the halfway point of the 21st Century. The year will be 2050, a decade when the last of my generation will pass the torch to our great-grandchildren. A decade when my friend in the Maze feared he would return as an old man to visit his great-grandson. What do we hope can be in place by the mid-point of the next Century?

THE MEANING OF RECONCILIATION

Compared to conflict handling mechanisms such as negotiation, mediation, adjudication, and arbitration, the approach called 'reconciliation' is perhaps the least well understood. Its meaning, processes, and application have not been clearly articulated or developed. A place to start understanding what it entails might be by trying to distinguish it from the other approaches used in peacemaking and peace-building.

If we were to look at the 'degree of mutual participation by the conflict parties in the search for solutions to the problems underlying their conflict' we could place these approaches in a spectrum as follows.

At the left end of the spectrum, we find approaches where mutual participation is minimal. The use of force by one of the parties to impose a solution would be an example of a mechanism that would be placed at this end of the spectrum. Further to the right of the spectrum, we could place mechanisms such as adjudication. Here a third party, instead of an adversary, imposes a solution to the conflict. However, the mutual participation of the parties in the choice of the solution is comparatively higher here than in the first. In the adjudication process, at least the parties have an opportunity to present their cases, to be heard, and submit their arguments for why their preferred solution should be the basis upon which the decision is made. Nonetheless, the choice of the solution is made by a third party, and the decision is backed by force (enforced) which ensures that the losing party confidence.

Arbitration is placed further to the right of 'adjudication'. Here, the participation of the parties is even higher since both adversaries can choose who is going to decide the issues under dispute, whereas in adjudication the decision maker is already appointed by the state. The parties in conflict can sometimes identify the basis upon which their case will be decided and whether the outcome will be binding or not. Although the mutual involvement of the parties in the decision making process is much higher than adjudication, the solution is still decided by an outsider and, depending on the type of arbitration, the outcome could be imposed by the power of the law.

Further to the right on the spectrum we find negotiation. Here the participation of all the involved parties in the search for solution is very high. It is the parties themselves who have to formulate the issues, and find a resolution that is satisfactory to all of them. In this situation, however, particularly in bargaining type negotiations (as opposed to problem-solving type of negotiations), the final choice of the solution might depend on the relative power position of the adversaries rather than on what might be the most satisfactory solution to everyone involved. The party with the higher bargaining leverage might end up getting the most out of the negotiations.

Mediation is a special type of negotiation where the parties' search for mutually satisfactory solutions are assisted by a third party. The third party's role is to minimize obstacles to the negotiation process including those that emanate from power imbalance. Unlike adjudication, however, in the final analysis it is the decision and agreement of the conflict parties that determines how the conflict will be resolved.

Towards the far right of the spectrum we find reconciliation. This approach not only tries to find solutions to the issues underlying the conflict but also works to alter the adversaries' relationships from that of resentment and hostility to friendship and harmony. Of course, for this to happen, both parties must be equally invested and participate intensively in the resolution process.

Before we move on to examine the insights that emerge from this spectrum, it will clarify our thinking if we quickly glance at one more issue of definitions and distinctions.

The conflict handling mechanisms illustrated in the spectrum can be categorized into three groups which we will call conflict management, conflict resolution, and conflict prevention approaches. Conflict management approaches generally tend to focus more on mitigating or controlling the destructive consequences that emanate from a given conflict than on finding solutions to the underlying issues causing it. On the other hand, conflict resolution approaches aim at going beyond mitigation of consequences and attempt to resolve the substantive and relational root-causes so that the conflict comes to an end.

While conflict management and resolution are reactive, they come into motion once conflict has surfaced, conflict prevention tries to anticipate the destructive aspects of the conflict before they arise and attempts to take positive measures to prevent them from occurring.

Most of the mechanisms identified on the left hand of the spectrum are conflict management approaches. The use of military force for deterrence or in peace-keeping (separating the conflict parties from each other so that they do not keep inflicting harm on each other) are typical conflict management strategies. To the extent that adjudication, arbitration, and bargaining negotiations do not become avenues to solve the underlying issues of the conflict, and in most instances they do not, they become mere stop-gap conflict management measures. But if they provide an opportunity to work out not only differences on substantive issues but also negative relationships, they can become conflict resolution mechanisms.

Observations

We notice that as we move from the left to the right on the spectrum, i.e., as the participation-of all the parties in the search for solution increases, the likelihood of achieving a mutually satisfactory and durable solution also increases. We know that solutions imposed by force will only last until the vanquished is able to muster sufficient force to reverse the situation. Solutions imposed by adjudication and arbitration, unless somehow the loser gives up, can always be frustrated by the latter's endless appeals or lack of cooperation in the implementation process. If, however, the parties are engaged earnestly in the search for the solutions and are able to find resolutions that could satisfy the needs and interests of all involved, there could be no better guarantee for the durability of the settlements. It would be in the interest of every one to see to it that they are fully enforced. This is what we believe problem-solving negotiations, mediation, and reconciliation can do.

What is noteworthy however is that as we move from the left to the right end of the spectrum, although the likelihood of effectiveness and durability of the solutions increases, our knowledge and understanding of the approaches to be utilized become sketchy, less developed and unsystematic. Our knowledge and methodology of conflict management approaches (the mechanisms on the left hand side of the spectrum) such as the use of force, adjudication, or arbitration are quite advanced. They are highly developed disciplines within institutions that command high respect and resources devoted to training and practice.

Military and police science, jurisprudence and legal studies, as well as the entire military and police academies, law schools, ministries of defence and justice, police departments, courts, prison systems, are examples of these disciplines and institutions that advance the practice of these approaches. In contrast, conflict resolution approaches such as problem-solving negotiation and mediation are less developed and institutions and resources devoted to their training, advancement and practice are meager. Whatever is in place is voluntary and adhoc. Then, when we come to reconciliation, let alone establish procedures and institutions charged with the application of the concept, there is not even much understanding of what it means, especially, among social scientists. Religious people and theologians are a bit better equipped to discuss the concept. But even there, there is a great gap between articulation and translation of the ideas into practice.

Healing and Reconciliation

Despite the lack of knowledge about how to operationalize reconciliation, there is however no question about the tremendous need for it. In fact, it could be said that the need in today's world is much greater than at any other time in the past.

One reason is that conflict management strategies are not adequate to deal with the kinds of contemporary conflicts raging in many parts of the world. Especially since the end of the Cold War, civil wars have replaced interstate wars as the most predominant large scale social conflicts. To a certain extent, in interstate conflicts strategies aimed merely at separating the conflicting parties might suffice. Even if the underlying issues of the conflict are not resolved, the separation could help avoid the recurrence of the conflict. Because states tend to isolate themselves from each other by their national boundaries, the task of separating them by peace-keeping forces is relatively easier.

However, in civil war situations the relationships between the protagonists is much more intimate and complex. In most cases, the parties share the same geographic area and even community, there might be strong economic interdependence between them, they usually have all sorts of social ties among each other including intermarriages. In these instances it is quite difficult to separate the protagonists since the boundaries between them are very difficult to draw. Even if it is possible to do it for a short while, it is not feasible to think of conflict management strategies such as separation as long term solutions. For that matter, even decisions imposed by adjudication or other such processes will not be solutions since the winning party cannot expect to enjoy its victory without facing the consequences of the loser's wrath. Therefore, in civil war situations conflict management strategies are not adequate. One has to move towards conflict resolution and reconciliation processes where not only the underlying issues to the conflicts are resolved to everyone's satisfaction but also the antagonistic attitudes and relationships between the adversaries are transformed from negative to positive.

Moreover, even in interstate relations, we are increasingly realizing that the components of the modern international system are no more the 19th century autarchic states. The globe is shrinking and the fates of peoples of the world are becoming more and more inextricably intertwined. Thus, it would be increasingly difficult to expect unilateral approaches to handling conflicts such as imposition of solutions by force as viable approaches. In an interdependent and closely interconnected world even those that are supposedly weak can have their own way of subverting or undermining the imposed order. Therefore, those groups must somehow be enabled to participate in the search for solutions in their conflicts even with the more powerful actors. In fact, the democratic values that the current international order is trying to promote as a universal value in all societies of the world necessitates movement more and more towards integrative negotiation, mediation and reconciliation as the predominant ways of dealing with conflict instead of unilateral measures that entail the use of coercion.

What Does Reconciliation Entail?

Reconciliation as a conflict handling mechanism entails the following core elements:

(a) Honest acknowledgment of the harm/injury each party has inflicted on the other;

(b) Sincere regrets and remorse for the injury done:

(c) Readiness to apologize for one's role in inflicting the injury;

(d) Readiness of the conflicting parties to 'let go' of the anger and bitterness caused by the conflict and the injury;

(e) Commitment by the offender not to repeat the injury;

(f) Sincere effort to redress past grievances that caused the conflict and compensate the damage caused to the extent possible;

(g) Entering into a new mutually enriching relationship.

Reconciliation then refers to this new relationship that emerges as a consequence of these processes. What most people refer to as 'healing' is the mending of deep emotional wounds (generated by the conflict) that follow the reconciliation process.

A very important aspect of the process of reconciliation and one that distinguishes it from all the other conflict handling mechanisms is its methodology. In most of the conflict handling mechanisms such as adjudication, arbitration, and for that matter even negotiation and mediation the method used for establishing responsibility for the conflict or its consequences is adversarial. In these processes, the parties present their grievances and make a case for the adversary's fault or responsibility, thereby demanding that it should be the latter that should make amends. Each party begins by defending its own behaviour and denying its own guilt or responsibility until the opponent proves it to his or her satisfaction or to the satisfaction of outside observers, be they judges or mediators. In such a process, one's behaviour is always explained as a reaction to the behaviour of the adversary. The typical pattern of the interaction is: 'I did this to you because you did such and such a thing to me!' The aim is to get the adversary to change his or her future conduct by proving the person's guilt. Of course, the expectation is that both parties will change each other in this way and will eventually transform their relationship from negative to positive.

On the other hand, the essence of reconciliation is the voluntary initiative of the conflict parties to acknowledge their responsibility and guilt. The interactions that transpire between the parties are not only meant to communicate one's grievances against the actions of the adversary, but also to engage in self-reflection about one's own role and behaviour in the dynamic of the conflict. In other words, in this kind of dialogue, as much as one attributes guilt and responsibility to the adversary for the damage generated by the conflict, one has to also be self-critical and acknowledge responsibility for his or her own role in the creation or perpetuation of the conflict and hurtful interaction. The aim of such interaction is that, in the final analysis, each of the parties acknowledges and accepts his or her responsibility and out of such recognition seeks ways to redress the injury that has been inflicted on the adversary, to refrain from further damage, and to construct new positive relationships.

It is true that in both reconciliation and other conflict resolution mechanisms the process of dialogue is expected to generate change and transformation. In reconciliation, however, the forces for change are primarily internal and voluntary; while in the other approaches they are external and to a certain extent coerced. In the situation where the source is external it is possible that it might be the adversary's skill in marshaling and presenting its arguments; its strong will and intransigence; or its capacity to manipulate, exert pressure, or administer punishment that might intimidate the other party into accepting responsibility and settlement. Under such circumstances, therefore, it is questionable to what extent reluctant acceptance of guilt can serve as a force for significantly altering the future conduct and relationship between the adversaries.

This is not to imply that it is not possible to induce change in behaviour and relationships by forces outside the person, nor that every person changes his or her behaviour and relationships wilfully or voluntarily. The point here is that unless the need for change is internalized, the change is likely to be only temporary. The relationship would not have been significantly altered, and the conflict would not have found enduring solutions. It would emerge again as soon as circumstances change. More enduring transformation is likely to emerge when motivated by an internal need to change, especially when it emanates from self-reflection and criticism.

RECONCILIATION AND JUSTICE

Here it would be important to clarify the often misunderstood relationship between reconciliation and justice. Especially in horrendous conflict situations like Rwanda,

Yugoslavia, Cambodia and others, many have argued that reconciliation is not appropriate because it is too soft on criminal conduct of offenders, and might even encourage it. They feel that justice (usually meaning the punishment of the offenders) precedes reconciliation. However, this argument presents a false dichotomy. An attempt at reconciliation without addressing the injustice in the situation is indeed a mockery and belittling the suffering of the victim. There cannot be reconciliation without justice. Justice and equity are at the core of reconciliation.

The central question in reconciliation is not whether justice is done, but rather how one goes about doing it in ways that can also promote future harmonious and positive relationship between parties that have to live with each other whether they like it or not. Justice is a necessary but not sufficient condition for reconciliation. Reconciliation takes the concern for justice a step further and is preoccupied with how to rebuild a more livable, and psychologically healthy environment between former enemies where the vicious cycle of hate, deep suspicion, resentment, and revenge does not continue to fester.

For this reason, the methodology used to arrive at justice in the reconciliation process is different from that used to arrive at justice in the conventional (juridical) approach. The aim of the latter processes (particularly of the criminal justice process) is primarily to identify guilt and administer the punishment that the law requires with little attention to healing the bitterness and resentment that exist between the parties in the conflict. Identifying ways in which offenders are assisted to redress the material and emotional damage they have inflicted through self-reflection, acknowledgment of responsibility, remorse, and compensation would be an important step towards establishing an environment of reconciliation. The approach known as 'restorative justice' as opposed to 'retributive justice' brings us closer to the point where justice can be done but at the same time the possibilities for reconciliation are enhanced.

Applying this concept in some of the catastrophic situations like Rwanda, Yugoslavia, Cambodia or Chile, reconciliation does not mean that the offenders are just pardoned. It means creating a process and an environment where the offenders take the responsibility to acknowledge their offense and get motivated to change the situation and relationship in a positive and durable manner instead of keep denying their guilt until it is proven to them by the juridical process.

The important thing to note is that to the extent the offenders keep denying their guilt, even if their responsibility is proved juridically and they are punished, the internal change that needs to take place to change the relationship from destructive to constructive, from hate to cooperation and harmony may not happen. Particularly in group conflicts, the punishment of the offenders alone does not prevent them or their followers and (at times, even their descendants) from continuing to hate and desiring to retaliate against those that punished them or their forefathers. Reconciliation has a much better chance of stopping the cycle of violence and hatred that sometimes transcends generations than any other conflict handling mechanism.

Although flawed in many ways, this is what the experiments with Truth and Reconciliation Commission in conflict-ravaged societies are trying to do. In a number of instances, these commissions have been able to go as far as obtaining voluntarily acknowledgment of guilt by offenders. But they have not gone far enough to get them to demonstrate sincere remorse, or take active steps to compensate and repair the relationship vis a vis their victims.

6

Telling the Truth in the Wake of Mass Violence

Since the mid-1970s, a growing number of states have tried to come to terms with a legacy of gross human rights violations committed in their recent history, whether during military or authoritarian rule or in the course of an armed conflict. An approach which has steadily gained prominence in this respect is the investigation and recording of past atrocities by so-called truth commissions. Some twenty such commissions have operated across the world in the last fifteen years of which those in Chile, Argentina, and South Africa, have become the most widely known.1

Without much international attention, a truth commission recently completed its work in Guatemala and investigations continue in the southern provinces of Sri Lanka. The establishment of a commission is being discussed in Suriname, where violations committed in the 1980s continue to haunt society. In Indonesia, the fall of Suharto has allowed civil society to take up the issue of confronting the past. A commission has been proposed for Bosnia-Herzegovina, one suggested for Northern-Ireland, and one called for in Namibia and Sierra Leone.

The recent proliferation of truthtelling bodies warrants a closer look as their establishment generally relates to addressing old conflicts and preventing new ones. This chapter introduces the concept of truth commissions and some of the major issues related to their use. It clarifies the rationale behind them, sets out their practices, and seeks to shed light on their role in furthering reconciliation. Attention is also paid to the challenges that truth commissions may encounter and to factors that might affect their impact and effectiveness. Given the complexity of the issues involved, an in-depth examination of these matters is, however, beyond the scope of this chapter.

BACKGROUND

When countries move out of protracted periods of violence, societies and leadership alike need to decide whether and how to deal with the widespread human rights violations that have been committed. In considering whether to close the book on such abuses or to investigate and hold individuals accountable, ethical and political considerations need to be balanced: the demands of justice must be weighed against what is politically feasible. A tension is then often perceived to exist between the pursuit of both justice and peace, given the precarious nature of a political transition. It is feared that the former may jeopardize the latter when a democracy or peace agreement is still fragile.

Yet experience has shown that justice is part of the positive contents of peace and that addressing justice-related issues contributes to reconciliation in the long term. Consequently, accounting for past abuses is increasingly deemed important for the development of an enduring democracy or a lasting peace. Failure to do so may well lay the foundation for renewed violence by reinforcing a sense of impunity and resentment, allowing for conflicting versions of the past, and perpetuating enemy images. Redressing past violations, on the other hand, might reassert the rule of law, create respect for human rights, and legitimize structures of governance, thus altering the conditions in which serious crimes occurred.

Telling the truth originally surfaced as a way to deal with a legacy of abuses because the political circumstances often preclude prosecuting perpetrators. 'Bringing truth to light' at least ensured that knowledge of past crimes would be preserved. Truth is also viewed as a direct response to human rights violations because many of those evolve around secrecy and denial (disappearances, torture, killings by anonymous death squads.) Public acknowledgement of the truth is therefore as important as knowledge itself, for it counters the atmosphere of silence and deceit that facilitates such crimes.

Internationally, a 'right to truth' is now recognized for both societies and individuals. For the former, it is considered essential to avoid the repetition of crimes in the future. For the latter, it is part of an effective remedy for violations. This right is included in a set of principles prepared for the United Nations with a view to combating impunity (hereinafter the 'Joinet-principles.')2 Serving this right to truth, truth commissions are increasingly considered valuable in their own right, rather than a second-best option to prosecution. Their broad scope of inquiry, inclusive character, impact on victims, and forward-looking nature add greatly to this appreciation.

FORMS AND ACTIVITIES: VARIATIONS ON A THEME

Truth commissions are remarkably flexible bodies. They appear in a wide variety of forms and sizes and new models continue to evolve as each situation presents its unique set of circumstances, constraints, and demands. The historical, political, and cultural context of a country is of major influence on the shape that a commission will take, precluding any easy categorization of the truth commissions existing to date.

Features

Truth commissions can be defined as official bodies that investigate, within a limited time-frame, past human rights violations in order to establish a comprehensive record of abuses that occurred in a particular country over a specific period of time. Their mandate is generally limited to serious violations. These are specified in detail or set out in broad terms, in which case the commission is left to interpret which abuses to include in its investigation. The Salvadoran Commission on the Truth, for example, was charged with investigating "serious acts of violence that have occurred since 1980 and whose impact on society urgently demands that the public should know the truth." Commissions may investigate violations by the armed forces of the state, those committed by the opposition, or both. Commissions are also charged with making recommendations aimed at reparation and prevention of future abuses.

Sponsorship

Most commissions to date have been state bodies, set up by parliament or the head of state. In El Salvador and Guatemala, commissions were established under auspices of the United Nations in the context of peace agreement between government and guerrilla forces. At times, human rights organisations or church institutions have undertaken projects that resemble such official commissions in the absence of any government effort.

Focus

The primary focus of truth commissions is on victims and relatives. As a result, few restrictions are placed on participation and much emphasis is placed upon on providing opportunity to victims to relate their accounts. In fact, only in South Africa did the commission receive significant information from perpetrators, owing to its capacity to grant amnesty in exchange for disclosure about past crimes.

Activities may be conducted in public or private depending on security considerations, the mandate of a commission, and the national context. While increasing the transparency of a commission, publicity may draw it into the political arena more easily.

Quasi-judicial

As quasi-judicial bodies, truth commissions do not make findings of criminal responsibility, their reports do not have judicial effects, and their powers are limited. Two issues have been particularly controversial: whether to name names, and whether to investigate abuses by both governmental and oppositional forces.

Traditionally, the concept of human rights violations has been restricted to acts of the state. Critics charge that investigating crimes committed by the state and by non-state actors (such as armed opposition forces) equates them, thus downplaying the gravity of the former. On the naming of perpetrators, many consider the truth to be incomplete without individualizing responsibility and argue that it is the only way to break a cycle of impunity. Others are concerned over due process protections for those named. Generally, the terms of reference have left it to commissions to decide whether to name names.

Reporting

Truth commissions compile comprehensive final reports which usually are widely released to the public. These reports establish the societal and political context, explain the historical background, indicate the overall pattern of abuses, and lay out institutional responsibilities. Some list all cases brought to a commission's attention, others detail some cases illustrative of general trends. Extensive recommendations are made, outlining needed reform (such as restructuring the police, strengthening civilian command over the military, human rights education) and suggesting reparation measures (compensation, access to health care and education, renaming of public spaces.) Most commissions have made recommendations regarding the prosecution of perpetrators, irrespective of concurrent amnesty measures.

Follow-Up

Following the publication of a report, some heads of state publicly accept responsibility for past wrongs and apologize to victims.

President Aylwin of Chile, for example, made a televised apology appealing for forgiveness and sent a copy of the report to the family of each victim named. A commission may also set other efforts to deal with the past in motion. In South Africa and Guatemala, a process of exhumations and reburials has begun, going some way in addressing the grief of relatives. The record of judicial follow-up is generally mixed. The evidence gathered by a commission may allow for the criminal prosecution of perpetrators. Yet in several countries, blanket amnesties were declared before a commission came into being; elsewhere, they were promulgated after the publication of a report. Individual perpetrators and the (former) military and political leadership often fail to take responsibility for past crimes. Nevertheless, in most cases society at large has acknowledged the abuses.

Limitations

The tense political environment in which commissions operate often place serious limitations on their activities. The balance of power between different political and societal actors during the transitional period determines the scope and depth of the truthtelling process. In Namibia, the government has resisted the establishment of a truth commission to avoid having its past behavior be scrutinized.6 The continuing dominance of the military in Guatemala ensured that the Historical Clarification Commission could not individualize responsibility nor provide the courts with the material it collected, despite strong pleas from national human rights organisations. Challenges truth commissions may face include lack of power and/or resources, intimidation of witnesses, and restricted access to information. The political parameters may also impede the implementation of recommendations.

Enhancing the Prospects for Reconciliation

While the contributions of truth commissions to reconciliation cannot be established in any precise manner, experiences to date suggest a number of ways in which commissions can enhance the prospects of reconciliation. These exist on social, factual, political, and moral levels.

- *Social:* Breaking the silence about the past and officially acknowledging what happened can be essential for healing the wounds that exist in society. It breaks through the fear and isolation generated by serious violations and undermines denial and deceit by those responsible. On victims, the official recognition of their pain can have a profound psychological impact. A truth commission gives them the opportunity to relate their experiences and be heard, which is a form of redress and rehabilitation. The process of truthtelling is therefore increasingly considered as important as its final product (the written record) as it allows people to become actively involved and to regain some authority and dignity. Thus, a commission can play a cathartic and empowering role.
- *Factual:* A commission can work towards a collective understanding of the past by creating a factual record

that impedes future distortion or manipulation. It is not so much that one, definitive, account of events can be established which everyone shares; rather, a framework is established in which further discussion can take place. In evaluating different claims in light of the information gathered, a commission will find that some cannot be upheld while others are validated. In Argentina, it is a matter of public record that people were thrown into the sea from helicopters while still alive. In South Africa, it can no longer be denied that a systematic practice of torture in detention existed. Yet a truth commission is also valuable in exposing the many accounts that exist of what happened, thus revealing the complexity of reality. Challenging perceptions, it undermines a rigid black and white picture of the past.

- *Political:* A truth commission can help lay the foundations for a democratic culture of dialogue and participation in which disagreement is tolerated and dealt with through non-violent means. Commissions offer a voice to those previously voiceless and encourage pluralism by juxtaposing different versions of history. Addressing a legacy of violence draws people into debate-about citizenship, the organization of society, and the governing of the state. Establishing facts about particular events or prominent cases can also facilitate interaction in the public sphere between opposing parties by dispelling suspicion and discrediting old lies. The official nature of the commission serves to restore the state's legitimacy, signaling its commitment to break with the past and respect human rights.
- *Moral:* A commission can contribute to an awareness of fundamental values as it evaluates the past on the basis of a normative framework that evolves around human dignity and integrity. Investigating the past becomes a way for society to discover anew moral imperatives-to base itself on the very values it needs to survive, allowing for the recognition of a common humanity. "The tales of war," Krog puts it, become "part of an ethos relating

to how people should behave towards one another."8 Truthtelling involves an examination of how conditions could arise that nurtured mass violence. Ultimately, it challenges people to reflect on their own role and responsibility, whether direct or indirect.

The positive impact of a truth commission in these areas can be significant. Yet a process of reconciliation is a complex one involving many aspects and taking place on a number of levels. A commission will encounter challenges in furthering reconciliation, three of which are discussed below.

Impartial?

The interpretation of principles such as 'impartiality' and 'evenhandedness' which guide a commission in its work, often prove divisive. 'Evenhandedness' means treating all violations fairly, but not necessarily apportioning equal blame across the board nor refraining from criticizing a political cause in the name of which abuses were committed. On the contrary, a commission cannot escape making moral judgements on the past as it makes its findings in light of human rights norms. It determines what was wrong and who was responsible. Findings may reveal one side to the conflict committed more abuses or was disproportionally victimized. Thus, while a truth commission can-and must-be impartial, it cannot be neutral. Those responsible for violations, anxious to protect themselves against adverse findings, point to this approach as proof of bias and argue that commissions should simply acknowledge that 'all sides committed abuses.' The tense environment in which a truth commission operates accelerates accusations of bias, thus intensifying the political wrangling around the body as some seek to trumpet its findings while others denounce them.

Coping with Conflict?

Truth commissions are most apt to deal with conflicts that have already been resolved politically; they cannot really function in an on-going conflict. A truth commission may be caught between two contradictory roles: a non-partisan facilitator, supposed to bring different actors together to set forth and discuss their version of the past, and an advocate, expected to attribute responsibility and judge the severity of abuses. In their origins, however, truth commissions are more the latter than the former, which limits their role in the actual resolution of conflict. For the same reasons, intercommunal violence may be more complicated for a truth commission to deal with than state-sponsored violence. In cases of communal violence, the abuses may not be concentrated on one side and a commission cannot invoke the specific responsibility of the state to respect the right of its citizens.

Reconciling the Personal?

The primary contribution of truth commissions to reconciliation is on the national level, rather than on the individual or community level. Interpersonal reconciliation would involve bringing people together-which commissions are generally unable to do given their temporary nature, the numbers of people involved, and the sheer enormity of their task of compiling a comprehensive record within a short period of time. Also, such reconciliation requires repentance and acknowledgement of the harm inflicted by those responsible. Yet only to a limited extent have truth commissions to date been able to elicit genuine remorse from perpetrators and to prompt them to own up to their acts.

Affecting the Impact of a Truth Commission

If anything, experiences to date teach us that there can be no standard model for a truth commission nor a recipe for success given the extent to which a commission is shaped by the particular national context. Nevertheless, past experiences do offer insight into the factors which might affect the impact and effectiveness of a truth commission. Of these, the political parameters during the transitional period are probably the most fundamental. They may further include the following:

- Willingness to deal with the past and to share a common future (or a recognition of a need to do so.) Genuinely coming to terms with the past is an inherently difficult undertaking which raises controversial issues and poses painful questions. As such, external actors cannot impose a truthtelling process on a society; they can only support it once it is embarked on from within. It is important to note that one cannot simply assume popular support for dealing with the past. Neither is it sufficient that one part of a society supports such an initiative. In order for a commission to be legitimate and successful in its efforts towards reconciliation, it must enjoy the support and participation of all major constituencies.

- Support by the political and military leadership. This enhances the commission's authority and reach, and will influence the resources at its disposal, its ability to access information, and the extent to which effect is given to its findings and recommendations, whether judicial, institutional, or reparational. Such backing must not, however, affect the independence of a commission. Even in the absence of active support, a commission may still function effectively so long as outright interference or obstruction is avoided. The Chilean Truth and Reconciliation Commission, generally regarded in a positive light, operated despite Pinochet's continued command of the armed forces.
- Legitimate and feasible mandate. Several issues arise in this regard. The mandate of a commission should cover the most frequently experienced violations. The Uruguayan truth commission had a mandate limited to disappearances while torture and illegal detention were far more common during the period under investigation. Flexible terms of reference allow a commission to investigate abuses as it deems fit. The mandate of the South African Truth and Reconciliation Commission specified killing, abduction, and torture as gross human rights violations, yet also included the undefined category of 'severe ill-treatment.' This enabled the commission to look into crimes not covered by the other categories, such as rape and poisoning. Further, the Joinet-principles advocate that all abuses ought to be investigated, whether committed by governmental or non-governmental forces.9 A practical consideration regards the proportion between the period under investigation and the period of operation. The fact that

the Accord on the establishment of the Guatemalan Historical Clarification Commission only provided six months (with a possible six-month extension) to investigate a 36-year period of armed conflict undermined the commission's credibility before it even came into being.

- Composition and procedures. The impartiality and representativeness of the commissioners will influence the acceptance of the commission amongst the public and political groupings. The Joinet-principles suggest that the public be informed of the criteria used for the selection of commissioners. The consultative procedure adopted for the appointment of commissioners, which included public nominations and public interviews of the nominees, enhanced the credibility of the South African TRC. Fair procedures are also important for ensuring just treatment of all parties.
- Public participation and strength of civil society. Involvement of the public and of civil society in designing the mandate ensures a general understanding of what commission is supposed to do. It also increases the democratic value of the truthtelling process. Thus far, South Africa has been the only country to undertake extensive public debate preceding the establishment of a commission but a trend may have been set, considering current developments in Indonesia and Suriname. Non-governmental organisations often have a wealth of information that will aid investigations. They can further be involved in collecting statements, providing information to the public, and supporting witnesses. The role of the media is also relevant in this regard, especially when a commission conducts its activities in public. While having the potential to extend a commission's influence and accessibility, reporting may undermine the truthtelling process if the media lack independence.
- Broader program of reform. Whether a commission can help overcome a legacy of past abuses is strongly

influenced by the extent to which it is embedded in a broader process of social, economical, and political transformation. This is particularly so when large scale violence was accompanied by structural repression. In such situations, many consider reconciliation to be directly related to the division of resources and opportunities; truthtelling must then be complemented by a focus on socio-economic justice. While not able to institute change itself, a commission can contribute to reform through recommendations. These may encourage changes in the long term if the political and economical context do not allow for immediate implementation. For example, despite the fact that all members of the Salvadoran Supreme Court-which the truth commission had recommended be dismissed-refused to step down initially, parliament re-elected none of them when their term had ended. President Menem of Argentine may have first downplayed the report of the national truth commission in public, he later silently slashed the military budget.10

- Timing. Establishing a commission early on in a transitional period may allow it to seize the momentum for dealing with past violations to the full extent. However, then the political situation is still fragile and emotions easily run high. In Northern-Ireland, for example, some feel that the situation has not sufficiently stabilized yet for a truthtelling process to be undertaken at this point.11 At the very least it seems that the violence should have abated before initiating a truth commission. The South African TRC has been less active in KwaZulu-Natal (where a large threat of violence remains), in part owing to fears that truthtelling might jeopardize the situation in the province.

The above are but a few of the factors that influence the effectiveness and impact of a truth commission. An evaluation of these may indicate whether a truthtelling process represents a genuine commitment on the part of a government to deal with the past or is merely window-dressing, being a substitute for real change or used as an instrument to relieve international pressure to address human rights issues. Other factors of influence include logistical and practical matters, international support, access to outside sources of information, the level of fear amongst witnesses, and the role of external actors in the violence. (While possibly fraught with difficulties, the investigation of the latter could be particularly important in situations like Northern-Ireland.) The relative strength of such factors and the way in which they are linked together will depend on the specific circumstances of each case.

CONCLUSION

Truth commissions have become very popular in the last fifteen years and their prominence is unlikely to abate in the near future. As more insight is gained in their functioning and the ways in which they may affect societies, commissions are increasingly deployed in coming to terms with a legacy of violence. Truth commissions can set a longer-term process of transformation in motion, especially when accompanied by a program of reform. They generate a process of reflection that blurs the hard edges of perceived reality, highlights the need for addressing relationships and attitudes, and forces people to contemplate the organization of society and the governing of the state. The increased level of public involvement in establishing truth commissions is valuable in this respect, signifying how dealing with the past is a collective effort. A truth commission cannot institute change alone nor can it bring about reconciliation. Yet it may create an environment in which change and peaceful coexistence become possible. The past is here to stay, but truth commissions offer a way for society to process and manage it non-destructively based upon the recognition of human dignity and integrity.

7

Europe: From Warfare to Coexistence

Emerging from World War II, whether victorious or defeated, we experienced as individuals or as groups the total annihilation of peoples, riches, institutions, values. Naturally we shared, with the same intensity, the same desire that it should never happen again. Total war led to a resolute quest for peace.

We knew that peace could not be established merely through the rhetoric of speeches or through good intentions. To build peace we had first to understand war. Why and how had our European civilization fallen into destruction on such a scale that the very fabric of our societies had almost collapsed? This meant undertaking a fundamental critical review of our history and its effects on individual and collective psychology. After this review we would be able to make concrete suggestions and take the necessary steps. Change would result from facts as much as from ideas or perceptions.

In order to exist, all living entities must fulfil three functions: they must find 'their' place, learn to survive, and to receive and transmit life. None of these functions encourages a passive attitude: to exist is to fight.

If one of the three functions is denied, the intensity of the fight increases to a level where violence becomes unavoidable. Consequently, we must recognize that fight is a natural instinct, an element of human culture. From the schoolyard, to the football stadium through to war and the battlefield.

The first step towards coexistence is existence itself: an awareness of one's identity with neither a superiority or inferiority complex, acceptance of the other within a system which guarantees not only one's equal acceptance, but is considered by all as legitimate and fair to each of its components' interests. To reach coexistence, channels providing adequate and lasting answers must be developed. Acceptance is only workable if at each level there exists a corresponding institutional and symbolic framework which is mutually accepted. If such a context does not exist, each group will try to prevail according to its own logic. Violence then becomes the ultimate resource. Through the centuries our societies have prepared for such eventualities by awarding war and the warrior a special place and prestige within their organisation, by according them a moral and even religious recognition.

The man of peace encounters great difficulties in competing with the traditional heroic, epic, romantic image of the soldier. The peacemaker must choose his circumstances, project and conditions very carefully if he is not to be perceived as an appeaser, a de facto agent of the enemy, a traitor. If peace is a universal human dream, its quest and implementation are extremely complex and hazardous. It is only if society feels itself to be secure and that its dignity is fully recognized that any peace initiative is workable.

The challenge is therefore to go against instinct and tradition, in order to demonstrate that war does not pay; that many means exist which can help to reach peace. This effort requires not only an individualised psychological approach and a sense of history but a thorough understanding of the influence of context on people's behaviour, and an ability to change the overall context through social engineering.

Discrimination between victors and defeated breeds future conflicts. Without full, free and equal access to the economic, political and cultural order resulting from victory, the defeated do not feel involved in its preservation. Under a surface appearance of acceptance, revenge awaits its opportunity to bring about change. A new peaceful order cannot prevail if its legitimacy is not as fully recognized by the defeated as by the victor. This poses a difficult challenge which can be met only when the victor offers principles which by their own nature are common to both parties. Sovereignty of the people-democracy-is the only principle which, by its very nature, finds legitimacy equally rooted in both existence and dignity.

The psychological ability to overcome the past, recent or ancient, is of cardinal importance as practically all organized human groups were at one moment of their respective history in a master-victim relation. To ask them to forget or to forgive is asking the impossible. People remember. The past cannot be changed. But it can be placed in a new dynamic process, and even transformed into a driving force for peace if the will to build the future together prevails. In post-War Europe, in freeing ourselves from an obsession with the potential enemy we also freed ourselves from the curse of past history and were able to join forces to discover and manage our new awareness of common interest.

The attraction of realizing this common future became for all of us the driving force for peace manifest in the creation of the European Community. It was and remains the most concrete answer to this challenge.

In one of the early texts of modern political theory, The Federalist issue no. 10, James Madison wrote:

'The latent causes of faction are....sown in the nature of man. Since the causes of faction cannot be removed....relief is only to be sought in the means of controlling its effects.'

We did not share that view and felt that in changing the causes we could find the relief.

So in order to establish the context which was able to change the psychology of individuals and nations alike, we looked for limited but decisive areas where fundamental and competing interests could be objectively recognized as common: coal and steel for Western Europe, (or, one day, water for the Middle East).

Common institutions based on the principle of non-discrimination were established in order to help recognize and manage such potentially divisive interests as common to all.

From this joint awareness and administration, a confidence building process emerged which demonstrated progressively the practical rewards of peace. Gradually the construction of this new context gathered momentum. A feeling of security began to replace the ancestral fear of the other. Through new habits and perceptions and the existence and work of common institutions, the partnership was enlarged to new areas and more and more potential conflicts were put into the category of those which could be prevented by being channelled into a process, which we all recognized as effective, practical, fair and legitimate.

This strand of recent European history shows that institutions can build peace. The more distant past also shows that without effective institutions, no lasting peace is possible.

However, it requires a special kind of institution to fulfil this role. It must be able to make and enforce decisions. It cannot be a coalition created by the victorious side in order to impose their will, because this would provoke a growing feeling of resentment among the defeated and a corresponding desire for revenge. Neither could it be a system where each participant would enjoy equal sovereign power or its effectiveness would be restricted by the constant risk of veto. The possibility of creating an authority which would give its orders to different national entities seemed to be the most efficient answer. But this would also involve ignoring the new and powerful trend which sees all types of human communities fighting for recognition. Coexistence today involves more and more actors. Accordingly, through trial and error, we came to understand that a new type of governance had to be invented. Despite the lack of a precedent, we succeeded. One day the European Union may be recognized not only for its role in solving nineteenth-century problems but also for having helped to create harmony between diversities in need of recognition and the universalist logic of modern technologies in the twenty-first century.

This is now the central issue confronting national bodies of every kind.

Through a process which was in many cases very dramatic and chaotic, national orders prevailed. In order to allow coexistence between them, the European union had the choice between adopting a traditional international method where all governments enjoy an equal veto right or the more effective approach in which an independent authority imposes its ruling over the member States-the supranational method.

The latter alternative was used at the beginning of our unification process. It worked and was accepted because it involved a limited sector with limited functions. But its adoption became more problematic when more and more-and finally all-aspects of economic, social and political life were incorporated in its jurisdiction.

The way out of the dilemma was to create a pragmatic balance between each of the participants' respective sovereignty and the group representing the common interest of the 'collective' sovereignty. The answer was found in adopting a horizontal model of decision making in place of the traditional vertical chain of command. In the vertical model, proposal for action is submitted to a superior authority whose executive authority is exclusive. In the horizontal model there is no hierarchical authority between those making proposals and decisions. Both enjoy equal but different sources of legitimacy, one European, one national.

The European Commission enjoys the exclusive right to make proposals. It represents the common European interest and has no link with any Government or coalition. At the same time, while it is designated through the joint action of the member States, it is confirmed by, answerable to and can be dismissed by the European Parliament which is democratically elected by the people of the Union, on the basis of direct universal suffrage. Thanks to this dual legitimacy and independence, the Commission can consult with all interested parties in the official world and civil society.

It can then investigate and submit proposals, which are by definition representative of the common interest. The fate of these proposals then becomes the responsibility of the different national sovereignties as expressed through the deliberations of the Council of Ministers. At this stage the Commission takes on the additional role of facilitator.

For national governments concerned about losing face, it is far easier to accept a proposal elaborated through a process grounded in common-interest-legitimacy, which by definition, also represents part of the national interest, than to bow to the will of other national sovereignties.

I had an opportunity to present this new form of governance in a more systematic form at a workshop chaired by the hon. Harlan Cleveland in Aspen, Colorado, in 1975. I gave it the name: 'extranational' to distinguish it from international or supra-national institutions.

The extra-national experience of the European Union might help elaborate a method for the prevention of conflicts.

If a danger of conflict arises or even when the conflict already exists, the first step to be taken should be to find an authority which both sides recognize as legitimate and well intentioned.

Then through its help, to find out what the potential opponents share in common. To make them aware that they share the fact that they are in opposition; that their conflict might escalate; that their joint challenge is to weigh how a peaceful approach might be more productive than war.

To share this recognition is almost impossible without the help of a third party. Arbitration of all kinds is a well known method used on an adhoc basis where the situation is tense, or under the pressure of an outside element or when both sides freely agree to abide by its conditions, hoping, as in war, that they might win.

If a permanent institutional framework or body were to exist, which potential opponents could recognize as legitimate and fair, they might more easily share the same willingness to understand what each party is trying to achieve and finally conclude that peaceful approach might bring about better results.

Then, but only then, as a third stage, negotiation on the contested subject could start with a reasonable chance of success.

In most recent conflicts, in Yugoslavia, the Middle East, and Rwanda etc., the mutual interest of the opposing parties did not get a chance to be explained in a manner acceptable to the antagonists because the legitimacy of the so called 'international community' was always challengeable and challenged by the main powers. The mandate and legitimacy of the third element which should have been the UN, was in fact the product of the different and even conflicting agendas of the five permanent members of the Security Council. The Secretary General who was trying to resolve the conflict, saw his authority challenged when he was about to become the independent facilitator that the situation required. Finally he ended up as a ping pong ball between opponents and major international actors alike. He was effectively reminded that he was in the final analysis merely the highest ranking civil servant in the organisation. A change in his statutory position is imperative if we intend to prevent or end conflicts worldwide.

This is where the value of the European Union's example lies. It comes from the fact that almost 50 years of practical experience are available to be studied as a realistic precedent because it managed to establish the conditions of a lasting peace between old sovereign states after centuries of wars and at the end of the most destructive conflict of all. This is a tried answer to conflict prevention for all to emulate.

The new extra-national approach can be used at any level where tensions occur. With proven credibility, this system could be used on global, regional, tribal, or local levels, as a non utopian answer to aspirations for peace common to the human race. It would transform the necessary fight for existence into a civilized process.

Jean Monnet instinctively referred to this institutional solution in the very last sentence of his Memoires:

'the sovereign nations of the past no longer provide the framework within which today's problems can find their solutions. And the Community (today the European Union) itself is no more than a step towards the types of organization of tomorrow's world'.

I would like to conclude with the comment that the world of tomorrow needs peace to survive. We have the means, we need the will.

I hope that among those who happen to read this text somebody somewhere will take up the challenge and make a difference in considering the extranational solution. We all need it. The bottle at sea might not be lost, after all.

WHAT IS COEXISTENCE?

Learning to live together, to coexist, to learn to accept difference, and make the world safe for difference will be one of the great challenges for the 21 Century. Coexistence is a term that has been used synonymously in several contexts and used as a key phrase in the emergence of a number of great social and political movements. The key characteristic in the definition of the word coexistence is its relation with its 'others' and the acknowledgement that an 'others' exists.

Coexistence means learning to live together, to accept diversity and implies a positive relationship to the other. Our identities are defined in relation to the other. When relationships are affirmative and equal it enhances dignity and freedom and independence. When relations are negative and destructive this undermines human dignity and our own self worth. This applies to personal, group and interstate relationships. After experiencing two world wars and countless wars of destruction and genocide the promotion of coexistence at all levels remains an imperative for the 21st Century.

One of the basic conceptions in the history of Western culture in general, and of modern philosophy in particular is that the actual validity of a certain entity with its specific qualities exists only when it is recognised by another subjectivity. According to Hegel, the essence of his conceptualisation of the term is that 'existence' is already, fundamentally 'coexistence'. This is true for individuals, groups and classes. Mutual recognition is required as a necessary condition (even as a constitutive one) for freedom and independence. There are many excellent examples of the struggle for recognition, and the assertion of independence in the history of social movements. A significant example is the struggle for coexistence between men and women from Patriarchy to the struggle for the emancipation of women and gender equality. The struggles against slavery, and against feudal bondage are well known.

Today the struggle for coexistence continues with the transformation of the former Soviet Union, the peaceful revolution in Eastern Europe.

In the modern political vocabulary the term 'peaceful coexistence' has been conceptualised as a strategy of survival and existence between war in the literal sense and peace in the ideal sense. Peaceful coexistence in this sense means the peaceful relationship between states. With the development and the centralisation of the state, coexistence between states and the non-interference in the internal affairs of other states has been a central tenet of state diplomacy. It was Lenin who first articulated peaceful coexistence as a state policy of the revolution. During the early phase of the Russian revolution he used it to describe periods in which Soviet policy would abandon the all-out attack on every front against the non-communist world and replace it by the more subtle tactics of concluding agreements with some governments in some areas, while keeping up intense pressure elsewhere. The purpose of coexistence, according to Lenin, was purely tactical and the phase strictly temporary. By changing the nature of the attack and relaxing the pressure, divisions in capitalist states, which were always inherent, would be allowed to develop and thus weaken the enemies of communism.

However in the Cold War context 'peaceful coexistence' enunciated by Khrushchev made a strategic shift in focus where it was explicitly recognised that the continued conflict between the two systems would lead to the mutual destruction of the entire system. coexistence according to Krushechev meant continuation of the struggle between the social systems-but by peaceful means, without war, without interference by one state in the internal affairs of another. It will be a competition of the two systems in a peaceful field.

Another shift in meaning came with the Bandung Conference where the concept of 'coexistence' was used with the aim of creating a more peaceful international environment. Nehru outlined his conception of peaceful coexistence between the two superpowers in terms of the Five Principles, or the Pancha Shila: mutual respect for territorial integrity and sovereignty, non-aggression, non-interference in one another's internal affairs, equality and mutual benefit.3 Nehru was convinced that India might contribute to bringing about reconciliation between the United States and the Soviet Union through this 'bridge-policy' which was rooted in the Gandhian strategy of satyagrahya, or non-violence. Although these principles may now be regarded as aspirations of the newly emergent independent nations of a number of Asian and African states, the fact remains that they brought to the forefront the acknowledgement of this concept in international policy making.

Coexistence as a paradigm should not only relate to inter-state relations but intra-state relations as well. Coexistence between different peoples, races, religious groups, clans, tribes within a spectrum of identities is the great challenge for the 21st century.

Coexistence between peoples has become an imperative in the next phase of evolution of civilisation. On the one hand the struggle for self-determination of peoples, a major factor in nationalist wars of the 20th century culminated in the completion of the decolonisation process. Currently the civil wars and ethnic identity conflicts are challenges to the existing state system.

There is a continuum of struggles for recognition of new identities and, of contestation and challenges to the unitary state. In some cases such contestation and war has led to the separation of states.

Recent examples abound, such as the separation of Pakistan from the Indian polity, the separation of Bangladesh from Pakistan and the recent breakdown of Yugoslavia. On the other hand there has also been the expansion of larger entities, where the expansion of the European Union is only one classic example. The formation of the European Union is a good example of the decision to suspend warfare, between the Great Powers. The work of Jean Monnet and others in crafting a normative framework, to develop peaceful coexistence between France and Germany, through economic co-operation and then to extend the concept to Europe as a whole provides an excellent example of recognising diversity and maintaining coexistence.

Identity, Ethnicity and Coexistence

When closely examined, the overwhelming majority of the nation states in our global community reveals significant internal cleavages based upon ethnicity, race and religion. The significance of these differences in the social and political process varies widely, as does the degree of saliency, intensity and politization of communal segments both within and between states. The most fundamental proposition after the proliferation of ethnic and identity conflicts, particularly after the cold war is the realisation that cultural pluralism is an enduring attribute of contemporary political life. There is no longer any justification for clinging to the belief that the array of processes commonly known as 'modernisation' would automatically lead to a notion of a single nation, or lead to the erosion of cultural solidarity, ethnicity or religion.

Rather the reverse may happen. Social change tends to produce stronger communal identities. Studies, which focus on the individual as the primary unit in the analysis of conflict, point to the need for identity as fundamental to the survival and well being of the individual and the society in which that individual exists. Burton for example points to such complex and protracted conflicts as the Arab-Palestinian conflict, the Cyprus conflict and the Northern-Ireland conflict as being based on the need for identity which humans will seek to satisfy irrespective of contextual circumstances or degrees of coercion.4 The 'basic human needs approach' therefore sees the recognition of identity both as a universal need and as an essential requirement for individual development.5

There are of course detractors who are sceptical about the value and operational viability of using the concept of coexistence. One school of thought would argue that relations between contending groups couldn't be changed, that they are primordial and not transformative. Others would argue that coexistence means accepting the status quo. A more powerful variant of this argument is that coexistence is a term used by majorities to assert dominance over the minorities.

They would argue that hegemonic majorities would wish to retain their dominance by proposing forms of coexistence, which do not undermine their dominance. I would argue however, that coexistence between communities and groups is fundamentally a transformative relationship, which is dynamic and positive. The term implies that identity is a fundamental driving force in human development and that coexistence evolves from a minimum condition of recognising difference and accepting diversity and the mutual recognition of the other to a transformative relationship where communities over time may find appropriate mechanisms and institutions to coalesce and a higher level of meaning.

Approaches to Promoting Coexistence

There are a variety of approaches, which are currently being used in the promotion of aspects of coexistence between peoples. Some social movements have defined themselves as promoting conflict resolution or conflict management. Conflict resolution or management is normally defined as bringing parties to the negotiating table. Other variants of conflict resolution refer to the various methods and approaches developed in two track diplomacy where the efforts have been developed to support the formal negotiations process by complimentary approaches such as promoting problem solving approaches and working towards building peace between communities. Numerous efforts are being made, largely by citizen based groups to create space for dialogue to improve coexistence between communities. The environmental movement for example is a classic example of extending coexistence to nature so that nature is seen as an aspect of our planetary existence. The gender movement is another example where the focus is on recognition, emancipation, and the struggle for equality and freedom. Typically, the concept of conflict resolution means the steps taken to promote political coexistence between different parties to a conflict.

Conflict Resolution was however too narrow for those who felt that the concept implied merely a negotiated settlement between parties to a conflict. This approach it was felt did not involve peace building between communities. Often negotiated settlements would fail if due care is not taken to sustain building efforts between the communities. This is why another concept was then introduced, called conflict transformation. Conflict transformation implied a wider concept where the critical aspect of conflict resolution is the transformation of social relations between groups and identities in society. Another concept, which came into vogue immediately after the Cold War, was the concept of conflict prevention. Concerned with the proliferation of internal conflicts and civil wars within states and wars between peoples within a state, conflict prevention was introduced to mean the prevention of conflict before violence actually occurs. A more sophisticated variant of conflict prevention was the reduction of violence in any point in the conflict cycle. However this concept was also confronted with terminological difficulties. There are those who argued that the term conflict prevention presents a negative connotation, suggesting that conflicts are endemic to human coexistence and therefore necessary in the course of human evolution. However, what the concept was meant to imply was the prevention of violent conflict.

POLITICAL COEXISTENCE AND COMMUNITY COEXISTENCE

Policy initiatives that have been presented to stem conflict between communities have been directed towards institutional management in the highest echelons of governments and in the hands of the political elites. The biases and prejudices of party politics and populist policy often entangle these policies. Policy initiatives to address community coexistence have been far less a priority. Much of the inter communal conflict that exists in society today are due to policy makers resorting to the easier and less resourceful method of initiating policy directed at the centre with the hope that the 'trickle down effect' would reform community institutions in grassroots levels as well.

They address only the needs of political coexistence through the implementation of constitutional safeguards and side stepping policy making with regard to community coexistence. A distinction needs to be made between the promotion of political coexistence and community coexistence. Political coexistence means the development of systems of governance which can better accommodate ethnic diversity and pluralism. This means the search for constitutional forms of governance ranging from federalism to forms of autonomy and self-governance. It may also take the forms of different types of electoral systems, which can best accommodate and balance ethnic groups in a society.

What is however distinctive about community coexistence is that often different groups, whether they are ethnic, or religious share a common living space, and thereby have to define their relationship to each other. How these relations are developed, sustained and nurtured is a major challenge for the 21st century. For it is at the community level that perceptions are developed transmitted and socialised to the other. According to Mari Fitzduff, 'Earlier definitions of the objective of community relations work seem to have primarily concerned themselves with emphasising the idea of a harmonious existence between differing groups with the intended goal of integrating the minority groups into the wider community as quickly as possible. Later definitions of objectives have put a far greater emphasis on the idea of equality of basic rights and opportunity for all groups, whilst simultaneously encouraging cultural diversity, as being preferable.6

In an assessment of Community Relations Work in Northern Ireland Mari Fitzduff argues, 'It is increasing recognised that such work focusing on differences e.g. of a political or theological nature in some instances is likely to be limited, unless work designed to facilitate free discussion within communities is carried out productively. If such intra-community work is not done, which is often the case because of fear and intimidation and lack of available structures through which to do the work-mutual understanding work is more likely to produce defensiveness and be therefore less effective.'

Building the Basis for Coexistence: Education

An attempt to release the child from the confines of the ethnocentric straightjacket and to awaken him to the existence of other cultures, societies and ways of life and thought. It is intended to decondition the child as much as possible in order that he can go out into the world as free from biases and prejudices as possible and able and willing to explore its rich diversity. As the twenty first century draws to a close, countries the world over are preoccupied by the challenge of finding new and improved ways to educate their citizens for living in diversity in the next millennium. There are over 2 billion children who will inherit the earth.

The right to education is a fundamental right recognised by all countries. It is however a fact that still a majority of our children is without proper schooling and facilities. Therefore building a basis for coexistence is that every child has to have access to education and participate in making decisions about her education. Education and learning is a principle means of learning to live together. This means that the school becomes a major institution for teaching coexistence, multicultural learning. The International Commission on Education for the 21st Century in its report on education for the 21st century outline the 4 pillars of education, of which Learning to Live Together is identified as a central challenge.

How can we inculcate the respect and need for existence and the need for coexistence amongst school children? The process of educating about coexistence needs to occurs on every level, from the informal level ranging from teacher's colleges, to schools themselves; to community groups; governmental organisations to media and corporations; and all the informal modes including families, celebrities, writers and poets. It is clearly challenging in culturally diverse societies to reflect satisfactorily the needs of all socio-cultural groups in the curriculum. Adapting a common core curriculum to local needs and traditions is of vital importance, but potentially divisive. If social sciences and humanities curricula are to adequately reflect international, national and local concerns in today's increasingly pluralistic, multicultural societies, curriculum development processes need to become more democratic, adopting decentralized approaches which permit input and participation by all interest groups.

Multicultural education is a viable means of social engineering drawing students to appreciate the plural societies from which they come.8 Teaching and learning are always cultural processes in that they encompass the dynamics of a particular social fabric. Although students learn better using examples drawn from their own cultures-retaining their own culturally specific examples-9 .there is a growing need for multicultural education as an agent for helping to defuse deeply held mindsets, biases that have been infused by the conditioning of the environment of a particular culture as being an integral part of that person's perception of self and others. However, if multicultural education is to succeed in its aims it cannot be a mere ad hoc program implemented at critical junctures of a conflict in a lame attempt to reconcile differences between conflicting social groups but should be a long-term project. Multi-cultural education deals directly with identity. Just as peace education was a reaction to Cold War politics, multicultural education should be looked as an essential tool developed to stem ethnic conflict.

An important instrument in promoting coexistence education is the curricula. At the end of the 20th century, it is more or less universally recognised that curricula should be open, active, flexible and intercultural. But the translation of this ideal into meaningful reality into schools and classroom is an enormous challenge in all countries. A core curricula needs to be adapted to local conditions and take account of local identities. It also requires a participatory approach to curriculum development. The stakeholders need to be enlarged beyond the policy makers in the Ministries of Education and be included and specialised education personnel, parents, teachers, community leaders, religious leaders and the students themselves.

The Need for a Policy Shift

Conflict exists on every level of human behaviour-however this is not always reflected as a determinant in policy making. The fact that conflicting perspectives exist need to be legitimised and ways of living together must be found despite these differences. Whilst many people are involved in coexistence work, these initiatives are not always reflected at the policy level. Politicians, governments and opinion leaders must accept that coexistence is a legitimate goal. One suggestion is to set up a special department or Ministry of Coexistence in all countries as Ministries of Environment were set up in the 1970s.

Learning to live together does not fall from the sky. It is clear that coexistence is learnt behaviour, which requires a sustained process of learning both at school, within the communities and in society as a whole. This requires structures, and institutions which sustain and enhance coexistence through a multitude of projects and programmes. Further, it requires financing such efforts and a commitment by the central government. An excellent example of such efforts is the work of the Community Relations Council in Northern Ireland. Here the government commits resources to the Council to promote community coexistence. Such a model needs to be repeated in other countries. There needs to be government commitment and resources provided for the Council to be effective.

Another form of legitimation is through the work of municipalities and local government bodies. These institutions are in the front line of coexistence work. They are located in spaces where many communities live together. Here much can be done to develop understanding, through a variety of schemes and programmes. They can range from the provision of resources for supporting community centres where all communities can come to learn and play. They could be in the provision of encouraging games and sports amongst the various communities. There can be programmes for learning other languages, to encouraging encounters between the two communities and learning about each others history. Municipalities and local government bodies are also democratically elected bodies, which have the power and the resources to provide substantive support for community building work.

Donor organisation and foundations need also to be sensitised. The Abraham Fund is one of the leading foundations doing this work, supporting over 200 hundred initiatives on coexistence between the Jewish and Arab populations each year. (see case-study)

The principled method used by the programmes of the Abraham Fund seems to be to encourage encounters between the two peoples and two cultures. These encounters are encouraged at a variety of levels. Given the level of hostility, misperceptions, and trauma that the peoples have experienced these encounters are not easy and have to be managed with great facilitation skills.

It has been very clear to me in my very brief visit to Israel that the support for these grass roots efforts and initiatives has influenced the politics of coexistence. In fact these grass roots efforts will be the necessary building blocks for the politics of coexistence.

These encounters between the two peoples are not easy. Although the two peoples have lived as neighbours, many do not know or understand each other's history, culture, and traditions. Therefore these encounters may result in the following dynamics:

- o Confrontation: stating ones grievances and complaints;
- o Understanding that each side has a point of view which needs to be recognised;
- o Reconciliation where a higher understanding may be reached and friendships begin to be formed;
- o Transformation where relationships of equality are manifested in the elaboration of joint projects at the level of the community.

The significance of the projects is that it promotes encounters and the two sides experience the transformation. A significant aspect of the projects is that the formulation and implementation of the project requires the participation of both sides. Therefore a prerequisite for funding a coexistence project is the requirement that both sides are represented in the decision making process.

CONCLUSION

Promoting positive coexistence between states and between peoples is a major challenge for the 21st century. There are fortunately today social movements, which have begun to grapple with these issues, both at the international and national level and at the political, and community level. What we are have argued is that political coexistence to be successful requires investment in coexistence at the community level. We need to accumulate the experiences, and the energies of a variety of citizen based movement, and build a multi-faceted approach to these issues. Social movements necessarily work on aspects of coexistence and it is the combination and the cumulative effects of these movements that will create the space for coexistence.

A principle pillar for coexistence is the education system. The education system requires a major paradigm shift in focus where living together in diversity becomes a principle value in the education of the child. We need to invest heavily in our children. This means that our attitudes towards education require fundamental reassessments where education should be seen as an interaction between the community, the school and the child. It is the relationship, which can create space for tolerance and the acceptance of diversity. Investments in the education of the child are a solid investment in ensuring a world safe for difference.

8

India-Pakistan: Nuclear Stability and Diplomacy

The conceptual discourse, contributed to in the main by Western scholars, on the security and strategic stability of new nuclear weapon states like India and Pakistan seems alarmist. In reality, however, India and Pakistan have been mutually deliberating on various aspects of nuclear confidence-building measures (CBMs). This article is an effort to identify the issues of nuclear security concerns in two spheres-academic and policy formulations. The emphasis is more on the nuclear thinking of the two countries and the diplomatic challenges ahead particularly on the nuclear CBMs.

Nuclear South Asia is a reality today. As soon as India and Pakistan conducted their nuclear weapon tests in May 1998, the debate-predominantly outside the Indian subcontinent-over nuclear security and stability assumed significant momentum. Many critics have questioned the rationale behind India and Pakistan possessing nuclear weapons. The strategic factors, especially those related to the nuclear-deterrence concepts, are being reviewed in the context of new nuclear weapon states by many diplomats, academics and strategic planners all over the world.

With the passage of time, on their part, both India and Pakistan have also been long deliberating on the security compulsions behind the development and possession of nuclear weapons at various international platforms. They are also trying, in their own ways, to cope with the international disarmament discourse dominated by the P-5 states who have refused to accord India and Pakistan de jurestatus in the elite nuclear club. At the same time, acknowledging the fact that nuclear weapons remain significant to strategic stability between the two countries, both India and Pakistan have been trying to evolve mechanisms for ensuring the long-term nuclear security of the region. Various nuclear confidence-building measures (CBMs) are being mutually discussed by the two nuclear neighbours with increasing determination.

This paper seeks to highlight the issues emerging out of available academic and policy debates concerning the security and stability of nuclear South Asia. Accordingly, it is an effort to broaden the understanding of the challenges before India-Pakistan nuclear diplomacy. The paper is divided into four parts. In the first part, an attempt has been made to understand the Western perceptions on India and Pakistan as states with nuclear weapons. The issues related to the risk of possible (pre-meditated, inadvertent or accidental) use of nuclear weapons in South Asia have also been identified within the conceptual elaborations. Part two includes a review of some key policy recommendations by US-based think-tanks. The third section reviews the nuclear postures of India and Pakistan, while the fourth provides an account of the initiatives taken by India and Pakistan towards nuclear confidence-building.

India and Pakistan as States with NuclearWeapons: ATheoretical Perspective Maintaining its commitment to work towards global nuclear disarmament, India believes: "The end of the Cold War had provided the opportunity to reduce the salience of nuclear weapons but we saw instead that most of the world acquiesced in the manoeuvres to perpetuate forever the right of a handful of nations to retain their arsenals. ...The search for unilateral advantage has led to measures that undermine the principle of irreversibility of committed reductions. There is no move towards collective renouncing of 'first-use'. Instead there are prospects of advocacy of pre-emptive use and a move towards developing new types of arsenals justified by new rationale."

Nuclear weapons have been a central element of the security discourse among American and Western scholars and policy-makers since the beginning of the Cold War. Possession of nuclear weapons by a state beyond the P-5 club is commonly described in Western academic and strategic communities interchangeably as 'spread' or 'proliferation' of nuclear weapons and they call it 'new nuclear weapon state'. By the end of the Cold War,in the course of the last five decades, a complex theology has evolved about the extent to which nuclear deterrence preserves or endangers world peace and security. Despite lacking universal acceptance at policy-making levels, "the debate over nuclear proliferation" in the Western world is instructive for its multiple intellectual inputs.

However, there appear two significant limitations in the prevailing debate. First, a lack of universal appeal is apparent in the inherent criticism by each group of scholars. They differ mainly over mutually contested assumptions and applications of each theory. Second, academic formulations on non-proliferation do not adequately advance the comprehensive nuclear disarmament approach. They fail to acknowledge the existing discriminating non-proliferation regimes. Instead, by and large while discussing 'deterrence' in the context of 'new nuclear weapons states', most of the academic writing legitimises the nuclear weapons of P-5 states and remain suspicious of the rationale of others. And, "there is little in the literature to tell us how a country should plan to use its nuclear weapons to deter its adversaries while denying the possession of these weapons."

There are two main streams of theorisation on nuclear proliferation, namely, Optimist and Pessimist. One more competing theory is also found in the writings of international relations-Political Relativist. Some prominent Realist scholars, classified under 'Proliferation Optimists', have argued that there is virtually no risk that nuclear weapons will actually be used if more countries obtain them. They believe that proliferation would result in lesser number of wars and greater peace and stability. Afew of them (Optimist scholars) believe that except from a slight rise in the probability of nuclear accidents, the increased deterrent effects of nuclear proliferation lower the likelihood of war among nuclear-armed states. Rooted in the assumption that states behave in a self-interested and rational manner, the pioneer among Proliferation Optimists, Kenneth Waltz, argues: "More May be Better"

He suggests the following six assumptions to prove his argument:

- International politics is a self-help system.
- Balance of terror is indestructible.
- 'Uncertainty' about controlling escalation is at the heart of deterrence
- Deterrence provides a guarantee against accidents.
- Nuclear weaponry makes miscalculation difficult due to greater awareness of possible damage and sensitivity to the cost of war.
- New nuclear states will feel the constraints of old nuclear states (meaning new nuclear states will learn lessons from the maintenance of deterrence during the Cold War).

Related to the issue of nuclear weapons and regional stability, however, for the states sharing common borders, Waltz says: "Where states are bitter enemies one may fear that they will be unable to resist using their nuclear weapons against each other. This is a worry about the future that the past does not disclose."

But, he indicates that nuclear weapons caused China and Soviet Union to deal cautiously. Political relativists, who give primacy to the character (political structures, ideology, culture, system of governance, etc.) of the possessor state over the technicalities involved in the existence of arsenals, challenge the optimistic view.

Political relativism is an approach that stresses more on the internal structure of states, rather than the international political environment in which the states act.

Political relativists believe that deterrence can fail when required the most, and that nuclear weapons are not secure in the hands of "bad states". Criticising the rationality factor in Waltz's argument, Robert Jervis, one of the 'political relativists' argues: "Proliferation among strongly dissatisfied countries would not necessarily recapitulate the Soviet-American patterns of stability."

While suggesting that mere possibility of nuclear use causes extreme caution all around the world, Waltz believes that preventive attacks are more unlikely to take place. Instead of creating large arsenals, based on the Cold War experience, for better survivability, Kenneth Waltz says: "Though large and complex nuclear arsenals are hard to control, the relatively small and simple forces of new nuclear states are not." In contrast to Proliferation Optimists, the Pessimists believe that the spread of nuclear weapons to other states beyond P-5 will make the world more dangerous. Opposite to Waltz's theory of 'More May Be Better', Scott D. Sagan, also known as a 'conditional pessimist', believes that 'More Will Be Worse.'

Against Waltz's rational theory, pessimistic assessments of Sagan are based on the organisation theory. The organisation theory implies that whereas the government (civilian) leaders may behave rationally, the final implementation of policy decisions is influenced by powerful groups/forces within the country.

Since the military organisation of any country is finally responsible for operational requirements of nuclear weapons, Sagan assumes that it determines the behaviour of the state. He argues: "professional military organisations-because of common biases, inflexible routines, and parochial interests-display organisational behaviours that are likely to lead to deterrence failures and deliberate or accidental war." While elaborating on how the United States and the former Soviet Union faced difficulties in handling issues like deterrence, deployment, safety and security of nuclear weapons, Sagan raises doubts as to how the new nuclear weapon states will follow the necessary precautions to avoid escalation, preventive wars or accidental hazards. Sagan in his thesis 'More Will Be Worse'provides the following pessimistic assumptions:

- Spread of nuclear weapons to new states will make the world more dangerous. Deterrence failures are more likely in the new nuclear states;

- o Military biases can lead to larger arsenals but not necessarily more survivable weapons;
- o Opaque (covert) nature of nuclear proliferation exacerbates nuclear weapons safety problems;
- o Poorly designed operating procedures can undermine survivable nuclear forces;
- o Lack of organisational and financial resources can result in inadequate mechanical safety devices;
- o Accident-prone nuclear operations will be more prevalent in states with volatile civil-military relations;
- o The most worrisome case in point is Pakistan;
- o Efforts should be made to assist the new nuclear states in making their nuclear forces safe, secure and survivable.

Describing the nature of the nuclear problem in South Asia, Sagan argues that the greater danger is the risk of nuclear war arising through deliberate escalation of a conventional war started over Kashmir. And, in addition, there is the risk of an accidental nuclear war, caused by a nuclear weapons accident, i.e., the unauthorised use of a nuclear weapon, or a false warning of an attack.

Among the Pessimists, the Abolitionists hold the view that all nuclear powers should dismantle their nuclear arsenals and put their stockpiles of military and civilian fissile materials under the control of an international agency.

Developing the argument that the United Nations would not indulge in nuclear weapons production, others have proposed an operational nuclear force or static nuclear stockpile under the command of an international body like UN.

And some, who believe that wisdom derived from the revulsion of war lies only with European and the North American societies, hold the notion that the possible use of nuclear weapons exists only in other parts of the world. They believe that "weapons of mass destruction could yet become a turning point, indeed a final point, of human history in a catastrophe beyond imagination."

Both Waltz and Sagan have provided a persuasive framework to academics in terms of policy-making of states. The policy prescriptions reflect on the responsibility of states, which nuclear weapon states may acquire, by virtue of possessing such arsenals. However, no analysis can be said to be complete because of their selective interpretation of facts and events. Each has interpreted the events of the Cold War period to justify an individual theoretical formulation: "The strategic arms race after both the United States and the Soviet Union secured second-strike capabilities is a mystery to nuclear optimists." Sagan's theoretical emphasis is pointed more towards weapons seekers (so-called nuclear proliferation) and is less critical about the lack of disarmament efforts.

Peter R. Lavoy has brought out 12 specific concerns about nuclear proliferation:

- Incomplete nuclear weapons systems invite preventive military attack;
- Vulnerable nuclear forces invite pre-emptive military attack;
- Primitive command and control raises the risk of nuclear accidents;
- Unstable command and control risks the loss of control over nuclear forces, raising the possibility of unauthorised nuclear use or nuclear terrorism;
- Nuclear arms racing is inevitable and raises the risk of war;
- Nuclear proliferation could increase the likelihood of conventional military conflict;
- Conventional conflict could escalate to nuclear war;
- Nuclear forces might be used for coercion and aggression;
- New nuclear states might assist proliferation elsewhere;
- Successful nuclear proliferation could induce further nuclear proliferation;
- Nuclear proliferation raises the risk of cataclysmic nuclear war; and,
- New nuclear states could limit the political and military influence of major powers.

A preventive strike refers to an attack on the adversary to forestall acquisition of nuclear weapons facilities, implying waging a war before the adversary acquires weapons capability. Israel's attack that destroyed the Osirak reactor in Iraq in 1981 can be cited as an example of such preventive strike. The possibility of preventive military strikes has little or no relevance for India and Pakistan after both nations signed an agreement in 1988 on the 'Prohibition of Attack against Nuclear Installations and Facilities'of each other.

Pre-emption includes military action when an attack by an adversary is imminent. This attack may include targeting of the opponent's strategic arsenals or decapitate its command channels to prevent the adversary from launching a retaliatory strike. India and Pakistan have already established nuclear command authorities. However, due to lack of adequate information currently available in the public domain, there remains some scope for analysts outside the official establishment to debate on the operational issues of command and control and communications.

The willingness shown by both India and Pakistan towards nuclear confidence-building is indicative of their concern for mutual understanding to minimise threats that go with possession of nuclear weapons. The possibility of conventional conflict escalating to the level of nuclear exchange may remain a concern for all till Pakistan comes out with a declaratory 'nuclear doctrine'. India is already committed to no-first-use (NFU) in its defined nuclear doctrine. It could be a point of discussion among strategic analysts as to why India and Pakistan would not follow the Cold War-like deterrence postures and why one should not worry that India and Pakistan too would refrain from using nuclear weapons. Both India and Pakistan have adequately expressed in respective threat concerns that impelled them to go for the nuclear choice. Pakistan's security formulations are India-centric, whereas India has a more comprehensive national security outlook that is not country specific.

Yet, in a significant assertion both the countries have recognised "that the nuclear capabilities of each other, which are based on their national security imperatives, constitute a factor for stability." The history of the development of nuclear weapons is linked with MAD-i.e., mutually assured destruction, a concept evolved during the Cold War.According to the MAD concept, the use of nuclear weapons by one against the other is apprehended in final destruction of both the attacker and the defender. The inducement aspect of proliferation, that successful nuclear proliferation could induce further nuclear proliferation, as averred by Western scholars, may be placed within the larger debate in answering two pertinent queries. First, why does a country seek nuclear weapon capability? And second, why is it so difficult to relinquish possession of nuclear weapons? Answers to these two questions remain contested in the light of progress towards global nuclear disarmament.

The Nuclear Non-Proliferation Treaty (NPT) includes a provision under Article VI: "Each of the Parties to the Treaty undertakes to pursue negotiations in good faith on effective measures relating to cessation of the nuclear arms race at an early date and to nuclear disarmament, and on a treaty on general and complete disarmament under strict and effective international control." This provision however does not provide any time frame for achieving the disarmament objective. At the same time, P-5 states also lack any serious commitment towards making the world free from nuclear weapons. The US abrogation of the 1972 Anti-Ballistic Missile Treaty (ABM), its pursuit for National Missile Defense and Nuclear Posture Review, none of these indicate reduction in stock of missiles and elimination of nuclear weapons in the near future. Potential US nuclear policy strategies seem to be at odds with its commitment to the NPT.

The new "Nuclear Posture Review" of December 2004 of the US Department of Defense envisages establishment of a 'New Triad'of defence including-offensive strike system (both nuclear and non-nuclear), defences (both active and passive) and a revitalised defence infrastructure. Russia still holds a huge stockpile of nuclear weapons. China's drive for modernising its force capabilities may seriously undermine its role in nuclear disarmament. Like China, the United Kingdom and France have shown little interest in joining any international arms reduction dialogue. Whether the new nuclear states can limit the political and military influence of the major powers is an issue that has not yet been tested in the international security environment. Ever since the two countries conducted nuclear tests in May 1998, India and Pakistan are being seen in the Western world as two potential users of nuclear weapons in any war-like situation. From the geo-political perspective, India is located between two-front nuclear capable states-China and Pakistan. Such a two-front security challenge did not concern the two Superpowers in the Cold War.

But do the debates over nuclear weapon states and associated concerns for stability address the comprehensive security realities in the region? Most literature on nuclear proliferation draws ideas from the Cold War experience. It either describes the protracted nuclear peace in the past or shows concern about a scary nuclear future. Western theorists have largely tested the assumptions against Cold War binary oppositions like the Warsaw Pact and the North Atlantic Treaty Organisation (NATO), balance of terror or mutual assured destruction and an uneasy peace.

Except the underlying disquiet about possible unauthorised use of nuclear weapons or accidental hazards, that are partially valid for any nuclear weapon state, most of the theoretical prescriptions are overstated in terms of 'new nuclear weapon states'. Since the beginning of the 1990s, India and Pakistan have shown interest in bilateral diplomatic communication to build upon the momentum of mutual concern for evolving a framework of mutual confidence and nuclear and missile threat reduction between the two nuclear weapon states. Relevant to the discussion on nuclear stability and security in South Asia, let us examine how reputed think-tanks view the future of nuclear peace and stability in South Asia.

Case Studies on NuclearThreat Reduction in South Asia

The Carnegie Endowment for International Peace (CEIP) published a draft report, 'Universal Compliance: AStrategy for Nuclear Security', in June 2004. The report proposes a strategic blueprint for US leadership to rethink international nuclear non-proliferation and global nuclear security. In this report, the recommended measures for nuclear risk reduction between India and Pakistan include:

- o Establishment of national risk reduction centres in both countries to administer agreed upon confidence-building measures.
- o Acommitment not to develop, produce, and use 'tactical' nuclear weapons.
- o Agreement not to flight-test missiles in the direction of the other country.
- o Agreement to flight-test missiles only from designated test ranges.
- o Provision of advance notification of the movement of missiles for training purposes.

The Henry L. Stimson Center'sreport, 'Reducing Nuclear Dangers in South Asia', argues that: "The stability-instability paradox that was formulated in the West to characterise the dangers of nuclear deterrence is alive and well in South Asia. This paradox holds that, while offsetting nuclear capabilities might indeed prevent a full-blown conventional or nuclear war, the presence of these fearsome weapons could also encourage the use of violence at lower levels in the expectation that escalation would be contained by a mutual desire to avoid the nuclear threshold." And that, "Kashmir has been inflamed since the advent of covert nuclear capabilities on the subcontinent, and tensions have grown even more pronounced with the demonstration of overt nuclear capabilities in 1998. The region is now experiencing crises with greater frequency and severity."

The report includes extensive deliberations during two workshops, November 14-18, 2002, and May 20-23, 2003, with participants from the US, India and Pakistan, convened by the Stimson Center to discuss escalation control and scenarios that could lead to crossing of the nuclear threshold. It provides the following 'doable' steps in the near term:

- o Establishment of national risk reduction centresto serve as focal points for the administration of confidence-building measures.

- o Missile-related measuresto formalise and properly implement the agreement concerning prior notification of missile launches; to formalise and extend the time-line for such notifications; to forego missile flight tests in the direction of the other country; to flight test missiles only from designated test ranges; and to provide advance notification of the movement of missiles for training purposes.
- o Clarifying terminology or developing common terminologyon nuclear-related programmes, deployment, and doctrine could reduce misunderstanding and increase crisis stability.
- o Leadership declarations affirming responsible nuclear stewardshipcould help defuse nuclear dangers and facilitate an improvement in bilateral relations.
- o Increased awareness of nuclear dangers, particularly with regard to the possible acquisition of nuclear materials by terrorist groups, would be advisable.

In the Stimson Center'sreport, the proposals collected in the workshops on escalation control are grouped in five categories: improving bilateral relations; nuclear risk reduction and strategic restraint; safety and security measures; and, improving intelligence through communication.

Both the reports, by CEIPand the Stimson Center, have his presumption that 'deterrence'may not work between India nd Pakistan as similar to the Cold War experience. Such ssumptions are not completely invalid for the two countries di resort to nuclear rhetoric during the 1999 Kargil conflict and indulged in 'nuclear signalling' during the period of crisis in 2001-2. In addition, the absence of a doctrine without no-first-use policy and repeated calls from the Pakistani side to lower the threshold could have a certain bearing on the thinking of Western analysts. Already, the strategic debate had reached a slightly higher level than was normally prevalent in the subcontinent when the Indian Army Chief stated that a limited war with Pakistan is possible. Thereon, escalation control came into the purview of discussion in a more focused way.

For any future war in the subcontinent, the two most likely scenarios discussed in the Cooperative Monitoring Center Occasional Paper of Sandia National Laboratories, are: a breakdown along the common border in Kashmir, and failure of nuclear policy. The authors propose an alternative approach through which India and Pakistan can begin to cooperate in managing their common border to prevent a breakdown. The ultimate concern in the report about the existence of nuclear weapons is the possibility of their use in a time of conflict. The following are the enumerations in the Cooperative Monitoring Center Occasional Paper that focuses on the monitoring of nuclear safety, security, and stability:

- The ability to assess the current operational and deployment status of nuclear weapons is perhaps the most critical factor in near-term crisis prevention.
- Developing measures to prevent escalation.
- National decisions to include both technical and procedural mechanisms to restrict use of weapons and delivery systems will permit more time to attempt diplomatic solutions to conflict before initiating weapons use.
- Another element of nuclear stability is determining the readiness of launch systems. There may be a number of indicators associated with launcher alert status. These include: Flight parameters loaded, other software updates (if appropriate); Vehicle fuelled (missile or aircraft); Crews readied; Delivery vehicle in launch location (moved to launch point); Transporter system in ready position (e.g., transporter erector launcher [TEL] in raised launch position); Weapon armed. While most of these indicators of launch preparation are difficult to monitor, some, such as missile fuelling and launcher movements, might be monitored through electronic sensors.
- There is the possibility of use through miscalculation or misinterpretation.
- Sharing information on any of the concerns for safety, security or accident will require an infrastructure of

capabilities and procedures. These include methods for providing timely, reliable, secure, accurate, and authenticated communications.

- o Ensuring safety of nuclear weapons and materials will primarily be a state responsibility because of the highly classified nature of most safety issues. These issues involve detailed design, as well as material and handling details. An expanded mission for hotlines between the Directors-General of Military Operations and between the Heads of State might be established to address this critical issue.

Acknowledging the fact that only the Indian and Pakistani governments can decide whether and on what basis, to establish new risk reduction measures, the 'Working Group Report of the Center for Strategic and International Studies (CSIS)' recommends the following steps for nuclear risk reduction:

- o A new communications mechanism-nuclear risk reduction centres (NRRCs) in India and Pakistan-should be established to complement existing bilateral channels.
- o The main functions of the NRRCs would be to provide each party a dedicated, secure means of: (a) notifying the other side about activities or events on its territory that might be wrongly perceived or misinterpreted that could lead to conflict, (b) sharing information that the two countries are obliged to exchange under existing security agreements, and (c) seeking and receiving clarifications about ambiguous events on the other'sterritory. Other functions could include the conduct of joint exercises of certain NRRC notification procedures, technical back-up during crises, and support for consultations on the implementation of existing confidence-building measures (CBMs).
- o Adequate infrastructure already exists in South Asia to support a wide range of secure communication options, including data, voice, video, or a combination of these.

  The approximate cost for a dedicated cable permitting teletype and voice communication would be US$10,000-50,000 annually. For a dedicated satellite channel permitting teletype, voice, and video, the annual cost would be roughly US$560,000.

o- The centres would operate on a continuous, round-the-clock basis. Written messages using agreed formats would be the norm, although voice and video capability would also be desirable. It would be the prerogative of each government to decide where it would institutionally house its NRRC and to determine how its NRRC would relate to other government organisations. The Indian and Pakistani solutions to these questions need not be symmetrical.

The Working Group Report concluded, that "the circumstances in South Asia today are very different from the circumstances surrounding the current US-Russian relationship and the relationship that existed when the US-Soviet Centres were brought into being. Totailor a new communications mechanism to the needs of South Asia, the mechanism could appropriately take on a wider range of functions than the US and Russian Centres."

Rodney W.Jones assumes that there lies intense political conflict over Kashmir and that the escalation in South Asia has the potential of becoming a nuclear war. In one of the papers presented during the fourth nuclear stability roundtable during March 12-13, 2002, in Washington on 'Military Asymmetry and Instability in Emerging Nuclear States: India and Pakistan,' he suggests the following conditions of nuclear stability in the region:

o High nuclear threshold (strong conventional defence)

o Secure second strike capabilities (robust C4I)

o Rough parity in size and defence space

o Neither falling behind the other'sfirst strike edge (good early warning?) Supposing that "nuclear deterrence might provide the security that allows a general improvement in security relations" in South Asia, the UNIDR (United Nations Institute for Disarmament Research) research paper depicts various aspects of nuclear confidence-building measures between India and Pakistan. Commenting on the current conflict situation between the two countries, the authors of the paper subscribe to developing CBMs in connection with the 'central issue-Kashmir'. An interim suggestion is made to work on the possibilities of addressing the 'central sore-cross-border terror raids' from Pakistan.

With regard to nuclear CBMs, according to the UNIDR paper, India and Pakistan should share the development of respective nuclear doctrines and security concepts to have clarity over 'red lines'; develop mechanisms on notification of ballistic and cruise missile tests; create nuclear risk reduction centres with robust safety systems to deal with the issues of accidental or unauthorised use; and install a secure and dedicated line of communication including safe command and control systems between the national authorities (the nature or constitution of national authority remains undefined). The paper categorically puts the 'Kashmir issue' to be discussed as in the final stages of CBMs between the two countries.

The UNIDR study concludes that the two countries should seize the ripe moment (that has begun since the two countries agreed to peace talks during the sidelines of the SAARC summit in January 2004) in the context of possibility of conflict. "Any future terrorist incident might provoke India into punitive action, which in the worst case might lead to uncontrolled or accidental responses, all the way to a nuclear exchange. This suggests that, although the nuclear aspects will have to be part of the general discussions on security, it might also be worth considering whether they can be made separable, in case the moment passes too quickly."

The aspect of geographical proximity of the two countries is also discussed in one of the reports dealing with nuclear threat reduction measures. Based on some hypothetical South Asian launch point-target combinations, the missile travel time between India and Pakistan is estimated between 8 to 13 minutes.

Taking account of the danger of false alarms and miscalculations, the Pugwash Discussion Paper of 2002 suggests that a posture of De-alert (most basic measures would be to keep the weapons de-mated from delivery systems; use of locking devices), and installation of best available safety measures into the weapons, like use of Insensitive High Explosive (IHE) and fire-resistant pits would significantly reduce the risk of inadvertent or unauthorised use of weapons. From the above discussed strategic policy recommendations, there emerge two sets of proposals that could draw attention of the diplomats and strategic planners of India and Pakistan. In the first set, one can identify mechanisms for escalation control and nuclear force management within each state. The second set includes possible measures of nuclear CBMs by the two countries to work towards long lasting stability in the region.

Issues Related to Escalation Control and Nuclear Force Management

- o Leadership declarations affirming responsible nuclear stewardship (avoidance of shrill rhetoric).
- o Developing strategies to avoid escalation of conventional confrontation to nuclear exchange level.
- o Avoiding sensitive targets in the event of a conventional war.
- o Raising the level of nuclear threshold (strong conventional defences).
- o Securing second strike capabilities.
- o Review of decision-making to develop, produce, and use 'tactical' nuclear weapons.
- o Regular assessment of each other'scurrent operational and deployment status of nuclear weapons (missile fuelling and launcher movements might be monitored through electronic sensors).
- o Determining the readiness of launch systems.
- o Improvements in intelligence to avoid miscalculation or misinterpretation.
- o Acquisition of technology to help provide prompt and accurate information concerning missile launches and nuclear detonations.
- o Advancement in respective command and control mechanisms including establishment of effective early warning systems.

- o Refraining from giving pre-delegation of authority to use nuclear weapons.
- o Effective physical safety of nuclear materials and installations.
- o Ensuring safety and security of nuclear weapons and materials.

Steps Required for Nuclear CBMs

- o Improving bilateral relationship.
- o Sharing knowledge of decision-making processes.
- o Agreement on advance notification of missile testing and movements.
- o Flight test missiles only from designated test ranges.
- o Provision of advance notification of the movement of missiles for training purposes.
- o Review of policy decisions related to tactical nuclear weapons (including development, production, or use).
- o Establishment of multi-layered, reliable, secure, accurate, and authenticated communication mechanisms.
- o Establishment of Nuclear Risk Reduction Centres (NRRCs).

Most of the above-mentioned studies on South Asia suggest that problems related to Kashmir may be the spark to trigger a nuclear exchange between India and Pakistan. Linking of the Kashmir issue with Indo-Pak nuclear strategy is quite complex. In fact, such an assumption indirectly endorses (and is born out of) Pakistan's nuclear blackmailing. In reality, it is the Pakistani military that has crossed the Line of Control (LoC) in the past to provoke Indian defence. Pakistan does not adhere to no-first-use (NFU) and keeps making frequent calls to lower the nuclear threshold in the apprehension of India taking reprisal measures to stop Pakistan-sponsored terrorism in Indian territory.

Pakistan insists on Kashmir being the 'core' issue of stability/ instability between India and Pakistan. India maintains that the scourge of 'terrorism'in South Asia has adverse implications for both regional and international security. In between the two exclusive views, remains a pertinent question unanswered-who is to guarantee that if the issues related to Kashmir remains resolved, towards which India has already been making significant efforts, Pakistan's military-ISI sponsored terrorist activities in other parts of India would end? In such a complex security environment, bilateral confidence-building measures alone would keep the escalation under manageable limits.

PAKISTAN'S NUCLEARPOSTURE

Pakistan is considered to have as many as 50 nuclear weapons and enough highly enriched uranium (HEU) stock for 50 more, including the additional capacity to produce five to ten bombs a year.

According to a more recent estimate, Pakistan is said to possess 55-90 weapons of highly enriched uranium and 20-60 plutonium bombs.

No definitive information at official levels is available on such speculative assessments. The possible delivery systems for weapons are aircraft and missiles.

Pakistan President Pervez Musharraf has gone on record to say that the weapons are in a "disassembled state."

Few other terms have also been used to project the deployment status of Pakistan's nuclear weapons such as "operationally deployed" or "in the component form."

While the term component form has not been spelt out, it seems that "the situation in Pakistan may be murky and may in fact best be described as partial deployment."

Replying to the question of an interviewer, "Can you say, are the nuclear weapons ready to go as they are, or are they, as I have heard, in different parts, have to be assembled first?", Musharraf said: "Yes, you are right. They are not mated (inaudible). And there is geographical-they are geographically apart. They cannot be-they are not ready to be fired. So really, it's not the concept that NATO has been having (inaudible) United States system, where your finger has to be on a button and then finally can be pushed. That's not the condition there."

As far as the doctrinal aspect is concerned, Pakistan has not announced any comprehensive doctrine document. However, two basic elements that emerge from statements by the country's leaders are: "a rejection of the NFU policy, and the role of nuclear weapons as minimum credible deterrent."

Realising the gap between the military strength in conventional terms, there is a view prevalent in Pakistan that an NFU posture of Pakistan could provide India the leverage of conventional attack. In the backdrop of such military planning, by asking for a 'no-aggression-pact' Pakistan seems to preclude even an Indian reprisal for its misadventures like the one in Kargil in 1999 and support to cross-border terrorism against India. Also, another factor of security complications for India vis-à-vis Pakistan is that "country's chief patrons, principally the US and China, are bound to try and [set] right the inherent imbalance in power by assisting it in ways inimical to Indian interests."

The implication for Pakistan being designated a 'major non-NATOally'of the United States is being seen in India as more American military assistance to Pakistan.

Pakistan's Ambassador to United Nations has argued: "We have to rely on our own means to deter Indian aggression. Wehave that means and we will not neutralize it by any doctrine of no first use."

Pakistan's doctrinal declaratory policy is kept deliberately ambiguous. And, in terms of ability to ensure survival, Pakistan wants to have sufficient number and types of assets to create 'reasonable doubt'.

Relevant to the current discussion is the bottom line for use of nuclear weapons by Pakistan. This has been spelt out by Gen. Khalid Kidwai, Head of Strategic Planning Division (SPD) under the National Command Authority (NCA), to a delegation of Italian Scientists. Toquote him: "Nuclear weapons are aimed solely at India. In case that deterrence fails, they will be used if India attacks Pakistan and conquers a large part of its territory (space threshold); India destroys a large part either of its land or air force (military threshold); India proceeds to the economic strangling of Pakistan (economic strangling); or

India pushes Pakistan into political destabilization or creates a large scale internal subversion in Pakistan (domestic destabilization)."

In other words, without defining any limits Pakistan intends to use its nuclear weapons to counter even a primarily conventional conflict situation if it feels threatened with military, political or economic defeat. However, there is a feeling in Pakistan that a nuclear response cannot be involved to deal with local contingencies and the nuclear threshold should be maintained at a high level.

Aformer foreign minister of Pakistan has opined that the destruction of even a single city would be an unacceptable risk for another country that contemplates a pre-emptive strike.

In an interview to CNN on June 1, 2002, Pakistani President Pervez Musharraf tried to allay the growing international fear of any nuclear war in the subcontinent by saying that, "I would even go to the extent of saying one shouldn't even be discussing these (nuclear war) things, because any sane individual cannot even think of going into this unconventional war, whatever the pressure."

Afew months earlier, while chairing the meeting of the NCAin October 2001, Pervez Musharraf reaffirmed the Pakistani strategic assets as the cornerstone of country's national security and that there will be no compromise on the nuclear programme.

The statement had come in the light of increasing international concern about improving security and installing new safeguards on Pakistan's nuclear weapons after 9/11. Musharraf assured the world that the country's strategic capability was fully safeguarded. Such assertions need further examination, especially when Pakistan is considered as a potential source for terrorists to get access to technology and materials.

A. Q. Khan's televised confessional statement in February 2004 of being involved in international nuclear black-marketing drew unprecedented media attention. However, "A.Q. Khan got off lightly, sending disturbing messages about US and Pakistani attitudes toward proliferation."

And, "the most troubling question of all remains how and to what extent Pakistan's free-market approach to proliferation has allowed terrorist groups like Al Qaida to acquire nuclear materials and technology."

INDIA'S NUCLEAR POSTURE

Judging by the official pronouncements in the wake of the May 1998 tests, India appears set for a pragmatic course of action, including three basic components-construction of minimum deterrent with a NFU policy, participation in a possible Fissile Material Cutoff Treaty (FMCT) negotiations and the pursuit of arms control rather than disarmament.

The Cabinet Committee on Security headed by the Prime Minister while approving the establishment of Nuclear Command Authority and 'alternate chains of command for retaliatory nuclear strikes in all eventualities', on January 4, 2003, summarised the nuclear doctrine as:

(i) building and maintaining a credible minimum deterrent;

(ii) a posture of NFU and nuclear weapons to be used only in retaliation against a nuclear attack on Indian territory or on Indian forces anywhere;

(iii) nuclear retaliation to be massive and designed to inflict unacceptable damage;

(iv) authorisation of retaliatory attack rests with the political leadership through the National Command Authority;

(v) non-use of nuclear weapon against non-nuclear weapon states;

(vi) in the event of a major attack against India, or Indian forces anywhere, by biological or chemical weapons, India will retain the option of retaliating with nuclear weapons;

(vii) a continuance of strict control on export of nuclear and missile-related materials and technologies, participation in the Fissile Material Cutoff Treaty negotiations, and continued observance of the moratorium on nuclear tests; and

(viii) continued commitment to the goal of a nuclear weapon-free world through global, verifiable and non-discriminatory nuclear disarmament.

As early as in 1994, India had proposed that India and Pakistan should jointly undertake not to be the first to use their nuclear capability against each other. Even after conducting the nuclear tests India expressed its readiness "...to discuss a 'no-first-use'agreement with that country, as also with other countries bilaterally, or in a collective forum."

However, Gen. Musharraf thinks otherwise. Interviewed on NBC television in Washington on January 23, 2002, General Musharraf was asked to explain Pakistan's reluctance to follow India in adopting a policy of no-first-use of nuclear weapons. He replied: "When you talk of no-first-use, Pakistan has been offering denuclearisation of South Asia...so we are going far, far beyond them.

It is not an issue of no-first-use, but far beyond that... Wewant to denuclearise South Asia. Wewant to sign a No War Pact with them. Isn't that better? I think the world community should insist on that. Pakistan is offering a much bigger deal."

The Indian Prime Minister rejected Pakistan's suggestion for a mutual rollback of their nuclear programme as India's nuclear programme is not Pakistan-specific. In fact, "the rationale for Pakistan's nuclear weapons programme continuously harped on is that Pakistan has always been quantitatively and technologically weaker than India in military terms.

India's counter-argument is that, in terms of the ratio between defence responsibilities and the size of the armed forces, especially in terms of territorial defence from external aggression, this argument is not valid." As early as in 1974, Pakistan submitted a resolution at the 29th session of the UN General Assembly, which sought to endorse in principle the concept of a nuclear weapon-free zone in South Asia.

At that point of time, Pakistan was already running the nuclear weapon programme. It is worth remembering that then President Zulfikar Ali Bhutto had called a meeting of

Pakistani scientists in Multan in January 1972 and had expressed his willingness to acquire nuclear weapon for Pakistan.

But in the wake of India's May 1974 tests, Pakistan tried to gain an image of veiled peacemaker though lacking any sincerity. India itself had proposed a resolution in the same 29th session of the General Assembly in which it recognised that, "in appropriate regions and by agreement among the states concerned, the creation of nuclear-weapon-free zones could promote the cause of general and complete disarmament under effective international control."

India also considered in that proposal that "the initiative for the creation of a nuclear-weapon-free zone in the appropriate region of Asia should come from the States of the region concerned, taking into account its special features and geographical extent."

In reality, South Asia could not be treated in isolation for the purpose of creating a nuclear weapon-free zone, as it is only a sub-region and an integral part of the Southern Asian region. Hence, it is necessary to take into account the security of the region in its entirety. Unlike Pakistan, India's adherence to a NFU policy and its strategic assets are not country-specific. Therefore, any effort towards creating a minimum credible nuclear triad, including qualitative improvement in missile systems or other technological advancements, seems related to India's national security perspectives beyond, but inclusive, of Pakistan.

The Indian perspective is both global and regional in nature. India believes that: "As long as nuclear weapons exist, the threat of use of nuclear weapons, accidentally or inadvertently, will remain. Only global and complete nuclear disarmament, within a time-bound framework, can totally eliminate the danger of a nuclear war.

This was the cornerstone of India's Action Plan for the elimination of nuclear weapons unveiled by late Prime Minister Rajiv Gandhi in 1988 at the Special Session of the General Assembly...While pursuing the goal of nuclear disarmament, it is desirable to take immediate steps for reducing nuclear danger. These could include measures to de-alert and de-target nuclear weapons, legally binding commitments on no-first-use of nuclear weapons and non-use of nuclear weapons against Non-Nuclear Weapon States."

India-Pakistan Nuclear CBMs

Recently, Indian External Affairs Minister Natwar Singh stated that: "Anew dimension has been added since 1998 when both countries became nuclear powers. And now it is absolutely essential that we have best of relations. And the Manmohan Singh government has already made it clear that we look forward to continuing the process, we will take it forward and it will be multi-faceted.

And the differences we have will be ironed out through negotiations, friendly talks and cooperation." And at the end of the meeting of Foreign Ministers of India and Pakistan in New Delhi on September 5 and 6, 2004, to review the status of the Composite Dialogue, the duo agreed to take further the expert level meetings on conventional and nuclear CBMs, inter alia,to discuss the draft agreement on advance notification of missile tests."

In 1988, India and Pakistan agreed to "refrain from undertaking, encouraging or participating in, directly or indirectly, any action aimed at causing the destruction of, or damage to, any nuclear installation or facility in the other country."

The term 'nuclear installation or facility' includes nuclear power and research reactors, fuel fabrication, uranium enrichment, isotopes separation and reprocessing facilities, as well as any other installations with fresh or irradiated nuclear fuel and materials in any form and establishments storing significant quantities of radioactive materials. And the two countries also agreed to inform on January 1 of each calendar year, of the latitude and longitude of its nuclear installations and facilities and whenever there is any change.

This practice is in regular use ever since it came into force from January 1, 1991, and the practice did not stop even during the crisis period of 2002. However, "each side has questioned the completeness of the other's list."

Subsequently, a forward movement in nuclear CBMs was witnessed during the Indian Prime Minister's visit to Lahore in 1999.

The memorandum of understanding (MoU) signed by the foreign secretaries of the two countries at Lahore in 1999 mentioned that "The two sides shall engage in bilateral consultations on security concepts, and nuclear doctrines, with a view to developing measures for confidence-building in the nuclear and conventional fields, aimed at avoidance of conflict." The two countries agreed to provide each other with advance notification in respect of ballistic missile flight tests, and envisaged a bilateral agreement in this regard.

India and Pakistan at Lahore also committed to continue to abide by their respective unilateral moratoriums on conducting further nuclear test explosions.

With a view to reaching bilateral agreements based on mutual deliberations and technical consultations, the two countries under the Lahore MoU included many significant issues such as national measures to reduce the risks of accidental or unauthorised use of nuclear weapons, notification in the event of any accidental, unauthorised or unexplained incident, prevention of incidents at sea in order to ensure safety of navigation by naval vessels and aircraft belonging to the two sides, review of the existing communication links (e.g., between the respective Directors-General of Military Operations), and periodic review of existing confidence-building measures.

The two sides would also engage in bilateral consultations on security, disarmament and non-proliferation issues within the context of negotiations on these issues in multilateral fora. The expert level talks, led by Sheel Kant Sharma, and his Pakistani counterpart, Tariq Osman Hyder, during June 19-20, 2004, culminated in a joint statement on nuclear CBMs with some repetition of important issues under the Lahore MoU.

The joint statement recognises "the nuclear capabilities of each other, which are based on their national security imperatives, constitute a factor of stability." This implies that the two countries have moved beyond the earlier differing ambits of threat perceptions, for holding nuclear weapons in the respective states. Instead of questioning the rationality of possessing nuclear weapons, the two countries now acknowledge nuclear weapons as a factor of stability in the region.

The important issues covered in the joint statement are: upgradation of existing hotline between DGMOs; new dedicated and secure hotline between foreign secretaries to prevent misunderstanding, reduce risks relevant to nuclear issues; to conclude an agreement with technical parameters on pre-notification of missile flight testing; unilateral moratorium on nuclear tests unless a country decides that extraordinary events have jeopardised its supreme interests; bilateral discussions and further meetings to work towards the implementation of the Lahore MoU of 1999, among others.

The provision in the joint statement of June 20, 2004, that "both countries will continue to engage in bilateral consultations on security and non-proliferation issues within the context of negotiations on these issues in multilateral fora" seems to reflect the shared view of India and Pakistan to work together against the existing discriminatory international regimes and policies of disarmament.

While agreeing to reaffirm a unilateral moratorium on further nuclear tests, the joint statement also shows consciousness for "their obligations to their peoples and the international community." It is perhaps indicative of the two countries endorsing international concerns related to nuclear security in South Asia.

The foreign secretaries of the two sides, Riaz Khokhar and Shyam Saran, who met in Islamabad during December 27-28, 2004, to review the progress made during the meetings of the Experts on Nuclear and Conventional CBMs, stated that they have, "narrowed further their differences on the draft agreement on pre-notification of flight testing of ballistic missiles, and agreed to work towards its early finalisation."

It is also reported that the Pakistani side has introduced 20 new proposals, including 'The Elements of a Strategic Restraint Regime (SRR)' comprising conflict resolution through a sustained, result-oriented dialogue; measures for nuclear restraint and conventional balance to be discussed at the political and experts level; objective of minimum credible deterrence; maintenance of nuclear weapons on low-alert status; no operational deployment of nuclear-capable ballistic or any other type of missiles/delivery systems; no acquisition or deployment of anti-ballistic missile systems; avoidance of a nuclear, missile, or conventional arms race; continuation of the national nuclear test moratoriums of both sides, as reaffirmed in the Joint Statement of June 20, 2004.

But, in the progressive mode of consultations and addition of fresh proposals at every next meeting of expert groups, there remains little hope for any definitive conclusion of the agreement soon. The issues involving the technical parameters of advance notification and deployment strategy, however, are tricky aspects.

CONCLUSION

The theoretical construct of the international security environment including India and Pakistan as states with nuclear weapons, is primarily based on the exclusivist assumption on the behaviour of 'the state' in times of crisis and peace. The international security discourse is dominated by the Cold War experience. The existing theoretical constructs does not acknowledge India's status at par with P-5 nuclear weapon states.

The prevailing international security discourse of the West on the rationale of possession of nuclear weapons for the P-5, seems hesitant to integrate the universal application of any change in the global security balance. While the policy projections of the P-5 reflect inclusion of its own security concerns in the international security environment, the 'new nuclear weapon states' face diplomatic challenges of conceptual contestation. The difference in perceptions is largely related to strategic stability and security at both the regional and international levels.

The apprehension of strategic stability being fragile in the region remains the cause of concern for many observers of South Asia across the world.

While both India and Pakistan believe in each other'sdeterrent capability, both of them have identified security vulnerabilities pertaining to possible accidental or unauthorised use of nuclear weapons. Toassuage international and regional concerns related to the risk of miscalculations and misperceptions, there is need for evolving mutually agreed frameworks of bilateral confidence-building.

The two countries' difference of perceptions related to nuclear security are likely to continue as long as Pakistan does not shed ambiguity in doctrinal formulations. By maintaining ambiguity, Pakistan wants to keep the nuclear threshold high in the region.

Any ambiguity in force preparedness is permissible to such an extent that it will not otherwise impede the process of ensuring nuclear confidence-building between the two countries. Mutual consultations on security concepts and nuclear doctrines may help bridge the gap of mutual mistrust.

Such consultations may be veiled under official secrecy, but they also accompany mutual assurance in public. Asignificant step in this direction could be to mutually develop some postulates on nuclear signalling at appropriate levels in the respective governments.

However, some bumps on the road ahead may be related to issues affecting stability in the region, like Pakistan's control over cross-border terrorism, its efforts to derail the peace process on issues related to Kashmir and its own internal domestic weaknesses. Against this backdrop, the linking of nuclear confidence-building to other issues of traditional hostility between India and Pakistan may slow down the process of nuclear confidence-building in South Asia.

It does not, however, exclude the fear of nuclear material and technology falling into the wrong hands in Pakistan. In essence, the issue of nuclear terrorism can be addressed effectively at multilateral levels rather than at the bilateral levels of India and Pakistan.

The earlier CBMs such as to provide advance notification of ballistic missile test-flights, maintain a unilateral moratorium on conducting further nuclear testing till the sovereignty right is not jeopardised, the joint declaration of August 1992 on the prohibition of chemical weapons, and existing communication links between DGMOs or Prime Minister'soffices, have shown workable precedents which lay emphasis on mutual benefits in security matters.

But a review of the effectiveness of past measures would help ascertain the authenticity of prevailing communication links to control escalation. There remains an element of uncertainty as to how Pakistan would react in case of a conventional military conflict. However, it can be said that despite rhetoric, neither side wants a nuclear conflict. Tore-ensure nuclear stability, the recent diplomatic initiatives by India and Pakistan towards confidence-building that have resumed under the composite dialogue process since January 6, 2004, are progressing well, but still have a long way to go.

9

Cyber-Diplomacy: A New Strategy of Influence

INTRODUCTION

Governments are developing a new form of diplomacy that they consider a central strategic element in the conduct of contemporary international affairs. As societies evolve, new scenarios arise in the realm of international relations that demand new methods and new priorities. Diplomatic practice keeps time with the changing world, evolving, as it has throughout history, to meet new challenges and respond to new sets of national interests. A crucial change has been the re-equilibration of the relative importance of 'hard' and 'soft' power. In other words, traditional coercive methods based on military or economic might are giving way to the more subtle diplomatic arts of persuasion and influence. This new balance is the product of a host of novel circumstances.

Complex interdependence, cultural globalisation, the empowerment of public opinion, the mass media revolution and the increasingly international flow of culture, ideas and information are all factors that direct mounting pressure towards national governments, urging them to remould their foreign policy structures and to develop mass diplomacy as a new focal point for their diplomatic efforts. In the light of this new global environment, governments come to view the ability to inform and influence foreign audiences as a strategic aspect of their diplomacy and as an indispensable condition for the pursuit of their goals. The reasons for the rise of conditions leading to mass diplomacy have been discussed in proceeding chapters.

It is fitting now to ask a few questions and consider states' potential uses for this new diplomacy. In what ways can mass diplomacy complete traditional state-to-state diplomacy? What is the utility of communicating directly with foreign audiences? Is it possible that mass diplomacy could create a more fruitful international environment, leading to better international footholds and greater facility in the attainment of national interests? Can mass diplomacy further specific security, economic and political goals?

It will be shown that a growing number of governments answer most of these questions affirmatively. In an attempt to explain this growing consensus, this chapter tries first to determine to what extent the task of informing and educating foreign populations can favourably influence the international context and secondly, to see how mass diplomacy can help advance specific goals.

Benefiting States in the International Arena

The rationale of mass diplomacy is threefold: first, to engage foreign populations in relationship of trust and empathy; second, to create an enabling international conjuncture and third, to facilitate thereby the achievement of national interests.

a. Generating an Atmosphere of Trust

It is interesting to consider both why states disseminate information and cultural values across international society, and why they believe that in so doing they advance their interests. A few decades ago, Karl Deutsh observed that "directly linked to the interests of each state [...] is the policy of diffusion of its own ideological propaganda in foreign countries, and the policy of support for cultural and scientific exchanges compatible with this goal". An implicit assumption among a growing number of leaders is that the promotion of a set norms and values viewed as preferable for one's own society as well as for the world in general is an important national goal. In the past few years, this foreign policy approach has become more resolutely inscribed in states' international agendas.

For Iranian, Japanese and Russian foreign policies it has become, respectively, an 'indispensable line', a 'pivot', or else, a 'pillar' on the same level as other more conventional fields. French diplomacy has made it a priority to make France's voice heard in the world by diffusing and sharing its preferred values, beliefs, norms and practices. U.S. public diplomacy, consisting of disseminating American values and ideas internationally constitutes today one of the two main focuses of the Department of State's Strategic Plan. For U.S. diplomats, this is a natural adaptation to the mass media revolution, the growing influence of culture and its greater relationship to politics and social change.

Foreign Policy in the 21st Century New Era', New Vision, New Diplomacy, Task Force on Foreign Relations for the Prime Minister, November 28, 2002.

In the eyes of German decision makers, as in those of most of their counterparts, cultural relations policy is not just a matter of "the good, the beautiful, the true" or "some kind of frilly extra"; rather it is an integral part of foreign policy aimed at completing and sustaining it. There are a number of reasons for this.

The first reason why the mass media information and cultural propagation programs occupy a central place in modern foreign policy systems is that they are viewed as effective instruments for fostering trust and understanding in foreign countries. This is particularly true in the American case. Over the years, promoting mutual understanding between the people of the United States and the peoples of the world through international information and cultural exchanges has become a "distinct and vital goal" for the State Department.

The intention is to project a more favourable image and in doing so, to reverse entrenched misconceptions and deeply rooted antagonism. In the short term, this goal is advanced through the dissemination of information in support of U.S. policy and in the longer term, through a multitude of educational and cultural initiatives. By combining information with education, mass diplomacy contributes to the familiarisation of foreign audiences with American norms and values allowing the construction of strong relationship based on confidence and trust. Cultural programs in particular are a top priority to the extent that they allow the modification of the value structure of targeted societies.

Secretary of State Madeleine K. Albright made the following remark in this respect: "many of our other more officials ambassadors have told me of the value that cultural programs have in improving perceptions about America." This certitude is based on a certain number of program evaluations showing that foreign populations exposed to mass diplomacy develop more empathy for their host country. U.S. mass diplomacy outreach capacity is of course greatly enhanced by strategic communications programs specifically designed for foreign audiences and conveyed by a vast array of technological facilities such as Internet, print publications, travelling and electronically transmitted speaker programs, and information resource services.

The same logic holds true across the globe. In every corner of the world, countries rely increasingly on mass diplomacy and mass media to create an atmosphere of understanding and peaceful dialogue with foreign societies. Adopting Wilfrid Laurier's idea that "the only way to defend one's ideas and principles is to make them known", Canadian policy makes a considerable investment in the dissemination of Canadian pluralist values throughout the world. This allows them to express and promote Canada's unique identity to foreign populations and to build genuine relationships. Creating understanding, goodwill and convergence are viewed as indispensable goals in the process of establishing a relationship with solid foundations with partner countries. In a nutshell, those are the fundamental goals of mass diplomacy.

One of the central tenets of the German policy is to teach values and norms to 'learning communities' in order to get them to know and understand Germany better. In doing so German mass diplomats hope to create networks and dialogue across ideological and cultural fault lines. For Joshka Fisher, the head of the German Foreign Service, to develop cultural relations with civil societies abroad is today one the "real hard issues that foreign policy is all about". Iranian foreign policy makers are convinced that chances for Iran's success lie in a mass diplomacy capable of changing world public opinion and of bringing into agreement with Teheran.

They believe in particular that a policy of détente, 'answerable' to people and based on the 'dialogue of culture and civilisations' holds the potential to improve the generally negative image of the Islamic Republic worldwide. The Japanese consider that the new communication and information technologies make possible a strategy of cultural public relations aimed at attenuating ideological, cultural and ethnic differences, thus creating inter-societal rapprochement. Japan is actively promoting its culture abroad as a means of engendering trust among nations and building truly friendly relationships.

Like their Italian, Turkish or British counterparts, a growing number of foreign policy makers regard their diplomatic methods of information and cultural co-operation as a strategic lever of particular importance in affirming a favourable national image abroad and in maintaining a proper basis for establishing deep-rooted and solid relations with foreign societies.

Engaging with Key Peoples and Creating a Facilitating Conjuncture

By targeting foreign populations, including both the general public and opinion leaders, mass diplomacy allows states to engage with key people and influence their government more or less directly. Far before the rise of the telecommunication tools that render mass diplomacy possible today, Hans Morgenthau had envisioned the potential of this subtle diplomacy that "aims not at the conquest of territory or at the control of economic life, but at the conquest and control of the minds of citizens".

According to top British mass-diplomacy strategists, this approach can achieve a wide variety of results. A few of these include increasing people's familiarity with one's country, increasing their appreciation of one's country (by creating positive perceptions and manipulating others into seeing issues from the same perspective) and finally by enabling them to engage with one's country (by getting them to buy British products, understand and subscribe to British practices and policies).

In turn, bringing foreign masses to share a common vision of the world is viewed as an indirect means of applying pressure to their governments. In other terms, mass diplomacy allows a country to secure a partner's consent or support by modifying the will of significant segments of its population. A Canadian specialist makes the point very clearly: "If there is initial resistance from the target government, it will be through public diplomacy that new alliances will be shaped with local groups to attempt to change policy". U.S. decision makers observe that in providing foreign audiences with a better understanding of the United States, cultural exchange are strategic activities that build a corps of informed opinion leaders in the national political, economic, cultural, and social infrastructures of their countries. The impact of mass diplomacy is magnified, when, as German specialists suggest, it targets in particular individuals exercising more influence within society. Similarly, for Americans, what is central is mass diplomacy's capacity to engage emerging and current societal leaders on cultural and ideological issues. Information initiatives and strategic communications programs created strictly for key international audiences, such as the media, government officials and opinion leaders, are of course an additional condition for success. This is why direct communication with foreign audiences is an increasingly essential responsibility of twenty-first century foreign policy.

Another shared postulate is that by building relationships based on trust and sympathy, mass diplomacy facilitates diplomatic conjuncture and provides states with a stronger international position. By benefiting from emotional ties, a country will prosper more by gaining a position from which it is easier to draw international opinion in a direction to national advantage and to frame international issues to its own advantage. Public diplomacy cannot force partner governments to co-operate, "but what public diplomacy can do is change the environment in which the debate takes place, and this has a real effect on its outcome." With that in mind one can better understand why the Belgian anthropologist, Constantin von Barloewen, considers that "intercultural dialogue, (...) will become the existential problem of tomorrow's Realpolitik."

Foreign policy advisors from around the globe today admit that mass diplomacy is an excellent means of creating a favourable context for political action thereby providing countries with more control over the outcome of their diplomatic manoeuvring. American analysts, to begin with, believe that the task of fostering a consensus on American values and norms, in other words, making the world a more congenial environment for American interests, is a crucial step in developing a facilitating context for the United States.

State Department strategists consider that creating empathy among foreign audiences builds a platform of international support from which it is easier to address issues of global importance. For them, "such understanding provides a sensible context in which the United States can articulate its policy, intentions, and actions abroad." A U.S. congressman remarks that, "public diplomacy-which consists of systematic efforts to communicate not with foreign governments but with the people themselves-has a central role to play in the task of making the world safer for the United States". At the Canadian DFAIT, there is no doubt that a country's success on the international scene depends in large part today on how it is perceived abroad and therefore on the ability of its diplomacy to project its values and culture globally.

For France, mass diplomacy conducted "in the public space" is one of the best guarantees for the expansion of national influence internationally, a 'base' for one's presence abroad. Mass diplomacy is a central tool of soft power diplomacy thanks to which Paris hopes to, once again, play a major role in international affairs. Iranian foreign minister, Dr. Kamal Kharrazi, describes cultural diplomacy as the basis for Iran's credibility in the international arena and for the creation of a durable atmosphere of understanding and peaceful cohabitation with other countries. He states that "the need to expand cultural relations with other

countries is as pressing as that of enhancing classic diplomatic ties". As suggested by the Japanese and Germans, for a country to play an enhanced part in the international community it is crucial to implement cultural public relations activities sustained by communication means. International media policy makes a valuable contribution to shaping a good image and building global networks that generate good will and voluntary co-operation.

A Soft Diplomacy for Hard Goals

By increasing dialogue with foreign audiences and creating an enabling international context, mass diplomacy represents a strategic means of advancing concrete national interests in international affairs. As Leonard and Stead explain, it is more than simply enchanting publics and engaging government for the sake of it-"it is about getting results." An increasingly widespread belief among today's leaders is that this soft policy is essential to success in paving the way for a wide array of hard goals.

At the start of the twenty-first century, it has become evident to American leaders that mass diplomacy has a vital contribution to make to United States foreign policy. For the State Department, "public diplomacy has value as a strategic element of power in the information age." The belief is that it significantly promotes the national interest of the United States through educating, informing and influencing foreign audiences. Working very much in co-ordination with and in parallel to traditional diplomatic efforts, the new diplomacy is officially presented as a 'sine qua non' or 'indispensable' instrument for addressing such critical objectives as increasing global economic growth, promoting democratic principles of government and securing a sustainable global environment.

As the State Department emphasises, "without mutual understanding and the trust it engenders, it would be virtually impossible for American diplomacy to pursue successfully [its] Strategic Goals." Secretary of State Colin Powell considers consequently that it is crucial that deepening contacts be developed at all levels to maintains United States leadership on the global stage and to compete effectively with its European partners in an area of strategic importance. A valuable aspect of public diplomacy is that it is not concerned solely with the attainment of specific time-defined goals but holds the potential of maintaining an ongoing process benefiting all international affairs goals. It is stipulated in the funding document of the Bureau of Cultural Affairs that: "Essential to promoting the strategic goals outlined in the Department of State International Affairs Strategic Plan, cultural exchanges seek to establish trust, confidence, and international co-operation with other countries that sustain and advance the full range of American national interests." Again, major U.S. foreign policy goals are reinforced in critical ways by mass diplomacy information programs and America's comparative advantage in information and soft power resources.

In the present context, other international actors are increasingly aware that mass diplomacy holds the potential to improve their standing in international society and to facilitate the attainment of their goals. Realising that they cannot match U.S. hard power at this point in time, second tier and middle powers increasingly rely on this soft power diplomacy to assume a key position.

- Like many other middle powers, Canada counts on its mass diplomacy to make a difference on the international scene despite relatively modest hard power assets. It is believed that given the new realities of global affairs and the growing vulnerability of national borders, ethical diplomacy consisting of disseminating a set of preferred values and norms will advance Canada's economic and security interests. The DFAIT stated it clearly when it announced that: "the projection of Canadian values and culture is important to our success in the world." This form of middle power international diplomacy is crucial in addressing a wide range of issues including straightening social cohesion and forging national identity domestically.
- Major European countries also understand that they can promote their influence and interests by investing effort in mass diplomacy. British leaders believe that public diplomacy and the promulgation of the United Kingdom's image, values and policies overseas are effective ways to promote and protect Britain's national interests. For the British diplomat Michael Butler, "the

purpose of public diplomacy is to influence opinion in target countries to make it easier for the British Government, British companies or other British organisations to achieve their aims". As regards the question of knowing to what extent mass diplomacy can maximise national gains, Germany's answer is clear: cultural policy abroad is "part and parcel of foreign policy". By building trust, mass diplomacy "directly supports and serves general foreign policy goals and aspirations." Although it is difficult to quantify its results, it makes a valuable contribution in paving the way for international co-operation. "By winning partners and friends for our country", declare German leaders, "cultural relations policy directly serves vital national interests." There is little doubt on their part that this approach represents a powerful diplomatic channel: a pipeline serving simultaneously 'soft' and 'hard' political issues.

- Many other governments consider mass diplomacy to be a medium through which they will be able to enhance their international standing and have greater impact than their present status suggests is possible. Notably, it is viewed by Chinese officials as 'an all-dimensional opening up axe' of its 'grand strategy' serving long-term national goals. For Indians, winning international understanding and support plays a central role for the defence of national interests, priorities and aspirations. Italians, Turks and Iranians agree that cultural policy helps champion national interests by contributing to the improvement of economic, trade and political relations with the rest of the world.

10

Mass Diplomacy and Preventive Security

Mass diplomacy increasingly represents an essential element of a modern security policy. According to traditional perspectives, defence and even security are matters best dealt with through brute military might. But in an era of global interdependence, of closely interconnected societies and intertwined of communications, it becomes more difficult for states to increase their security by constraining rivals through force or military dissuasion.

In this new context, security policy has been constantly broadened beyond the narrow classic definition to include non-military factors such as social, cultural and communication considerations. New factors, among which feature prominently the mass media revolution and the growing political weight of public opinion, have led to the diversification of functions and levels involved in the definition and delivery of security policy. Culture, information and communication are strategic assets in this domain. According to the former German president Roman Herzog, they become "imperatives of security policy." The new communication and information facilities become as important to national security as political, military, and economic power.

Increasingly, a purely persuasion diplomacy based on culture, information and mass communication proves not only necessary but also feasible, cheap and easy. Mass diplomacy effectively prevents crises, resolves problems, establishes trust, builds alliances before aggression occurs and advances general national interests on the international scene. It functions as a first line of defence that promotes a better image among foreign publics, that instigates of a more favourable attitude from governments and creates a more stable and hospitable international environment. Mass diplomacy can also used as an offensive weapon designed to neutralise hostile groups or governments by depriving them of popular support.

Alternatively, it can anticipate and react against the development of hostile sentiment by attacking on a grass-roots level through a patient and resolute strategy combining education and the dissemination of information. Though mass diplomacy is not a substitute for the use of brute force it is becoming its unavoidable complement.

This policy of pre-emptive dissuasion occupies a more and more important place within states' international security agenda. To date, in spite of the lip service paid to them, little concrete attention had been given to the importance of cultural diplomacy and information programs. In these new circumstances, issues of 'transparency', moral legitimacy and accountability to foreign populations are likely to be central to the success of states' defence and security policies, even though they have traditionally been absent from classic approaches in these areas.

According to Canadians, there is a clear and growing utility for security policy to "go beyond simple military preparedness" and to include new approaches based on cultural and information relations. They believe that the successful promotion of peaceful values, such as multiculturalism and democracy, can make an important contribution to national security and international stability. It is a strongly held conviction that the dissemination of these values "will be critical to the struggle for international security in the face of new threats to stability." Italians do not doubt that this preventive diplomacy is a vehicle for peace and stability in the world.

French diplomacy is also founded on the assumption that such diplomacy, far from being futile, can reinforce security and facilitate the struggle against terrorism by allowing the patient development of exchange, legitimate relations and international solidarity. Joshka Fisher too shares the certitude that that by promoting dialogue and exchange, cultural diplomacy can play a critical role in preventing conflict by socialising 'difficult' partner countries and by drawing them closer to the international community. For the British, it is clear that "communication and building relationships do have a part to play if we are going to avoid slipping into a battle between the West and the rest." It is interesting to note that the quest for cultural and moral legitimacy among world populations is at the heart of the Common European

Security and Defence Policy project. The head of the Iranian Foreign Service also believes that "Iran's successful policy of détente and push for dialogue among civilisations to enhance relations has lowered significantly the cost of maintaining national security."

This is a perspective shared by its Indian, Turkish and Japanese counterparts for whom mass diplomacy holds a central place within a comprehensive security policy. They believe that mass diplomacy is becoming an essential component of international peace by helping to resolve ideological distortion and fostering cultural rapprochement.

By erecting a global psychological 'firewall', mass diplomacy has become America's first line of defence. While military strength and flexibility are vital to assure national security, the new international context has magnified the importance of communication with foreign audiences as a way to legitimatize and strengthen U.S. leadership in the world.

American leaders have come to realise that relatively small investments in mass diplomacy information and cultural propagation initiatives today can decrease the possibility of more costly conflicts later. Should mass diplomatic methods be ineffectually applied, military force might have to be employed prematurely but if it is undertaken in a timely and adequate manner it can help resolve emerging problems at low cost before they represent serious threats.

Thanks to its comparative advantage in the domain of communications, U.S. diplomacy is in a position to deploy a 'global cultural umbrella' of great strategic importance for its security. As J. Nye and W. Owen explain, the information edge acts as a 'multiplier' of American cultural diplomacy; of its capacity to reinforce emotional links with foreign nations and to prompt alliances and ad hoc coalitions.

It is believed that, "[i]n the information age, diplomatic influence and military power go to those who can disseminate credible information in ways that support their interests and effectively put public pressure on the leaders of other countries." The State Department's Strategic Plan insists on the importance of a sustained mass diplomacy promulgating American cultural values, norms and practices (ranging from democracy to mass consumption to pop music) for building a secure and friendly environment.

This policy is of critical significance in engaging populations, especially in fragmenting states and unstable regions, and in cultivating feelings of sympathy and trust instead of hostility and hatred. Another security goal that mass diplomacy is designed to achieve is to "promote and strengthen international norms and principles that formalise and help verify non-proliferation commitments." Now it appears that in establishing an international consensus on such moral norms as the 'no-first-use pledge' and the 'nuclear taboo' it has greatly contributed to reducing the menace emanating from weapons of mass destruction (WMD).

One of the primary contributions mass diplomacy can make is in the struggle against terrorism. Although it may conflict with some aspects of short term military action, the pursuit of a long term policy of pacification through mass diplomacy can be of great utility in persuading opinion leaders and the general public in priority countries to the danger of support for and public apathy toward terrorists.

The American example offers a good illustration. With 9-11, fostering mutual understanding, respect and long-term relationships with the peoples of other countries through information programs and cultural exchanges has assumed a sudden urgency. Many specialists came to conclude that military force was not enough to eradicate the terrorist menace unless it was combined with a concerted mass diplomacy campaign attacking its roots. A ranking member of the U.S. Foreign Policy Committee put it clearly: "Strong public diplomacy is critical to winning the war against terrorism. If we are to prevent future terrorist attacks, we must launch a concerted campaign to win over people across the globe who are subjected to anti-American misinformation and hate."

By the same token, the U.S. Under Secretary of State for Public Diplomacy declared that "[i]t is extremely dangerous to ignore groups of people who are busy creating misperceptions about the United States so that it becomes part of a cause of fanatics." It is became strikingly evident among U.S. officials that mass diplomacy is now crucial to the goal of generating a global anti-terrorist coalition among allied nations, to win the hearts and minds of the people exposed to hostile influence, and to diminish the underlying conditions that allow terrorism to take root and flourish. The struggle against terrorism through initiatives designed to inform and educate populations of young men and women in potentially dangerous countries is now the number-one mission of the U.S. public diplomacy.

Its specific contribution to U.S. psychological warfare is fixed by White House's National Security Strategy and State Department's National Strategy for Combating Terrorism. These official documents stipulate that mass diplomacy has the task of serving 'a war of ideas' the goal of which, as explains U.S. Secretary of State Powell, is to eliminate the conditions in which terrorism is bred and lies dormant before erupting violently.

In waging this war of ideas, we will be equally resolute in maintaining our commitment to our ultimate objective. The defeat of terror is a worthy and necessary goal in its own right. But ridding the world of terrorism is essential to a broader purpose. We strive to build an international order wheremore countries and peoples are integrated into a world consistent with the interests and values we share with our partners-values such as human dignity, rule of law, respect for individual liberties, open and free economies, and religious tolerance. We understand that a world in which these values are embraced as standards, not exceptions, will be the best antidote to the spread of terrorism. This is the world we must build today.

As emphasised by Charlotte Beers, this is a war about a way of life, a vision of the world and the set of beliefs, values and norms that sustain it. It is a war that America did not expect to ever have to fight again after the defeat of communist ideology but a war that has become essential for the preservation of its global interests.

However, one would be wrong to conclude that mass diplomacy is the monopoly of Western powers. As Noble and Leonard remind us, they are not alone in harnessing the power of public opinion and technology to promote their interests.

So will their adversaries. Terrorist and criminal organisations, extremists and rival powers are also increasingly becoming sophisticated in using technology to get their message across and recruit followers. This means in the future, conflict prevention will become a main driver of public diplomacy, since governments will have to play extremists at their own game and counter their messages using the same tools.

It must be recalled that this competition for cultural leadership and global mind space need not take the form of a 'clash of civilisations'. Mind space is open to all. Spheres of influence can be superimposed without automatically generating armed conflicts. Without reducing its strategic significance, this is what makes ideological and cultural action so very attractive to so many governments.

Spearheading Economic Interests

As observed by Italy's former Minister of Foreign Affairs, Lamberto Dini, the time when states could pursue their economic interests through economic means alone is now over:

"Culture and economics, sentiments and signs, practices and values can no longer be dissociated." In the age of interdependence and global communications, cultural values suddenly acquire a primordial importance for international trade and financial flows. In this new environment, a growing number of states adhere to mass diplomacy to increase their influence and competitiveness in the world economy. The reason is it permits the alteration of domestic conditions within partner countries.

Firstly, states rely on mass diplomacy to shape favourable macroeconomic structures by influencing political and economic leaders into adopting norms and practices that they view as preferable for their own economy and for the world economy in general. The assumption is that information and cultural exchanges forge close cultural links with economic leaders on the private level which in turn foster economic co-operation between governments. U.S. State Department's strategists are convinced that public diplomacy can achieve a wide array of goals in this regards. Information programs targeting economic and political leaders help persuading governments to adopt or maintain market-oriented macroeconomic, trade, investment, exchange rate, legal, and regulatory policies designed to support economic growth.

When combined with long-term cultural and educational programs, they favourably predispose future leaders to support global efforts to strengthen the international financial system and to adopt domestic policies, such as appropriate exchange rates and improved banking regulations, consistent with these improvements. Another claim is that they encourage broad-based reforms, critical for clearing the path for effective economic partnerships, particularly with developing and transitional economies.

They are designed to promote the transition from state protectionism to market-based economies, good governance, accountable leadership, fiscal responsibility, and financial market development. Their role is to persuade foreign decision-makers to observe the rule of law (civil and economic codes) as well as a certain number of preferred norms and practices. The purpose of cultural and education efforts is also to foster domestic growth and stability in stimulating transformation to more socially stable, free market-oriented regimes.

Secondly, mass diplomacy information and cultural programs are believed to serve a national economy on the world stage by stabilising world populations, by educating and informing them and by promoting a culture of mass consumption.

Like many others, U.S. foreign policy clearly integrates humanitarian issues and world population regulation into a comprehensive economic strategy in which educational and cultural initiatives play a key role:

> Achieving healthy and sustainable world population growth is vital to US interests. Economic and social progress in other countries can be undermined by rapid population growth, which overburdens the quality and availability of public services, limits employment opportunities, and contributes to environmental degradation. Not only will early stabilisation of the world's population at sustainable levels promote environmentally sound economic development in other countries, it will also benefit the US by improving trade opportunities and mitigating future global crises.

Population stabilisation policies incorporate information, educational and cultural programs, such as family planning and other reproductive health programs, targeting women and adolescents in emerging countries. At the same time, cultural diplomacy complements efforts to prevent humanitarian crises (disease, starvation, and conflicts) by providing necessary education to remedy them or early warning to mitigate their consequences. Mass diplomacy and more specifically human rights and democracy diplomacy have the capacity to stabilise partner countries and to turn them into "good investment environments." Finally, mass diplomacy can contribute to the emergence of vibrant mass consumption societies by enhancing communication with business sectors and foreign populations, by increasing social awareness, by providing access to new sources of information and education and by attenuating socio-economic disparities.

Thirdly, mass diplomacy significantly contributes to foreign trade policy by opening foreign markets and stimulating exports. It occupies a central place in the U.S. trade liberalisation strategy by promoting core liberal standards, increasing trade and freeing the flow of U.S. goods, service and capital. For American foreign policy makers there is little doubt that cultural and information efforts are central to building popular support for further trade liberalisation through domestic outreach efforts in the domains of information and culture. The State Department's Bureau of Educational and Cultural Affairs (ECA) prides itself on fostering America's economic prosperity by expanding world trade and by enlarging the area of vibrant open-market economies94. Mass diplomacy supports trade policy by contributing to export promotion efforts.

For example, Washington relies among other things on the capacity of its cultural and information diplomacy to reach and engage consumers overseas in order to expand U.S. exports from $930 billion to $1.2 trillion by early in the twenty-first century. Canadians also believe that the projection of their values and culture combined with their expertise in the domain of mass media technologies is essential to their economic success. According to recent analysis, Canada's strategy in this domain rests on a niche diplomacy, which prioritises the 'economic pillars' of comparative advantage, efficiency, and maximum impact in the national interest rather than broader popular targets. For Italians, "the promotion of culture abroad does not only mean mobilising Italy's ingenuity and credibility abroad but more specifically, preparing the ground for greater economic and commercial penetration of products and companies." For Germans too, informing and educating foreign audiences is an increasingly important element of their trade strategy. For instance, Joshka Fisher admits that German schools abroad not only communicate German culture and language but also serve as "base camps for Germany's export industry" by engaging future leaders emotionally.

Strengthening Political Influence

Among the vital interests that mass-diplomacy can serve, one of the most important is the increase of ideological influence through the export of one's political culture and institutions. Athenians, the Fathers of the U.S. Constitutions, French Revolutionaries, Bolsheviks and Islamists have all considered the export of their political regime as a crucial foreign policy goal. The reasoning is quite simple: if populations share values and political culture they will be more likely to have friendly relationships based on trust. A perfect illustration is offered by the projection of the democratic regime by democracies. This example also illustrates the central role that mass diplomacy can play in spreading a political system internationally.

- o The propagation of the democratic regime constitutes a leading political and strategic goal. Immanuel Kant was one of the first thinkers to envisage the spread of the republicanism as source of legitimacy, concord among nations, stability and international prosperity. More recently, the Democratic Peace School led by Michael Doyle has admirably systematised this line of thought: like-minded democracies develop quasi-fraternal relations and form an almost absolute sphere of peace. It is therefore the prime interest of democratic powers to co-opt other nations into the democratic club. Lucid in this regard, Kant had affirmed that 'moral politics' designed to spread republicanism is a matter of interest as much as authentic idealism and altruism. He had also specified that it requires politicians and governments to be 'innocent as a dove' but also 'wise as a serpent' designated to expand the democratic zone of peace rests on the capacity of democratic powers to shape a normative environment that impregnated non-democratic societies with their socio-political values and standards and fosters political reforms. Among the concrete measures designed to spread "democratic tastes across borders" and instigate democratic norms, Doyle prescribes an "active democratic right diplomacy", incorporating information programs, educational exchanges, tourism and scientific meetings101. In many regards, mass diplomacy is therefore the instrument which, in the twenty-first century, should allow the reconciliation of idealism with traditional realpolitik.

  A growing number of governments rely on public diplomacy to export their political system together with their specific values, norms and practices as a way of expanding their authority in the international arena.

- o A crucial task given to the U.S. mass diplomacy is to integrate other nations and governments into a democratic network consistent with U.S. values and norms. As stipulated by the State Department Strategic Plan, by supporting liberal democracy, public diplomacy "not only promotes fundamental American values," but also helps create a more secure and prosperous world in which the United States can advance its national interests. The chairman of the House International Relations puts it rather clearly: "in addition to genuine altruism, our promotion of freedom can have another purpose, namely as an element in the United States' geopolitical strategy." The ECA Bureau confirms that a stable community of democratic nations respectful of U.S. values serves all of America's strategic interests; from enhancing security to promoting economic prosperity.

- o The strategic targets of a campaign designed to further the spread of democracy are of course foreign populations. American officials estimate in this regard that their democratic crusade will be more likely to succeed by targeting the masses, those that Henry J. Hyde calls "America's silent allies." U.S. 'democratic rights diplomacy' supports the transition process of non-liberal countries by communicating directly with populations and by impregnating them with American liberal ideology. The State Department takes advantage of a vast array of international forums, cultural exchanges and information programs to promote the emergence, from the bottom up, of robust civil societies. It also promotes the development, from the top down, of democratic political systems respecting human rights, the rule of law, liberal constitutionalism, freedom of opinion, the independence of media and the free flow of ideas. U.S. mass diplomacy also takes advantage of the United States' superior information assets and the increasing access of foreign audiences to global media to undermine illiberal propaganda but also to diffuse on a massive level its own ideological campaign.
- o Other democratic states count on such "democracy diplomacy" to expand their moral influence and serve

their geopolitical goals. Japan, like many of its partners is convinced that the preservation of its interests lies in a policy aimed at expanding the community of democracies. The Italian Prime Minister, Silvio Berlusconi reminds us though that "[i]n the modern world, democracy cannot spread with the use of weapons, except under exceptional circumstances." There is little doubt that it can only move forward when driven by a complex initiative including economic means but also, to large extent, the use of culture, information and communication to educate populations in emerging democracies.

Although democracy is a universal idea and although democratic states generally join forces in this domain, each of them tends to promote a version of this idea that is saturated by its own social values. Thus they not only stress their distinctiveness, but also serve their own interests. In other words, each of them attempts to champion democracy by giving to it a national cultural character. They do so by strategically linking the promotion of democracy with key cultural messages about themselves. U.S. leaders recognise that "democracy will continue to advance internationally, but democratic practices will vary among states and will be subject to countervailing influences and interests." In other words, democracy is both a universal concept and an ideological tool that states try to appropriate in order to spread their influence.

Washington brands America's image of liberal democracy as the universal model in an attempt to remain a major authority on the multilateral scene. Paris emphasises the distinction between the U.S. model and the French model of social democracy, in a bid to play a stronger role as a moral alternative in international society. These differences are reflected in the design of mass diplomacy. Ottawa puts forth the multicultural and federal quality of the Canadian political system through a "liberal internationalist" public diplomacy. Teheran and Ankara vie for the leadership of Central Asia by insisting on the distinct formulation of their democratic model. On the one hand, Turkey offers the appeal of a democracy inspired by the pro-western kemalist model, and on the other hand, Iran provides a democracy inclined towards Islam and theocracy.

CONCLUSION

Increasingly, political leaders and foreign policy-makers from around the globe have come to consider mass diplomacy as a necessary, pertinent, affordable and rewarding strategy for the twenty first century. It has become evident to them that culture, information and communication are essential tools for acquiring better international status and for maximising national interests.

- o They view it first as a relevant approach fully equipped to deal with both the downside of global interdependence and the new opportunities it presents. They are aware that deep and lasting changes to the global landscape, such as new technologies and increasing democratisation, have made it not only feasible but also increasingly essential to the success of states in the international arena. It appears to them a relatively simple approach for a complex age. Mindful that the lines between economic, security and cultural policies are blurred, they are increasingly seduced by this new diplomacy that allows them to deal with different diplomatic goals simultaneously and, at the same time, to contribute to each of them distinctly and significantly.
- o Mass diplomacy also suggests itself as a clever means to attain one's new international ambitions while involving a minimum of risk for national security. Mass diplomacy has the reputation of being able to combine daring and caution as it permits the exploitation of new opportunities and the promotion of national interests without irritating other countries. Indeed mass diplomacy often by generates friendly and harmonious relationships. In many regards, it is considered to be one of the less threatening ways to engage foreign audiences, build strong relationships and long-lasting alliances.
- o Mass diplomacy also benefits from the fact that it is perceived as a cheap way to frame the international

debate and to play a key role in world politics. In an age where the use of military force is increasingly costly (and inefficient), it constitutes an ideal palliative, exercising a growing appeal on governments. Relatively small investments in mass diplomacy hold the potential of creating the conditions for stability and economic growth while decreasing the possibility of future problems that might prove more costly to resolve later. This "diplomacy of the poor" has the potential to even out international interactions by allowing smaller players to compensate for their lack of hard power.

With each passing moment, mass diplomacy appears more indispensable to the conduct of foreign policy. By having the capacity of accomplishing significant goals in the medium and long terms, it tends to acquire a central position in the toolbox of diplomacy. Many decision makers see it as the tool par excellence for the conquest of hearts and souls on which more and more states depend for achieving their goals. In so doing, they increasingly swap the 'spirit of conquest' for the 'conquest of the spirit'.

Bibliography

Abbott, James: *Narrative of a Journey from Heraut to Khiva, Moscow and St. Petersburgh*, London, 1843.

Abd al-Razzak Ibn Najaf Kuli: *The Dynasty of the Kajars*, London, J. Bohn, 1833.

Ahmad, Imtiaz: *State and Foreign Policy: India's Role in South Asia*, New Delhi, Vikas, 1993.

Appleby, Paul H.: *Policy and Administration*, Birmingham, AL: University of Alabama Press, 1949.

Baddeley, John F.: *The Russian Conquest of the Caucasus*, New York, Russell & Russell, 1908.

Basu, Prahlad K.: *Governance and Public Administration for Poverty Reduction*, Salvador, Brazil, 1997.

Bearce, George D.: *British Attitudes Towards India 1784-1858*, Oxford, University Press, 1961.

Burnes, Alexander: *Cabool; a Personal Narrative*, London, J. Murray, 1842.

CCTA: *The Government Centre for Information Systems*, Norwich, CCTA, 1995.

Elphinstone, Mountstuart: *Account of the Kingdom of Caubul and its Dependencies in Persia, Tartary, and India*, London, Longman, 1815.

English, Barbara: *The War for a Persian Lady*, Boston, Houghton Mifflin, 1971.

Entner, Marvin L.: *Russo-Persian Commercial Relations 1828-1914*, Gainesville, University of Florida, 1965.

Fletcher, Arnold: *Afghanistan, Highway of Conquest*, Ithaca, New York, Cornell University, 1965.

Fraser, James B.: *Narrative of a Journey into Khorasan in the Years 1821 and 1822*, London, Longman, 1825.

Habberton, William: *Anglo-Russian Relations Concerning Afghanistan 1837-1907*, Urbana, University of Illinois, 1937.

Hambly, Gavin: *Central Asia*, New York, Delacorte Press, 1969.

Hans J. Morgenthau: *Politics Among Nations: The Struggle for Power and Peace,* New York, Knopf, 1960.

Hurewitz, Jacob C.: *Diplomacy in the Near and Middle East: A Documentary Record 1535-1914*, Princeton, New Jersey, 1956.

Huttenback. Robert A.: *British Relations with Sind 1799-1843; An Anatomy of Imperialism*, Berkeley and Los Angeles, University of California, 1962.

Imlah, A. H.: *Economic Elements of the Pax Brittanica*, Cambridge, Harvard University Press, 1958.

Keane J.: *Democracy and Civil Liberty*, London, Verso, 1988.

Kelly, John B.: *Britain and the Persian Gulf 1795-1880,* Oxford, Clarendon Press, 1968.

Majumdar, R. C.: *An Advanced History of India*, New York, St. Martin's Press, 1967.

Moseley, Philip E.: *Russian Diplomacy and the Opening of the Eastern Question*, Cambridge, Harvard University Press, 1934.

Norris, James A.: *The First Afghan War 1838-1842*, Cambridge, University Press, 1967.

Puryear, V. J.: *International Economics and Diplomacy in the Near East*, London, Oxford University, 1935.

Selden, S.: *The Promise of Representative Bureaucracy: Diversity and Responsiveness in a Government Agency*, New York, M. E. Sharpe, 1997.

Singh, Kushwant: *A History of the Sikhs*, New Jersey, Princeton University Press, 1966.

Singhal, D. P.: *India and Afghanistan: 1876-1907. A Study in Diplomatic Relations*, St. Lucia, University of Queensland, 1963.

Stoker G.: *The Politicals of Local Government*, Basingstoke, MacMillan Educational, 1988.

Index

□□□